# On the Autonomy
# of the Democratic State

*Written under the auspices of the
Center for International Affairs,
Harvard University*

# On the Autonomy

OF THE

# Democratic State

———◆———

## Eric A. Nordlinger

Harvard University Press
Cambridge, Massachusetts
and London, England
1981

*Library of Congress Cataloging in Publication Data*

Nordlinger, Eric A.
On the autonomy of the democratic state.

Includes index.
1. Democracy. 2. Autonomy. 3. State, The.
4. Social control. 5. Policy sciences. I. Title.
JC423.N65        321.8        81-1683
ISBN 0-674-63407-1             AACR2

This book is dedicated to my children—
Alexandra, who waited patiently for its appearance,
and
Oliver, whose impending birth helped speed up its completion

# Preface

THIS BOOK is the product of a question, a surprise, and an intuition. About three years ago I sat back and asked myself a very broad question: How can we best understand and explain the public policies adopted by the legislative, executive, and administrative officials who make up the democratic state? Within a short time I had the answer, more accurately, the kind of answer put forward in very nearly all writings on empirical democratic theory and public policy formation. It is the contours of civil society, the distribution of political resources, along with the policy preferences of those societal groups that control the weightiest resources that account for the authoritative actions and inactions of the democratic state. When the policy preferences of public officials differ from those of the politically best endowed private actors it is the latter that are almost invariably translated into public policy.

My surprise was not triggered by the substantive features of this societal constraint answer, but by the near unanimity with which it has been accepted, its barely questioned pervasiveness, in all variants of liberal and Marxist writing on democratic politics. It struck me as most implausible that the democratic state — the elected and appointed officials who populate this large, weighty, resource-laden, highly prized ensemble of offices — is consistently unwilling or unable to translate its preferences into public policy when they diverge from those held by the politically weightiest societal groups. This book is the development of that intuition.

In the course of writing it I incurred debts to several friends and colleagues. Their help was of inestimable value in all sorts of ways, from reassuring me that what began to appear patently persuasive had not, in fact, been said before, to offering incisive critiques that led to my rethinking some basic concepts and arguments. For their patience in reading through the entire manuscript I am most grateful to Brian Barry, Stanley Hoffmann, Stephen K. Krasner, Peter Lange, Robert Paarlberg, Sidney Verba, and Alan Zuckerman. For their warmly given help with particular parts of the manuscript I want to thank Roger Cobb, Charles E. Lindblom, Robert D. Putnam, and Nancy Rosenblum.

It is again a pleasure to be able to acknowledge my appreciation to the Center for International Affairs at Harvard University. Its director, Samuel P. Huntington, and its executive officer, Grant T. Hammond, have helped create a collegial setting where the time set aside for writing runs up against especially stiff competition from other activities. I am indebted to Brown University, and its provost, Maurice Glicksman, for providing the time in which most of this book was written.

At Harvard University Press, Elizabeth Suttell helped out the readers of this book by cutting down its length, without, it needs to be said, editing out anything in the way of significant content. Authors are understandably much concerned with the appearance of their books, yet only rarely is the designer thanked and complimented for an exceptionally attractive book. Perhaps Marianne Perlak will help begin a tradition.

Among the several typists who worked on the manuscript, I want especially to thank Lee Boileau and Carolyn Riley for the careful attention they gave to it.

Since my wife, Sam, is a rather private kind of woman I can say no more than this: she helped in all sorts of wonderful ways.

# Contents

# On the Autonomy
# of the Democratic State

# 1

## State, Society, and Public Policy

HOW CAN WE ACCOUNT for the authoritative actions of the democratic state, its public policies broadly conceived? To what extent is the democratic state an autonomous entity, one that translates its own policy preferences into authoritative actions? These two overlapping questions are the central concerns of this book. My answers are decidedly state centered: the preferences of the state are at least as important as those of civil society in accounting for what the democratic state does and does not do; the democratic state is not only frequently autonomous insofar as it regularly acts upon its preferences, but also markedly autonomous in doing so even when its preferences diverge from the demands of the most powerful groups in civil society.

Of course, these are not the only possible answers. According to the alternative, often incompatible society-centered perspective, these are very much the wrong answers. It is this other perspective that has a pervasive grip upon citizens, journalists and scholars alike.[1] If a measure of exaggeration may be permitted on the first page of a book, the conventional portrayal of democratic politics derived from the society-centered perspective is one in which the heaviest brush strokes are used to depict elected and bureaucratic officials constantly courting societal actors, continuously seeking pockets of support from voters, pressure groups, labor unions, corporations, and ethnic and regional blocs, always scanning the societal waters for currents with which to float along, cautiously testing the waters' temperature before entering them, carefully assessing the marginal gains and losses of support before taking one position or another, and then almost invariably acting to realize the marginal gains. The lighter brush strokes are reserved for public officials who enjoy predominant and secure societal support, or who are well entrenched in their positions, which occasionally allows them to take unpopular, losing positions and engage in arbitrary actions and inordinately self-serving behavior. But even these securely placed public officials are not portrayed as active, determined individuals, shaping the patterns of societal demands, political resources, and alignments, and most certainly not as policymakers acting contrary to the demands of the politically *best* endowed private actors, whether these are voters, well-organized "special interest" groups, the managers of huge corporations, or any other set of societal actors.

Few people would question the aesthetic, emotionally expressive, and artistic rationale for surrealist painting, which purposefully exaggerates and distorts objective and subjective realities. But whether surrealism speaks to our emotions or is simply an "interesting" art form, it is recognized as such, as pushing the limits of reality forward, asunder, or aside. The conventional portraiture of democratic politics is surrealistic without knowing itself to be so. Its hard-nosed, "realistic" depictions of public officials as consistently constrained by societal groups are unrealistic, not because they are inaccurate in and of themselves, but because they exaggerate without knowing it and paint on much too small a canvas without an awareness of the resulting distortions.

Each of the major variants of empirical democratic theory — pluralism, neopluralism, social corporatism, and Marxism — has as its central aim the explanation of the state's authoritative actions and inactions, the public policies that are and are not adopted. The explanations are not only decidedly society centered, they consistently rely upon a set of societal constraint assumptions. With public officials being heavily and diversely dependent upon societal support, with private actors controlling and effectively deploying a great armory of political and politically fungible resources, public policy is understood primarily as a response to the expectations, demands, and pressures of those who control the largest proportion of especially effective resources. The state, that is, public officials taken all together, is commonly seen as a permeable, vulnerable, and malleable entity, not necessarily in the hands of most individuals and groups, but in those of the most powerful ones. When state and societal preferences diverge, this society-centered model denies, ignores, or downplays the possibility of public officials acting on their preferences after engineering a shift in societal preferences or in the relative distribution of resources behind them, and strenuously denies the possibility of the state translating its preferences into authoritative actions when opposed by societal actors who control the weightiest political resources.

Accounting for what the democratic state does and does not do is also the central focus of American and comparative public policymaking studies. Here too there is a decidedly society-centered focus. Here too the societal constraint assumptions are almost pervasively accepted and uncritically applied. The study of public administration in America emerged from its formal-legal cocoon in the 1930s and 1940s to become more politically "realistic," and apparently did so by fully accepting the existence of the societal constraints to which the state is putatively so heavily subjected. In a highly regarded public administration textbook, the very survival of bureaucratic agencies is said to be in societal hands. "Government agencies cannot exist without appropriations or enabling statutes. They can survive only so long as they can continue to secure the support of politically effective groups in the community and continue through these groups to secure legislative and executive support. 'Bureaucrats' can wish to survive, but they do not determine the conditions of survival."[2]

This portrayal is admittedly somewhat overdrawn, but not

with respect to the major assumptions and motifs that have informed the study of politics in democratic regimes. There are certainly numerous studies of officials making public policy and the various factors that shape their policy views and behavior—from their educational backgrounds, through their bureaucratic interests, to their anticipated move into the private sector, to mention only a few among dozens. Yet almost all of these writings can be characterized in one of two ways: they sidestep or ignore the societal constraint assumptions, without ever questioning them. The general and specific situations that are analyzed from the perspective of the state do not include those in which the public actors' policy preferences diverge from those held by the politically weightiest private actors. Many other writings, especially those whose focus is upon the internal arrangements and structure of the state, ignore the societal constraints altogether by delimiting their concerns to the state alone. The former can afford to sidestep the societal constraints insofar as they are not thought to be operative, while the latter are justified in ignoring them given the perfectly suitable manner in which the research questions have been formulated. But neither belies the critical point that studies of the state, society, and state-society relations rarely assign public officials a substantial measure of independence in the face of politically weighty demands and pressures. There are some studies that do not take this position. Still, our portrayal of the literature on empirical democratic theory and public policy formation is only somewhat overdrawn. For this motif is of recent vintage and its products are minimal in number. The winds of change are beginning to blow, even if up to now they have done no more than occasionally flutter some of the hundred society-centered candles. These recent studies will, of course, be highlighted at the appropriate places in this book.

When working on the unquestioned assumptions and within the exclusive confines of the society-centered model, there is little point in drawing an analytical distinction between state and society. Organizing concepts that do not distinguish clearly and consistently, if at all, between state and society—such as the political process, elites, political elites, political parties, successful coalitions, political gatekeepers, and so on—obviously have suitable uses and important advantages. Yet there are disadvantages: the possibility that the state's preferences have at least as much impact upon public policy as do society's is ignored; the state's having certain distinctive interests and divergent preferences is not considered; the state's many autonomous actions are not calculated; the state's numerous automony-enhancing capacities and opportunities are not examined; and most fundamentally, the failure to differentiate state and society eliminates the possibility of validating or invalidating the societal constraint assumptions. They remain irrefutable even in principle; explanations for particular public policies are at the least broadly predetermined from the outset. No matter how compelling the societal perspective is thought to be, only by distinguishing between state and society does it become possible, even in principle, to establish the forceful and extensive impact of the societal constraints. To make the point in reverse fashion, only by drawing the state-society distinction does it become possible to assess the impact of the state upon public policy independently of the constraints and supports of societal actors, and thereby allow a case to be made for its autonomy.

The pervasive grip of the society-centered perspective helps explicate the common absence of a clear and consistent state-society distinction. It has also resulted in a conception of the state as little more than an arena within which societal conflicts are fought out, interests mediated, and the ensuing results authoritatively confirmed. State and society are conflated, the former even coming close to being incorporated within the latter. In America—except for some political scientists who came under the spell of Germanic scholarship in the late nineteenth century, including a later president of the United States, Woodrow Wilson—a concept of the state has been barely thinkable. For if America has had a state at all, it continues to be an inordinately weak, permeable, fragmented entity undeserving of the name itself. Extremist movements in Europe are generally "prostate"; in the United States, not only is the center "antistate," both the far right and left are supremely American in being even more "antistate."[3]

Until recently, a distinctive concept of the state has rarely been used and appreciated, not just because so little has been made of it, but also because far too much has been made of it. Since early in the nineteenth century—whether related or unrelated to an accurate or inaccurate reading of Hegel—the concept has often been inflated, mystified, and subjected to the reification and anthropomorphic fallacies. The inflation of the state concept has sometimes helped make for its distortion, it having occasionally become exclusively identified with authoritarian, reactionary, and fascistic regimes and ideas.

What is it then that we want to say about the democratic state? Most broadly, I hope this book will foster a greater appreciation for a state-centered model in accounting for the public policies of the democratic state—a model whose plausibility, applicability, and explanatory power is thought to compensate for the weaknesses, limitations, and omissions of the conventional society-centered model in its various forms. Some serious questions are raised about the society-centered model, in particular, the societal constraint assumptions upon which it rests. But it should be absolutely clear that my purpose is very far from denying its extensive applicability, explanatory power, and validity. Indeed, the adjective "centered" is used to imply that neither model focuses solely upon one sphere, that there is in fact a measurable overlap between them. What is at issue is the near pervasive, often total reliance upon the society-centered model, when it can be shown that the state-centered model offers at least as plausible a set of propositions for understanding the what, how, and why of the democratic state's authoritative actions. So despite the very different emphases and incompatible assertions that turn them into rival explanatory models at several critical junctures, the state-centered model is thought of as a complement to the society-centered model, compensating for its one-sided, partly problematic assertions by emphasizing important dimensions it ignores and propositions it denies.

Getting far ahead of the story, though serving as an introduction to it, what does the state-centered model look like? How does it interpret the making of public policy? This book attempts to establish the plausibility of the following six propositions that make up our state-centered model:

1. Among the panoply of state preferences many converge with, many are compatible with, and many diverge from societal preferences.
2. When state and societal preferences do not diverge, public officials invariably translate their own preferences into authoritative actions, and their preferences have at least as much explanatory importance as societal preferences.
3. When state and societal preferences do not diverge, public officials periodically capitalize upon their autonomy-enhancing capacities and opportunities to reinforce societal convergence, deference, and indifference so as to forestall the emergence of preferences that diverge from the state's.
4. When state and societal preferences diverge, public officials periodically capitalize upon their autonomy-enhancing capacities and opportunities to bring about a shift in societal preferences and/or the alignment of societal resources in order to make for nondivergent preferences, and they then translate their own preferences into authoritative actions.
5. When state and societal preferences diverge, public officials periodically capitalize upon their autonomy-enhancing capacities and opportunities to free themselves from societal constraints, and they then translate their preferences into authoritative actions.
6. When state and societal preferences diverge, public officials periodically rely upon the inherent powers of the state to translate their preferences into authoritative actions.

The propositions making up the model, as well as its fundamental, overall import, thus provide what are thought to be the most persuasive responses to the two overlapping issues that were raised at the outset—those having to do with the relative importance of state and society in the formation of public policies and the extent to which the state's authoritative actions are autonomous. Public officials have at least as much independent impact or explanatory importance as any and all private actors in accounting for the public policies of the democratic state. The democratic state is regularly, though by no means entirely, autonomous in translating its preferences into authoritative actions, and markedly autonomous in often doing so even when they diverge from societal preferences.

In his 1977 presidential address to the Canadian Political Science Association, Alan Cairns made several comments that encapsulate much in these introductory pages, underscoring the pervasiveness of society-centered analyses and pointing to a significant aspect of the state-centered model.

> The impact of society on government is a common theme in the study of democratic polities. Less common is an approach which stresses the impact of government on the *political* functioning of society . . . Although I do not doubt that government rides such a tiger of social change that the sweet smile of victory is often on the face of the tiger . . . I am convinced that our approach to the study of Canadian politics pays inadequate attention to the weight of the rider, and to his possession of reins to steer, whips to beat, and various inducements to make the tiger responsive to his demands.[4]

### State Autonomy as a Conceptual Variable

Immanuel Kant equated individual autonomy with free will. The autonomy of any social entity refers to the correspondence between its preferences and actions. A totally autonomous one, if there is such an entity, invariably acts as it chooses to act, and does not act when it prefers not to do so. An autonomous state translates its policy preferences into authoritative actions; it is autonomous to the extent that public policy conforms to the parallelogram (or resultant) of the public officials' resource-weighted preferences. This, our central concept, needs to be explicated, amplified, and defended as analytically appropriate and meaningful. Doing so involves a delineation of the three components of the state autonomy concept—the state, authoritative actions, and state preferences.

Whether found within a democratic or nondemocratic regime, the state has been variously conceptualized by using some combination of its functions, purposes, activities, personnel, organizational contours, legitimacy, legal norms, rules and machinery, sovereignty, near coercive monopoly, and territorial control. Some of these elements appear in this definition: "The modern state is perhaps best seen as a complex set of institutional arrangements for rule operating through continuous and regulated activities of individuals acting as occupants of offices."[5] The appropriateness of any definition depends upon the uses to which it is put and the validity of its empirical referents. In the present context, it is important that a definition of the state have certain characteristics.

First, the definition of the state must refer to individuals rather than to some other kinds of phenomena, such as "institutional arrangements" or the legal-normative order. Since we are primarily concerned with the *making* of public policy, a conception of the state that does not have individuals at its core could lead directly into the anthropomorphic and reification fallacies. For instance, if institutions were taken to define the state, these being viewed as stable and valued patterns of interaction, how could it be said that institutions have preferences, or that they somehow realize them after first purposefully overcoming the societal constraints? Only individuals have preferences and engage in actions that make for their realization. And only by making individuals central to the definition can Hegelian implications (substantive and metaphysical) be avoided when referring to the state's preferences.

Second, the state should include more than the government and/or the bureaucratic agencies that derive their authority from it. Although the executive and/or the bureaucracy have been said to constitute the "core" of the state, this in itself does not warrant a definition limited to them alone. Since we are concerned with all authoritative actions and all parts of the state as they relate to one another and to societal actors, the definition should include all public officials—elected and appointed, at high and low levels, at the center and the peripheries—who are involved in the making of public policy.

Third, variable characterizations can and should be avoided. Only those that encompass all states and all of their components at all times should be included. For example, the concept should not include a reference to something like centralized authority since it would then exclude some states, most especially the American national state. Nor should it refer to "continuous and regulated activities" since the actions of public officials are not consistently of this variety. The juristically perplexing notion of sovereignty should be avoided because it is empirically variable—both within the state since all of its units are not considered sovereign, and between state and society since society is sometimes viewed as sovereign. These and other variable characterizations of the state—such as the legitimacy of its authority—have their appropriate uses, but they can be introduced when and where applicable rather than being placed within the core definition.

Lastly, while recognizing that no definition is completely neutral in its theoretical and normative implications, the one adopted here should be as neutral as possible. While all scholars are not about to agree upon any one definition of the state, the one used here should prompt the fewest objections. This means not defining the state in terms of the bases of its authority—its near monopoly of the means of coercion, legitimacy to make binding decisions, or some variously weighted combination of the two. For this is exactly the problem: there is much disagreement about the relative importance of coercion and legitimacy as the bases of public authority in democratic (as well as in authoritarian and mobilization) regimes. Nor should *invariable* functions and purposes be attributed to the state, such as the preservation of political stability or the reproduction of capitalism, if the definition is to be as theoretically neutral as possible. Those who view the state in these terms can tack on specific functions and purposes to the present definition in the course of reading this book. In fact, we will be doing just this when using the Marxist variant of democratic theory to argue for state autonomy.

In this book the state is defined in something of a Weberian manner. It refers to all those individuals who occupy offices that authorize them, and them alone, to make and apply decisions that are binding upon any and all segments of society. Quite simply, the state is made up of and limited to those individuals who are endowed with society-wide decisionmaking authority. Public officials are distinguished from private officials — in churches, universities, voluntary associations, labor unions, corporations, and so on — in that their authority is more exclusive and comprehensive. Public officials alone can take actions that are binding upon any and all private actors. The present definition differentiates between public officials and public employees — those individuals who hold publicly funded positions that do not involve them in authoritative decisionmaking. Louis XIV may then have put forward the "correct" definition of the state when he reportedly said, "L'etat, c'est moi." On his implicit assumption that the hereditary noble governors had been denuded of their authority, they would be viewed as private individuals; on the premise that all officials other than himself, including the nobles at Versailles and the *intendants* in the provinces, were without decisionmaking powers, they would be seen as public employees, who consequently reside on the private side of the state-society fence.

Any definition that distinguishes between state and society is, of course, a simplification of reality. But it is appropriate, advantageous, and for some purposes, necessary to do so. The distinction between public and private actors is at least implicitly made in most studies of democratic politics, and provides the basic framework for those that deal with issues of representation. In denying the independent impact of public officials upon public policy when opposed by the most powerful societal actors, the conventional wisdom presupposes the very same distinction. Most important for our purposes, the differentiation between state and society allows for an inquiry into

the relative importance and interplay of public and private actors in the making of public policy. In a book concerned largely
with state-society relations, these two inclusive components of
the polity have to be distinguished, whatever the linkages and
interactions between them to which much of the analysis is
devoted.

While the drawing of a clear analytical distinction between
state and society is a necessary simplification, perhaps this
definition oversimplifies by circumscribing the state in an ex-
cessively sharp manner. In the United States in particular, individuals move back and forth between the public and private
spheres, and it is hardly uncommon to find two or more coalitions each made up of both public and private actors resolving
a public policy issue. In Norway many private actors could be
seen as quasi-public ones when they sit on the more than 1,000
public-private committees that are attached to all administrative departments, independent agencies, and public
corporations, with responsibilities for overseeing their activities, proferring advice, and formulating public policies. In
all democratic regimes political parties provide much of the ce-
ment that holds state and society together. In part, they do so
because political parties include both public and private actors.
But these empirical facts, and others like them, would afflict
any definition of the state, some all the more so. A Weberian
type definition allows for the state's relatively clear-cut empirical identification and delimitation. Moreover, it neither
denies nor prevents consideration of those instances in which
the state-society distinction is blurred. These can be treated as
variations, as in Chapter 6, which highlights just such differences in discussing the liberal, distorted liberal, and liberal
corporatist state. Once the democratic state is seen to feature a
high degree of autonomy, there will be more than enough time
and opportunity to drop the simplification, focusing instead
upon the subtle, specific, complex variations in the ways in
which the state is and is not differentiated from society. In fact,
when a broad-gauged study of state-society is written it will
probably identify an important secular trend among the ad-

vanced industrial democracies, elaborating upon the several ways in which the state has become less and less of a distinctive entity.

The applicability, explanatory power, and persuasiveness of any model that purports to explain what the state does and does not do depends upon the breadth with which its authoritative actions are defined. With one significant exception, these are given the broadest possible meaning. Authoritative actions encompass both the public policies that have been adopted and those that have not, including those whose consideration has not even been placed on the formal or informal agenda. Authoritative actions are not limited to highly visible ones that have a great impact upon many individuals, such as the enactment of new social welfare legislation; authoritative interpretations and applications of narrowly focused regulations are also included. Although distinctions are made between public policies and their implementation, the latter also falls squarely within the compass of authoritative actions. To be sure, there are significant differences in accounting for routine and nonroutine decisions, but many implementation decisions are far from routine, prescribed, foreordained decisions, and even precisely formulated legislative and executive decisions can be and often are altered when applied. Nor is the concept limited to decisions that have a direct and purposeful impact upon societal actors. The state is continuously making authoritative decisions with respect to its own internal arrangements, activities, and budgets. Most of them do have recognized and direct affects upon the interests of societal actors, but even those that do not have a discernible societal impact constitute authoritative actions.

With authoritative actions encompassing decisions and nondecisions and the adoption, application, and implementation of all manner of public policies, it will prove useful to differentiate among them. Here it is done in terms of their "targets," the economic, social, political, and public objects and relations to which they are directed. These include intrastate relations, such as the distribution of formal powers, programmatic responsibilities, operating procedures, and budgetary allotments among and within separate state units; state-society relations, such as the opportunities, rules, and channels that determine the extent and manner in which societal actors select, influence, and interact with public officials; and most important for present purposes, all aspects of the economy and society, the collective and noncollective values of private actors, and their interactions with one another.

As is now probably apparent, even this encompassing conceptualization of authoritative actions omits the impact they have on their intended targets, that is, their consequences and overall effectiveness. This patently important dimension of policy effectiveness speaks to a different set of questions than those raised here and involves many explanatory factors other than state and societal preferences. The now common observation that democratic states are currently confronted with exceptionally complex societal problems, with public officials experiencing great difficulties in policy design and societal guidance, consequently falls outside the scope of this book. The problematics of policy design and effectiveness should not be interpreted to mean that democratic states are currently lacking in autonomy, or that authoritative actions have been conceptualized in an overly narrow fashion to sidestep possibly unwanted evidence.

With the preferences of public officials referring to authoritative actions they are given an equally encompassing meaning. They include any and all realistic, nonutopian policy preferences, be they ideologically coherent or disparate, broad or narrow, durable or fleeting. They are genuine, societally unconstrained volitions, unaffected by the perceived need for support, the fear of opposition, the anticipation of sanctions, or the application of pressures and inducements by societal actors. Within these broad but critical limits preferences may derive from society, state, or self — from the wish to serve society as a whole, particular groups within it, a political party, certain state units, or the officials' private interests, from convenience to career advancement. They may be influenced by any unconstrained cognitive, evaluative, or emotional responses to the distribution of societal wealth, ethnic divisions, economic growth rates, the effectiveness of current public policies, or any type of information, from mass media advertising to new scientific discoveries. The overall features of policy preferences, where they come from, and how they are formed do not delimit them so long as they are not societally constrained.

State preferences refer to the resource-weighted parallelogram (or resultant) of the public officials' preferences — preferences as backed by variously distributed intrastate resources. State preferences, as distinct from the discrete preferences of public officials, are those with the weightiest support of public officials behind them, based on the number of officials on different sides of the issue, the formal powers of their offices, their hierarchical and strategic positioning relative to the issue at hand, and the information, expertise, and interpersonal skills at their disposal. The employment, effectiveness, and relative weight of these and other relevant intrastate resources are mediated by the norms and decision-rules governing the interactions of public officials. The resources of public officials are exclusively intrastate resources; the societal support they often call upon in pressing their views on other officials is not used in estimating state preferences.

Although the term "state preferences" is suggestive of unity and seems to include the preferences of all officials, it should certainly not be taken to mean that all officials have preferences on any given issue, or that all interested officials are in agreement. They usually do not, and are not. Later on in this chapter we will be discussing some of the major factors that help shape the preferences of public officials. Simply to mention some of them — the officials' career interests, organizational loyalties, and professional knowledge — makes it abundantly apparent that state preferences are rarely unified preferences. They are usually the product of all sorts of conflict, competition, and pulling and hauling. State preferences refer solely to those of a single state unit — for example, a city council in the United States, a committee of the Italian parliament, a *direction* in the French Ministry of Justice — when other officials are indifferent to the issue at hand or are without the intrastate resources to affect the final decision. At first glance state preferences might also appear to be a reified and anthropomorphic concept. But with the state being defined in terms of individuals — those whose occupancy of authoritative offices turns them into public officials — the term does not at all partake of the reification and anthropomorphic fallacies. It refers to some weighted aggregation of individual preferences. Just because of the several ways in which this shorthand term (and its counterpart of societal preferences) may be misinterpreted, these clarifications should be kept in mind in the course of reading this book.

Just as state preferences are based exclusively upon the weighted intrastate resources of those public officials who have an interest in the issue at hand, so too are societal preferences identified solely in terms of the relative weights or effectiveness of the private resources controlled by those who have a manifest concern with a particular issue. "Societal preferences" is a shorthand term for the parallelogram (or resultant) of resource-weighted private preferences as these bear upon both issues and nonissues (that is, those that have not found their way onto the political agenda). It would be relatively simple to identify a particular societal parallelogram if everyone's preferences enjoyed equal weight, if, in other words, the criterion of "one man, one vote" that obtains on election day were also applicable to the actions of elected and appointed officials during the hundreds of days between elections. A well-designed survey of a nationally representative sample would then often be sufficient. For example, if the issue at hand were that of the preferred minimum wage and 50 percent of the interest respondents preferred a $3 minimum wage and the other 50 percent a $4 one, then the resultant would be a societal preference for a $3.50 wage.

Political reality is obviously not quite so simple; the preferences of different individuals are backed by resources of varying weights or effectiveness. In fact, identifying the societal parallelogram presents a special difficulty. There are profound, accentuated disagreements about the relative weights to be assigned to different kinds of resources. In the next chapter it will be seen that the "great debate" in empirical democratic theory revolves around just this issue — the question of the relative effectiveness of numbers, votes, organization, expertise, information, social prestige, money, access to the mass media, and control over economic enterprises. This in turn means that there is little agreement on the question of whose preferences determine the resource-weighted societal parallelogram of preferences. Is it primarily the preferences of any and all sizable groups, of small well-organized groups with specialized policy concerns, of mass membership national "peak" associations representing labor, employers, and agriculture, or of the economically dominant class that controls the means of production?

One way to address this problem is to pursue the argument for state autonomy under conditions of state-society divergence separately with respect to the holders of each set of especially effective resources as identified in pluralist, neopluralist, social corporatist, and Marxist writings (see Chapter 6). Another approach is found in the systematic construction of judgmental measures and their sensitive application, as done by Gabriel A. Almond and his colleagues in comparing very different kinds of crisis episodes in variegated societal contexts. Although they chose not to differentiate consistently between state and societal "contenders," their study serves as a guide for the systematic measurement of two variables that are central to their concerns and ours — "the contenders' weights measured by their share of the effective political resources and the contenders' preferences, which are conceptualized and measured by the extent of their agreement or disagreement on issues."[6]

The fit or lack of fit between state and societal preferences constitutes the critical contextual variable within which state-society relations are played out. Variations in the patterns of state-society preferences go a long way in determining the outcome of authoritative actions. They also have an important bearing upon the manner in which the outcome is decided, the way in which winners win and losers lose. It then makes eminently good sense to use these patterns in ordering the central analytical context for an inquiry into state-society relations. In doing so, state rather than societal preferences serve as the reference point; these are taken as given, with societal preferences varying in their fit with the state's. It is patently appropriate for the state to constitute the vantage point. We are more concerned with the frequency with which the state acts on its preferences than with the frequency with which societal preferences are translated into public policy; we are more interested in how the state reacts to societal preferences than the reverse, especially when state-society preferences diverge. The questions of just how often the state acts autonomously and how it manages to do so can then be most directly addressed. There is a secondary advantage in adopting this perspective. The state is never neutral. At least some public officials have decided preferences with regard to every possible authoritative action and inaction, whereas practically all societal actors are indifferent to some issues. With state preferences serving as the reference point, the analysis can address all policy issues directly.

The basic distinction to be drawn is clearly the one that distinguishes between divergent and nondivergent state-society preferences. Divergent preferences obtain when there is a greater or lesser perceived distance between them, that is, state and societal actors have different or incompatible preferences. Perceptions may well be distorted; they are never entirely accurate to begin with. Yet perceptions are what matter in shaping consequent behavior. Just how public and private actors form their perceptions or misperceptions of one another's preferences is an important question, but it is not taken up here. Divergence refers exclusively to the perceived substantive incompatibilities and differences separating the positions of public and private actors; the consequentiality of the issue, for themselves or an outside observer, is not part of the concept. The assessment of intrinsic or extrinsic importance is fraught with ambiguities at best. For example, it has become a truism that ends are not necessarily more important than means, and that one person's ends are another's means; nor are the distinctions between policymaking and implementation and between goal setting and administration recognized as consistently viable ones. Moreover, the way in which state and societal preferences have been conceptualized already covers much, even most, of an issue's subjective importance. There is a good correspondence between the consequentiality that an issue has for any set of political actors and the proportion of their resources that they deploy in attempting to have the issue settled in a manner favorable to themselves. State and societal preferences are already defined as resource-weighted preferences.

Nondivergent state-society preferences include convergent (or congruent) ones; there is very little if any distance between them. Also included are societal preferences that are compatible (or consonant) with the state's. With the latter serving as the reference point, there is a compatibility of preferences both when society is indifferent, with virtually no private actors holding preferences that relate to the state's, and when the politically weightiest among them defer to the state's preferences. In the latter case, societal actors may or may not have distinct preferences with respect to the issue at hand, and if they do, these may or may not diverge from the state's. But whatever the subsidiary pattern, they want public officials to act on their own preferences, as is often the case in the midst of a national security crisis.

Having delineated what is meant by the state, authoritative actions, state preferences, societal preferences, and the fit or lack of fit between them—and, I trust, having provided a persuasive rationale for each—the meaning of state autonomy should now be fairly clear. The state is autonomous to the extent that it translates its preferences into authoritative actions, the degree to which public policy conforms to the parallelogram of the public officials' resource-weighted preferences. State autonomy may be operationally defined in terms of the overall frequency with which state preferences coincide with authoritative actions and inactions, the proportion of preferences that do so, the average substantive distance between state preferences and authoritative actions, or some combination of the three.

The generic definition of state autonomy does *not* refer to the fit between state and societal preferences. A state that acts upon its preferences under conditions of nondivergence is just as autonomous as one that does so under conditions of divergence. Yet the great differences and differential significance of state autonomy as it occurs in the context of varying state-society preference patterns are not about to be downplayed. Whether state-society preferences are divergent or non-divergent serves as the most important basis for distinguishing between the different types of state autonomy. Two further clarifying comments. Although the shorthand language might imply more than is intended when no reference is made to particular public officials or state units, it should be clear that state autonomy refers solely to legislatures, legislative committees, cabinets, presidents, bureaucratic agencies, mayors, district councils, prefects, and so forth, when other officials and units are either without preferences on the issue at hand or without the intrastate resources to affect their authoritative resolution. In the not uncommon scenario in which two (or more) coalitions, each composed of both public and private actors, confront one another, state autonomy is assessed independently of the private actors who support opposing public officials. State autonomy obtains to the extent that the policy outcome coincides with the latter's preferences in both (or all) coalitions as weighted exclusively by their intrastate resources.

Many concepts are imbued with more than one meaning. With state autonomy serving as the central one here, there is all the more reason to discuss some alternative meanings. Doing so should further clarify what is and is not included within its definitional compass, concomitantly showing how it avoids the questionable and disadvantageous aspects of other definitions while retaining what is viable in them.

Autonomy has recently come to be somewhat loosely used as

a synonym for the state's "strength" or "power," which is hardly surprising since autonomy implies something about the latter, and vice versa. A strong state is commonly said to be one with great capacities. The mixed-economy welfare state is strong because of the wide scope of its social and economic activities, its enormous regulatory, distributive, and (to a much lesser extent) redistributive capacities. But it is one thing to think about state strength in terms of capacities and quite another to equate or connect them with autonomy. Public officials do not invariably prefer to create or expand state capacities. Would it make sense to assume that the archetypical nineteenth-century "night watchman state," which in Britain actually began the century purposely contracting its capacities, is necessarily far less autonomous than its twentieth-century counterparts? And among the latter, to say that those with the greatest capacities are necessarily more autonomous is to sidestep the possibility that the expansion of state powers is primarily explicable in terms of societal rather than state preferences.

Much of the rationale for identifying autonomy with capacities derives from a seemingly persuasive hypothesis. Public officials with many policy levers to pull have decided advantages in confronting societal actors with divergent preferences, while the enormous resources at their disposal make societal groups especially dependent upon them. This hypothesis is overly simplistic, however, in ignoring two additional considerations—considerations that are even suggestive of an inverse relationship between state autonomy and capacities. All other things being equal, a state with wide-ranging, penetrative capacities is confronted with markedly greater private demands and pressures, and is thus more susceptible to societal constraints than one whose capacities tend toward the other end of the continuum. And the dependence of private actors upon a highly developed mixed-economy welfare state is at least partly offset by the state's need for societal cooperation in formulating and implementing its ambitious social and economic policies. These considerations are not meant to reject outright the existence of a positive relationship between a state's autonomy and capacities, but they do indicate that even if the relationship holds, it is far from sufficiently simple and straightforward to justify a definitional equation.

A far more acceptable notion of state strength is a relational one. The state is strong or weak in relation to society, as in the oft-heard assertion that America has a weak state and a strong society.[7] A strong state, an autonomous one, is able to overcome societal demands; the greater the resources behind the demands and the greater the societal resistance that the state is able to overcome, the more autonomous it is. This is basically the way that state autonomy is used in the Marxist theory of the capitalist state, in the one public policy study to claim that the democratic state does sometimes act on its preferences under conditions of divergence, and in the most significant recent contribution to the literature on social revolutions.[8]

In Stephen D. Krasner's public policy study, "the power of the state *vis-a-vis* its domestic society" is laid out along a three-part continuum. The state is "able to resist societal pressures, but unable to change the behavior of private actors"; the state is able to resist societal pressures and "change private behavior" but is unable to "change the social and economic structure"; the state is able to resist private pressure, change private behavior, and change the social and economic structure.[9] State autonomy serves as a central concept in Theda Skocpol's analysis of state-society relations before, during, and after the French, Russian, and Chinese revolutions. She limits the concept's applicability to instances in which there is a conflict between the state's interests and those of the economically and politically dominant class. An autonomous state then acts according to its own interests. Substantively, it often does so by "appropriating resources from the economy and society," "maintaining sheer physical order and political peace," "controlling the population and collecting taxes and military recruits," and pursuing its foreign and military goals. Autonomous actions are also undertaken to "strengthen the bulk and autonomy of the state itself." Skocpol's formulation parallels the Marxist "relative autonomy of the state" proposition. But she argues that the latter is un-necessarily and incorrectly limited in not allowing for state actions that run counter to the fundamental, long-run interests of the economically and politically dominant class. The reasons for doing so are often related to the state's international position.

> A state's involvement in an international network of states is a basis for potential autonomy of action over and against groups and economic arrangements within its jurisdiction — even including the dominant class and existing relations of production. For international military pressures and opportunities can prompt state rulers to attempt policies that conflict with, and even in extreme instances contradict, the fundamental interests of a dominant class. State rulers may, for example, undertake military adventures abroad that drain resources from economic development at home, or that have the immediate or ultimate effect of undermining the position of dominant socioeconomic interests. And, to give a different example, rulers may respond to foreign military competition or threats of conquest by attempting to impose fundamental socioeconomic reforms or by trying to reorient the course of national economic development through state intervention.[10]

Skocpol and Krasner think of the degree of state autonomy as the extent to which the state brings about behavioral and structural changes that are opposed by the most powerful societal actors. However, rather than being loosely conflated, it should be noted that the extent of societal change and the amount of societal opposition are, in fact, two analytically and empirically distinct dimensions. This two-fold conception of state autonomy is indeed a meaningful and ambitious one. Yet its very ambitiousness unnecessarily restricts both its meaningfulness and it applicability.

Defining autonomy in terms of the state acting according to its interests when these conflict with those held by the politically dominant actors is to exclude those cases in which the state acts on its preferences in the absence of such conflicts, that is, under conditions of nondivergence. Surely there is no a priori reason to refer to such actions as nonautonomous, heteronomous, or societally constrained; nor is it unreasonable to view them as autonomous actions. To find that a state is making the public policies that it prefers to make is patently significant, whether it does so in the face of massive societal opposition or with overwhelming societal support behind it. The state becomes all the more significant if, as will be suggested in Chapter 3, state-centered accounts of public policies adopted under conditions of nondivergence enjoy at least as much explantory power as society-centered accounts. Moreover, in some ways it makes sense, both intuitively and analytically, to view a state that acts on its preferences with enormous societal support behind it as stronger than one that has first to overcome societal opposition. Similarly, what is one to make of a state that acts on its preferences after purposefully engineering a shift in the societal parallelogram of resource-weighted preferences, turning a divergent into a nondivergent parallelogram? Is this not also an especially strong state, even though it does not translate its preferences into public policy until it is no longer opposed by the politically weightiest societal actors? The distinction between a state acting on its preferences under conditions of divergence and one doing so under conditions of nondivergence is hardly unimportant. But it is advisable to use the term autonomy inclusively, and then go on to differentiate among types of autonomy on the basis of the fit between state and societal preferences, as will be done here.

There are also reasons for not adopting the other dimension of the Krasner-Skocpol formulation. It too unnecessarily restricts the applicability of state autonomy, and it gives a biased cast to its assessment. State preferences do not always involve the alteration of private behavior or the socioeconomic structure, even when restricted to instances in which they diverge from societal preferences. Sometimes they do and sometimes they don't. Where they don't, the autonomy concept would be inapplicable or used to assume away the state's autonomy. It thus makes better sense to think of autonomy as the degree to which any and all state preferences coincide with authoritative actions, rather than focusing exclusively upon the scope or ambitiousness of the state's preferences. A state that brings about great changes in societal behavior and structure is thought to be much stronger than one that succeeds in preserving the status quo. This generalization presumably serves as the rationale for the Krasner-Skocpol formulation. Yet it is at least partly off the mark in identifying the critical variable, which is not the scope of change aimed for but the amplitude of societal support or opposition to whatever the state's aims happen to be. A reactionary state that maintains an unbearably distorted status quo against overwhelming societal opposition is not necessarily weaker than one that brings about great societal changes in the face of equally strong opposition. In fact, the former could be viewed as stronger than a state that succeeds in reconstructing society with the backing of the politically dominant groups. Although it is not especially appropriate as a definition of state autonomy, the scope of state engineered change could be included as one important dimension of a broader conceptualization.

One conception of autonomy is quite different from these others; it goes much beyond the identification of autonomy with strength. According to this conception, an autonomous social entity not only acts on its preferences, which is our definition; in addition, its preferences are internally or self-generated. This kind of autonomous state is at once behaviorally (or objectively) independent in acting as its chooses to act, and subjectively independent insofar as its preferences derive from its internal attributes. It would, however, be unrealistic to expect any social entity to come even close to being fully autonomous in this subjective sense, for as a social entity it learns from the others in its environment, especially those with which it has fairly close and frequent interactions. In fact, were its preferences exclusively self-generated, these might diverge so sharply and consistently from those of others as to threaten its survival.

A subjectively autonomous state is then one whose

preferences are largely but not entirely, derived from the characteristic and distinctive features of the state itself. The last part of this chapter sets out the major explanations for the appearance of state preferences that diverge from society's, and these provide good reasons for thinking that the democratic state is substantially autonomous according to this definition. However, this conception of autonomy will not be pursued beyond that point. For while it is indeed a meaningful one, the significance of a subjective conception of autonomy is largely premised upon or presupposes behavioral (or objective) autonomy. It would make little sense to view a state that generates most of its own preferences as an autonomous one unless it is able to act upon them. And since the behavioral autonomy of the democratic state has yet to be demonstrated, first things first. In addition, a comprehensive, systematic inquiry into the origins of state preferences would run up squarely against some exceptionally stubborn and difficult to circumvent analytical problems.

One other point is relevant. Each conception of autonomy is applicable to all states — those found in democratic, authoritarian, and mobilization regimes. But only our own is especially well suited for the study of the democratic state. It speaks to the central normative and empirical issue of representation, which is commonly treated as the fit between the authoritative actions of the state and societal preferences. "The congruence between the policy preferences of the represented and the policy decisions of the representative is the measure of good representation."[11] By defining autonomy as the translation of state preferences into public policy, and then distinguishing between autonomously adopted policies that do and do not match up with societal preferences, the subsequent analysis relates directly to the greater or lesser representativeness of the democratic state and the manner in which public officials carry out, ignore, and circumvent their representative responsibilities.

In comparison with other conceptualizations of state autonomy, the one presented here is at least as meaningful as

t.                                    stemming from unwarranted
as                                    ge of being more encompass-
in                                    f autonomy as a subjective
var                                   vs for the inclusion of these
nari                                  ensions of state autonomy,
and                                   upon more or less problematic
assun                    ossible explanations for variations in state
autonomy. It also happens to be the most advantageous one for the study of the democratic state's autonomy.

*NOTE: COMPARE HIS NOTION OF STATE TO ALMOND'S SUBSET OF THE POLITICAL SYSTEM*

### Public Policy: A Typology of State Autonomy and Societal Constraint Explanations

How can one account for the public policies of the democratic state? The broad answers to this central question are depicted in figure 1. It presents a typology of four kinds of explanations for the authoritative actions and inactions of the democratic state. The vertical axis represents the state autonomy dimension, as gauged by the frequency, extent, or proportion of instances in which state preferences match up with its authoritative actions. This dimension is simplified as a dichotomy: preferences and authoritative actions are coincident or noncoincident. The horizontal axis represents the degree of fit between state and societal preferences. This dimension depicts the critical context within which the state does or does not act on its preferences. It too is presented in simplified form as a two-fold division between issues on which state-society preferences are divergent or nondivergent. The latter encompasses convergent preferences and compatible ones, when societal actors defer to the state's preferences or are indifferent to them.

The upper and lower halves of figure 1 depict the fundamental distinction between the state- and society-centered perspectives, distinguishing between a state that does and does not act autonomously. The lower left-hand box represents the societal perspective's basic assertion: the state is constrained by society. Societal constraint explanations are those in which state-society

1. EXPLANATIONS FOR THE AUTHORITATIVE ACTIONS OF THE DEMOCRATIC STATE.

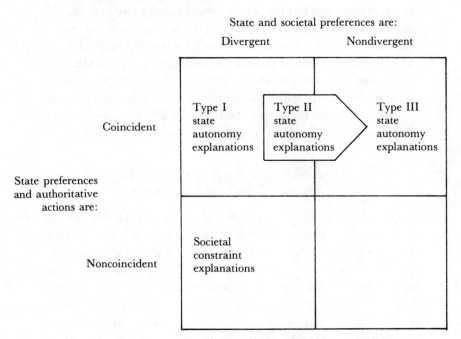

preferences are divergent and the state acts in accordance with society's preferences rather than its own. The anticipation, threat, or deployment of private resources and sanctions, dissuades public officials from acting on their own preferences or pressures them into translating private preferences into public policy.[12] The other box representing instances in which the state does not act upon its own preferences remains empty, which is exactly as it should be given the way in which authoritative actions are conceptualized. Having excluded the effectiveness of public policy and the actual impact it has on its intended targets, societal constraint explanations become the only ones capable of accounting for the state's inability to act upon its preferences.[13]

The upper half of figure 1 depicts three types of state-centered explanations. Type I state autonomy explanations are those in which state-society preferences diverge, with public officials being neither successfully pressured into translating societal preferences into public policy nor dissuaded by the threat of societal sanctions from acting upon their own. The representation of Type II state autonomy does not fit squarely within the figure because it includes a time dimension not found on the vertical or horizontal axes. State-society preferences are at first divergent. Public officials then purposefully bring about a shift in societal preferences to make them congruent or consonant with their own, followed by the translation of their now nondivergent preferences into public policy. Type III state autonomy explanations are those in which state-society preferences are nondivergent and the state acts upon its preferences. Although there are good reasons for interpreting Type III cases in a society-centered manner, with the state acting on it preferences because of societal support or nonopposition, the reasons for viewing them as state-centered accounts are at least as persuasive.

Strictly speaking, the different contextual conditions within which the state acts autonomously should not be used to refer to different *types* of autonomy. A logically correct formulation would refer to autonomous actions being taken under different kinds of conditions. However, so long as it is understood what the terms mean, there would seem to be no harm in using some shorthand language.

Here then are three types of autonomous actions, three very different ways in which public officials translate their preferences into public policy. Although not depicted in figure 1 so as not to make it overly complex, autonomous actions may be usefully distinguished in yet another manner, depending upon whether they involve one or two steps. Public officials may act autonomously by relying *solely* upon the inherent and exclusive powers of the state to make authoritative decisions. Here public officials translate their preferences into public policy without engaging in any behavior designed to alter societal preferences or to free themselves from societal constraints. They may also act autonomously by relying upon their inherent powers along with, or after engaging in, purposeful efforts to enhance their autonomy. Public officials capitalize upon what will be called the state's autonomy-enhancing capacities and opportunities to somehow forestall, neutralize, transform, resist, or overcome the societal constraints imposed upon them.

In applying this distinction to each type of state autonomy, Type I and Type III autonomy encompass both kinds of autonomous actions. Type I autonomy accounts include those in which the state relies solely upon its inherent powers to translate its preferences into public policy under conditions of divergence, and those in which public officials use their autonomy-enhancing capacities and opportunities to free themselves from the constraints imposed by those societally predominant actors who hold divergent preferences. This distinction relates to propositions five and six of the state-centered model set out earlier in this chapter. Type III autonomy accounts include both those in which the state simply relies upon its inherent powers in acting upon its preferences under conditions of nondivergence, and those in which it capitalizes upon its autonomy-enhancing capacities and opportunities to reinforce that nondivergence. Public officials take purposeful actions to forestall the emergence of societal preferences that diverge from their own. This distinction relates to propositions two and three of the state-centered model. Since Type II autonomy accounts are those in which public officials purposefully bring about a shift in the societal parallelogram of resource-weighted preferences, they are clearly not just employing the inherent powers of the state. They are also relying upon their autonomy-enhancing capacities and opportunities to alter society's policy views and/or the distribution of political resources between those whose preferences do and do not diverge from the state's. Only proposition four refers to Type II autonomy.

A final word about this study's central concept is needed to avoid a possible misunderstanding. Just as the prior concept of state preferences may be taken to imply unity within the state, that of state autonomy and the different types of autonomous actions is suggestive of public officials acting in unison. This kind of meaning should most certainly not be read into the concepts despite the shorthand language. For instance, Type II state autonomy refers only to the actions of those interested officials who control the weightiest intrastate resources in bringing about a change in societal preferences and then translating their own into public policy. These officials could constitute the entire state or all those with an interest in the issue at hand, but neither obviously obtains more than occasionally.

### Divergent State Preferences

The fit between state and societal preferences constitutes the critical context for distinguishing among different types of autonomy and for inquiring into the relative importance of state and societal actors in policy formation. It would therefore be patently desirable to determine the relative frequency with which divergent and nondivergent preferences appear. Yet no attempt will be made to estimate preference distributions. Doing so would hinge upon the resolution of a highly problematic and controversial issue—deciding upon the specificity with which discrete preferences are to be defined. Nor is it necessary to make the attempt. To discuss state autonomy under conditions of divergence and nondivergence all that needs to be established is that considerable variations in the fit between state and societal preferences exist, that there are numerous instances of divergence and nondivergence. At this point only the abundance of divergent preferences is discussed. The identification of nondivergent ones is set aside until Chapter 3.

It makes eminently good sense to explicate the appearance of divergent state preferences by focusing upon the characteristic and distinctive features of the state itself—those conditions and attributes that are common to many or most public officials and that differentiate them from the overwhelming number of societal actors. What public officials do, where they sit, whom they interact with, and what they see and know—these all tend

to generate distinctive interests, values, beliefs, and perceptions, and, as such, engender a goodly number of divergent
policy views. We can be more specific.

Most elected officials, and the overwhelming majority of appointed officials, are state careerists in a two-fold sense: the
state is their vocation and their career patterns are much more
influenced by other officials than by societal actors. The chief
reference groups for public officials are other public officials,
those with whom they closely interact and those they aspire to
succeed or replace. Promotions, assignments, responsibilities,
perquisites, professional reputation, influence, even tenure for
many elected officials are affected far more by other officials
than by societal actors. There are some exceptions — such as the
American president, whose reputation within the state is
largely a product of his societal standing[14] and whose reelection
depends far more on private than public actors — but not all
that many. Public officials very much turn to, look at, and allow their preferences to be shaped by other public officials.
They are professionals in the sociological use of the term.

The preferences of societal actors are determined by how the
policy alternatives are expected to affect them and other societal actors; as the targets of public policy they are concerned almost exclusively with policy consequences. Public officials, on
the other hand, attach additional process meanings and significance to public policies, since it is they who formulate, adopt,
and apply them. The processual costs and benefits associated
with alternative policy options are often given overriding
weight. They include the options' significance for relations with
other officials, rivalries between state units, existing routines
and practices, coordination, the scope of discretion, convenience, and predictability, not only in adopting but also in
formulating and applying public policies.

Public officials belong to one or more state units whose members share various "collective" or institutional interests. The interest of bureaucratic units in budgetary and staff expansion is
the one most widely remarked upon. Others include the maintenance of bureaucratic, executive, and legislative units, the

preservation (or expansion) of their formal powers, the absence of other units responsible for the same or overlapping "missions," noninterference of other public officials in the units' internal arrangements and decision processes, the maintenance of good morale and avoidance of friction, and their overall standing relative to other units with whom they are involved in the making of public policy. These institutional interests sharply impinge upon the relative attractiveness of policy alternatives.

Also relevant here are the distinctive, at times exclusive, information sources, skills, and experiences that help trigger certain preferences that are not yet on the issue agenda, and inform and shape those that are already there. It is too often forgotten that governing is in large part an intellectual exercise, and the knowledge of public officials and the criteria they apply are sufficiently different from that of most societal actors to make for a good number of divergent preferences. Public officials have a greater knowledge and appreciation of the available options' several ramifications, second-order consequences, implementation difficulties, and incompatibilities with one another and with existing public policies. This is by no means to suggest that public officials are in any way more competent decisionmakers than the ordinary voters among us, but rather that the decisions they make are sufficiently different in substance and kind to engender divergent preferences. Public and private actors tend to ask different questions and employ different frames of reference in answering them.

Charles W. Anderson stresses this point. What public officials know as state professionals — by seeing, training, expertise, and memory — is indeed used to confront, puzzle out, and form judgments about substantive societal problems and the effectiveness of the available options for dealing with them. "A policy is more than a state action or activity. It is a conscious contrivance reflecting human purposiveness."

Seen in this light, a policy cannot be satisfactorily "explained" simply as a product of certain socioeconomic conditions, or a given configuration of political pressures, or as the outcome of a particular political process, all of which are dominant motifs in contemporary policy study. It is also necessary to know what people *thought* of prevailing socioeconomic conditions, what claims and grievances interested parties brought forward, and how they debated and assessed these problems . . . The latent functions of politics are the capture and maintenance of power, the protection and advancement of self-interest, the preservation and expansion of institutions and offices. The modern social scientist frequently does not feel that he has produced an explanation of public policy until he has reduced the manifest justification to the latent function. In the eyes of most political scientists and sociologists, this is what policymakers *really* do. If one asks "What problems are these policymakers trying to solve?" a straightforward response might be that they are trying to stabilize prices without increasing unemployment. However, for most political scientists, what they are really doing is trying to get reelected, collecting IOUs for future logrolling, or contriving an expedient way out of the "fiscal crisis of the state" . . . [In contrast], we might look at policymaking as a creative, intellectual, problem-solving activity, wherein goals, puzzles, and problems are defined by certain frameworks of reasoning[15]

It is not necessary to go all the way with Anderson in saying that "We have, *first* of all, to understand what policymakers think they are doing on their own terms; what reasons they give for what they do."[16] Once state preferences are seen to derive not just from political pressures and reasons of self-interested expediency, but also from professional knowledge and "certain frameworks of reasoning," this suffices to give a partially divergent cast to the substantive content of state preferences.

The advent of the mixed-economy welfare state has increased the number of divergent state preferences by heightening the salience, expanding the scope, and increasing the frequency with which some of these just discussed considerations apply. The more burdened the state is with an overflowing agenda, the greater the importance of such process variables as convenience, coordination, predictability, routines, and relations with other officials in shaping state preferences. The larger the bureaucracy and the greater the interactions and interdependence of state units dealing with overlapping policies, the larger the impact of the units' collective interests upon state preferences. The heavier the state's involvement in social and economic guidance activities, the more do the special expertise, information, and policy experiences of public officials help form their preferences.

Not to be overlooked is a variously worded notion that the preferences of some public officials conform to the public interest, a conception of the public good that is not simply a summation of expressed societal interests. The idea has been subjected to sledgehammer attacks and analytical scalpels, but we need not become embroiled in the fray by claiming that the public interest constitutes a normatively defensible entity or some set of objective interests spanning time and space. It suffices to say something quite different. Because the self-image and role definitions of public officials are partly shaped by the responsible offices they hold and the prestigous institutions within which they are embedded, because of the "high" or strategically situated vantage points from which they view the world, and also because they can materially afford to be disinterested, some public officials come to hold long-term, broad gauged, inclusive conceptions of what constitutes the best interests of the societal groups who support them or of society as a whole. They perceive the public interest — correctly or incorrectly — to be something other than the summation, processing, or mediation of societal interests.[17] The public interest may refer to the interests of particular state institutions, the preservation of state legitimacy and political order, the avoidance of partisan extremes, the traditional norm of moderation, the application of exclusively rational, technocratic criteria in deciding among policy options, the reproduction of capitalism, special responsiveness to the preferences of politically disadvantaged groups, or the acceptance of present sacrifices for future gains.

To say that a larger proportion of public than private actors manifests long-term, encompassing beliefs about the best interests of particular societal groups or society as a whole is not necessarily to idealize the state. In fact, the present interpretation of the public interest notion is based on the recognition that individuals have a tendency, perhaps even a definite habit, of coming to believe in that which is advantageous for them. Public officials have several good reasons to believe in the palpability of the public interest, to develop a genuine commitment to it as a set of potentially realizable ideas.

As a phrase, the public interest and its equivalents — the best interests of all, the common good, the welfare of the country — have evocative meanings not only when voiced on great public occasions, in speechmaking before large audiences, and in other situations allowing for rhetorical flourishes, but also in materially consequential assertions, debates, and negotiations. To criticize a position that is adamantly said to be in the public interest necessitates a derision of the concept or an impugning of the proponent's sincerity; neither is easy, without cost, or regularly effective. The use of the term also offers a chance to exhibit personal commitment, firmness, and judiciousness to others, and if used often enough, it makes for psychic reassurance in the correctness of one's own position. It is, of course, public officials — those who are most responsible for the public interest, if not the monopolizers of the idea as in France and Italy — who can most effectively speak on its behalf. Doing so compels societal opponents to debate, negotiate, and discuss the issue at hand on the public officials' advantaged, even privileged grounds. Those who claim that their preferences are in accord with or shaped by considerations of the common good have some interpersonal and pragmatic leverage, a well-built platform from which to defend and impress their preferences upon society, for example, in pressuring reluctant labor and business associations into serious negotiations. It is the awareness of these considerations, be it conscious, dim, or subconscious, that reinforces the belief of public officials in the genuineness of their public interest preferences and the confidence that these are beneficial ones for society. In short, the public interest notion is "real" insofar as it has real consequences; it helps generate and reinforce divergent state preferences.

Lastly, there are the officials' preferences for the maximization of their autonomy, more specifically, their freedom from societal pressures and constraints, without, it needs to be said, a corresponding loss of societal support. There are those who choose to view themselves solely as representatives of constituent and client interests, thinking it appropriate and correct that they act solely according to the latter's preferences rather than their own, even when unconstrained to do so. Structured, regularized state autonomy is of little interest for these officials. They also happen to constitute a minority. For the others, a structuring of state-society relations that preserves, further secures, or enhances their autonomy serves several goals and interests. The preeminent feature of the state is its authority to make and apply binding decisions. The wider the decisionmaking freedom of public officials, the better able they are to act like and see themselves as "State" officials. Structured autonomy permits public officials to translate a larger proportion of divergent preferences into public policy, and they can do so in ways that involve less strenuous efforts and fewer risks. It also means that public officials are less pressured and inconvenienced, concomitantly allowing them to devote more attention to the state's internal relations which are of such importance to them. And hardly of small import, they can feel more secure in their tenure as elected officials. The strains of governing are eased.

Over and above bringing together the sources of divergent state preferences as a way of underscoring the many instances in which public and private preferences are different or incompatible, this discussion indicates that the democratic state is to some significant extent subjectively autonomous. Many of its preferences are self-generated rather than shaped by societal influences and conditions. State preferences derive from several characteristic and distinctive features of the state itself: the state is a career for most public officials and their colleagues generally serve as more salient reference groups than do societal actors; preferences for alternative policy options are affected by their attendant processual and decisionmaking costs and benefits; public officials subscribe to the collective interests of their own state units which often impinge strongly upon the relative attractiveness of policy alternatives; some policy preferences have an intellectualized component which is informed by the officials' more or less distinctive information sources, experiences, skills, and professional knowledge; a significant number of public officials hold public interest preferences that differ from some summation of societal preferences because of their role definitions, strategic positioning, and a more or less conscious awareness of the advantages attendant upon the holding of such preferences; and the distinctive attribute of the state, the making and application of authoritative decisions, directly and indirectly generates a preference for the state's structured autonomy.

No doubt state preferences are also to be understood in terms of societal factors. These would include the social backgrounds, socialization experiences, education, and professional training of public officials prior to their recruitment; the historical memories that form the traditions of numerous generations and the recent societal crises that affect the attitudes of current generations; the information produced and appeals made by all sorts of regional, ethnic, and class actors and specialized associations; and the economy's structural features as they impinge upon the intellectual and value laden components of state preferences. These could turn out to have a greater impact upon state preferences than do the characteristic and distinctive features of the state itself, especially with respect to the convergent state-society preferences discussed in Chapter 3. But in all probability they do not overshadow the state's internally generated preferences. The democratic state is significantly autonomous in this subjective sense.

### A Short Prolegomenon

The point will be made again, but let it be said clearly at the outset: this study does not purport to offer an empirical validation of the state-centered propositions. It does not pretend to provide sufficient evidence to substantiate the propositions in a direct, empirical manner. I cannot even hope to do so at this point because there are a distinctly limited number of case studies to draw on, and even fewer studies that address the broad issue of state autonomy versus societal constraint explanations in a direct and unbiased manner, largely due to the nearly unquestioned reliance upon the societal constraint assumptions. What this book does aim for is to demonstrate the persuasiveness of the state-centered propositions, their eminent plausibility. The persuasiveness of a generalized statement can be assessed in two ways, and these take on special importance when there is a scarcity of confirming or disconfirming evidence that bears directly upon it. Its plausibility very much hinges upon the manner in which the propositions have been developed, the methodology broadly conceived, and the persuasiveness of the underlying arguments. The concluding chapter summarizes the eight methodological considerations and eleven substantive ones that, when taken together, are thought to constitute a convincing case for the plausibility of the state-centered model.

In making as persuasive a case as I can for each state-centered proposition, it will never knowingly be forgotten that the subject of this book is the *democratic* state, the state within a regime featuring a democratic format. None of the authoritative actions or autonomy-enhancing capacities and opportunities identified here in any way contravene the democratic format — the rules, procedures, and prescriptions that guarantee and provide for open, fair, and regular elections, and the (minimally curtailed) freedoms of expression and organization upon which they depend. For example, although the state has a near coercive monopoly whose significance in intimidating and restricting its opponents should not be underestimated, the arguments for the autonomy of the democratic state do not even hint of coercion. Nor do any of the arguments refer to illegal actions or those whose substantive content is illegally secreted away. Had these been included the democratic state would appear more autonomous, especially in national security matters, than as portrayed here.

While this is indeed a state-centered study, nowhere is it said or implicitly assumed that public officials are fundamentally any different from politically involved societal actors, either as individuals or as the constituent elements of groups, associations, regional blocs, ethnic segments, social classes, labor unions, and corporations. Both public and private actors have as their most fundamental, and nearly all-embracing, goals the realization of both autonomy and support—the independence to act on their own volitions without a consequent loss of support, commonly along with some combination of respect, liking, and applause from others. Ideally, autonomy and support are present in full measure, allowing for the fulfillment of nearly all wants, interests, norms, and values. But the world is far from being an ideal one for either public or private actors; difficult choices often have to be made, trade-offs accepted between autonomy and support. It is therefore incumbent upon me to show that in choosing to translate their preferences into public policy under conditions of divergence, as well as in choosing to capitalize upon their autonomy-enhancing capacities and opportunities, democratic officials either are willing to suffer a loss of societal support, which is not all that rare, or more commonly, do not expect societal sanctions to be applied against them.

A substantial part of this study is devoted to a review, interpretation, and critique of the literature on empirical democratic theory and public policy formation broadly conceived. There are several reasons for doing so. Far more than any others, these two bodies of writings have as their core analytical problem the same one that forms the centerpiece of this book—the explanation of the democratic state's authoritative actions. As such, it is most appropriate to delineate the ways in which their analyses overlap with and depart from my own. Empirical democratic theory and public policy studies both evidence an inordinate reliance upon the societal constraint assumptions. This point is worth stressing in and of itself. It also directs us toward a critical discussion of the limits and limitations of the assumptions. More broadly, it

allows for the question: How plausible are state autonomy accounts relative to the alternative societal constraint explanations? Lastly, since some small part of these writings do in fact
provide support for the state-centered model, they will be fully
used—both substantively and in identifying the outer limits of
what are on the whole two decidedly society-centered bodies of
literature.

# 2

## Societal Constraint
## of the State

SOCIETY-CENTERED ACCOUNTS of the democratic state's authoritative actions focus on the distribution of private preferences in conjunction with the varying weights of the political resources that stand behind them. As such, they revolve around and decisively hinge upon a set of interrelated societal constraint assumptions. The state is continuously and inordinately dependent upon societal actors for a variety of specific and diffuse supports, from votes on election day to assistance in the implementation of public policy on a day-to-day basis. Private actors control a great armory of political resources and others that are readily translatable into political coin with which to importune, threaten, pressure, and levy sanctions against the state. Those who control a disproportionate share of the resources over time or with respect to any one issue deploy them effectively in exerting control over the state directly, and indirectly, by using them to attain a predominant position within civil society.

Several different, but only partly incompatible, interpretations of the democratic state are derived from these assumptions. The most unabashedly society-centered one is now largely outmoded. Here the state almost literally serves as nothing more than a "cash register" that accurately totals up the resource credits and debits of contending societal groups ("the balance of power") and then authoritatively "ratifies" the outcome of the societal competition.[1] According to a marginally different interpretation, the state is seen as little more than an arena in which societal interests are represented and societal struggles played out. In a significantly less one-sided one, the state aggregates and processes societal demands, mediating and arbitrating among and between societal groups, thereby adding something of its own to the resultant policies. In effect, the least society-centered interpretation of the state drawn from the societal constraint assumptions sidesteps them. They are implicitly accepted, certainly not questioned, in the course of highlighting the mutuality of interests between the state as a whole and those actors who predominate within civil society, or between separate state units and the societal actors who predominate within narrow issue areas. In the absence of divergent state-society preferences, the state acts on its own preferences and responds to society's at one and the same time.

Whatever view of the state is derived from the societal constraint assumptions, little if any acknowledgment is given to its independent impact in shaping societal preferences per se and in altering the distribution of societal resources behind them. Most or nearly all public policies are understood as responses to the politically weightiest societal expectations, demands, and pressures; the state is almost invariably unwilling or unable to act upon its preferences when these diverge from society's. If society does not literally predominate from a position above the state, it very much controls it from below. Being subject and subjected to the societal constraints, the state is vulnerable and malleable; those who predominate within civil society dominate the democratic state.

The societal constraint assumptions are central to empirical democratic theory and public policy studies. The conception of the state found in nearly all of these writings is drawn directly from them; their generalized and specific explanations of public policy very much depend upon them.

### Empirical Democratic Theory and Public Policy Studies
No single empirical democratic theory is embraced by nearly all or even most students of democratic politics. There are,

however, four well-subscribed theoretical variants, each of which presents a distinctive interpretation of the contours of civil society and patterns of state-society relations: the pluralist school, headed by David B. Truman and Robert A. Dahl;[2] the neopluralist interpretation, developed primarily by Grant Mc-Connell and Theodore J. Lowi;[3] the social corporatist variant, best exemplified by Stein Rokkan and Phillippe Schmitter;[4] and Marxist theory, as recently amplified by Ralph Miliband and Nicos Poulantzas.[5] Despite the variants' very different, often incompatible accounts of authoritative state actions, their competing explanations derive from the same core assumptions. The great debate in empirical democratic theory is not about the enormous and overriding impact that private actors have upon public policy, for despite some differences, all four variants are at one in looking primarily, often exclusively, to civil society in order to understand what the state does and why it does so.

The crucial differences among the variants have to do with varying depictions of the patterned relations among societal actors, the manner in which they influence public policy, the relative weight of different political resources within civil society, and most important, their differential effectiveness in constraining the state. Knowing which resources are exceptionally effective in influencing public officials and how these are distributed within civil society allows for the identification of what will be called the effective demand groups. These are the private actors who control most of the especially effective political resources, which means that they predominate relative to other societal actors and are most successful in constraining the state. The great debate then turns primarily on the question: Which societal actors constitute the effective demand groups?[6]

For pluralists, any and all sizable groups that attempt to influence the state are effective demand groups. Given the identification of a large and diverse number of especially effective political resources, along with their widespread, non-cumulative distribution, the effective demand group universe is indeed an encompassing one. The political marketplace is nearly coterminous with civil society. The especially effective resources encompass numbers, votes, money, organization, information, expertise, social status, professional reputation, access to the mass media, and control over economic resources among others. It is then hardly surprising that "virtually no one, and certainly no group of more than a few individuals, is entirely lacking in some influence resources."[7] Public policy is seen as the "resultant of effective access by various interests," as in Truman's compendious study in which not a single state unit is said to have acted contrary to the politically weightiest preferences. With public officials even evincing concern about the preferences of "potential groups," the possibility of Type I or Type II state autonomy is barely thinkable.

In neopluralism, the effective demand group universe is limited to particularly well-organized, financially well-endowed groups with primary interests in narrow bands of public policy. The especially effective resources are strictly limited to organization, money, and specialized policy concerns, which tend to cumulate among small groups with politically homogeneous memberships. Partly because of the effectiveness of their resources, along with the public officials' own ideology of "interest-group liberalism," the state enfranchises the "most interested and best organized" business, labor, agricultural, trade, and professional associations as the exclusive representatives of particular societal interests. Separate legislative and administrative units regularly consult with, take the advice of, and act according to the preferences of these clientele groups; indeed, public officials are "beholden" to and often are the "captives" of, the specialized demand groups within their narrow constituencies.

Social corporatism is most fully, but not solely, applicable to Sweden, Norway, Denmark, Finland, Austria, and the Netherlands. Here the effective demand groups are the numerous functional associations and, where present, the national peak associations that represent almost all of the labor, business, and agricultural sectors. Their especially effective resources include a high density of membership (the vast majority of functionally and sectorally situated actors belong to the associations), exceedingly large memberships in the case of the peak associations, centralized organization, control over critical economic resources, along with technical expertise and specialized information. These resources are deployed by association representatives in their interactions with one another and public officials at high and middle levels, not only in proferring and formulating, but also in adopting and applying most public policies. Public officials respond to associational preferences in accordance with the resources they bring to bear upon one another and the state, and the response is modified only by considerations of mutual advantage and a shared set of technical-managerial criteria. The possibility of the state acting contrary to the resource-weighted preferences of the effective demand groups is denied, ignored, or barely hinted at.

According to Marxist theory, the distribution of political power in capitalist societies is intimately and inextricably bound up with control over private property. It is first and foremost among the exceptionally effective resources. The effective demand group universe is made up exclusively of the economically dominant class, analytically specified as the bourgeoisie or capital. Marx draws a firm and unwavering connection between private property and the state. "Modern private property corresponds [to] the modern state, which, purchased gradually by the owners of property by means of taxation, has fallen entirely into their hands through the national debt, and its existence has become wholly dependent on the commercial credit which the owners of property, the bourgeoisie, extend to it, as reflected in the rise and fall of State funds on the stock exchange."[8] Private property, or the control over the means of production, also derives its special effectiveness from its exceptional fungibility. It is translatable into such diverse political coin as well-financed organizing efforts, contributions to party coffers, control over the mass media, and the threat of "investment strikes." It is these resources that at

one and the same time make for the bourgeoisie's predominance over other societal actors and the state's practically
unswerving dependence upon it. According to this, "primary
view of the state" in Marxist theory, the state is an "instrument"
in the hands of capital, compelled to act as the "agent" of the
bourgeoisie.

There are, of course, other differences among these variants.
The most pronounced ones distinguish Marxism from the three
variants of liberal political theory. For instance, in accounting
for political stability, Marxism assigns far greater weight to the
coercive domination of the subordinate class by both the state
and the bourgeoisie, while liberal theory accords more importance to the legitimacy of state authority. But despite such incompatibilities and some very different assertions about the formation and substance of public policy among the four variants,
scholars working within each would agree on one fundamental
assertion. Whoever has *correctly* identified the especially effective political resources within civil society can circumscribe the
effective demand group universe, with its resource-weighted
preferences then accounting for many or most authoritative actions, and almost invariably constraining the state from acting
on its divergent preferences. Although not equally so, each of
the three variants of liberal democratic theory and Marxism
thus offers decidedly society-centered accounts of public policy
formation; they are reductionist in looking to society for the
most basic, if not also for the immediate, explanations of public
policy.⁹

This overall characterization of empirical democratic theory
must immediately be modified in at least one important
respect. Although the proposition is not at the core of Marxist
theory and, more important, it is applicable only on occasion
at most, Marxism does make a powerful claim for the Type I
autonomy of the state in capitalist society. According to the
"relative autonomy" of the state proposition, the capitalist
state acts contrary to the demands of a shortsighted, narrow-
minded bourgeoisie in order to safeguard capitalist relations of

production and maintain political stability. This patently distinctive proposition about the democratic state is examined in Chapters 5 and 6.

Some Marxist scholars in particular would want to modify the society-centered characterization of empirical democratic theory in yet another way — stressing that structural Marxism is far more state-centered than is the primary, instrumental version. Rather than responding to the pressures of the effective demand groups as in instrumental Marxism (and the liberal variants of democratic theory), according to structural Marxism, public policy is made in response to objective, impersonal "constraints" — the "structural requisites" of the economy and polity. The state necessarily serves capitalist interests because it is solidly embedded, structurally and functionally, within capitalist relations of production. Its own viability depends directly upon the reproduction of capitalism, and both require authoritative actions to overcome capitalism's inherent economic and political contradictions. (These are discussed in Chapter 6.)

Although patently distinctive, structural Marxism does not seem to be any more state-centered than its instrumental counterpart. They differ primarily in explicating the state's preferences. Where structural Marxists look to the contradictions of capitalism and their impact upon the polity, instrumental Marxists look to the "social character" of state personnel — their recruitment from predominantly bourgeois class backgrounds, socialization experiences, education, business interests, professional contacts, social connections, and so on. Yet the upshot is basically similar: a powerful commitment to the reproduction of capitalism, based on some varying combination of structural necessities and capitalist values. With respect to Marxism's unabashedly state-centered assertion — the relative autonomy of the state proposition — the structural and instrumental versions are at one: whenever necessary the state acts on behalf of the long-run interests of capital and the capitalist state, even in the face of capital's overwhelming opposition. With respect to those policy issues that do not involve a divergence between the preferences of the state and capital and those that do not impinge significantly upon the preservation of capitalist relations of production and political stability, structural Marxism is silent or merges with the instrumental version.

Students of public policy formation in particular might be expected to focus upon the state, the public offcials who actually adopt, apply, and implement public policies, as Graham Allison does in his influential development of the "governmental politics" and "organizational process" models and their application to American decisions during the Cuban missile crisis.[10] There are, of course, many other public policy studies that explicate the preferences of public offcials and the processes involved in translating them into authoritative decisions. But nearly all of these — with a few exceptions that are discussed in later chapters — explicitly or implicitly accept the societal constraint assumptions. By and large, public policy is interpreted in terms of the resource-weighted parallelogram of societal preferences; when the explanatory focus is upon the state, it is not because public officials act contrary to societal preferences, but because the weightiest societal actors' preferences are congruent or consonant with the state's. Taken as a whole, the public policy literature is as much reliant upon and "constrained" by the societal constraint assumptions as is empirical democratic theory.

I cannot begin to review the abundant writings on each of the many policy areas — education, health, transportation, fiscal, monetary, defense, and so forth — in order to show that the societal constraint assumptions have a powerful hold on the field as a whole. But this can be accomplished in two other ways: by discussing what are the most commonly used typologies of policy issues and by reviewing the literature on the single most often studied substantive issue.

All typologies are premised upon one or more assumptions about political reality; many typologies are designed to engender explanations for variations in the phenomena being classified. Typologies of policy issues are premised upon the societal constraint assumptions and look to the preferences of private actors and the distribution of resources among them to account for public policy decisions. The three typologies most frequently cited and used are those developed by E. E. Schatt-schneider, James Q. Wilson, and Theodore J. Lowi.[11]

Schattschneider's *The Semi-Sovereign People* made a seminal contribution to what its subtitle refers to as "A Realist's View of Democracy in America." His central variable for distinguishing among different issues and for explaining the way in which they are decided is their scope — that is, the number of private actors who seek to influence the issue's authoritative resolution. "The outcome of all conflict is determined by the *scope* of its contagion. The number of people involved in any conflict determines what happens; every change in the number of parti-cipants, every increase or reduction in the number of partici-pants affects the result."[12] Using the issue's scope as the central dimension, Schattschneider distinguishes between "two con-trasting kinds of politics, *pressure politics* and *party politics,*" one involving small- and the other large-scale organizations. In the course of elucidating the characteristics of pressure politics we are given the often-quoted remark about its consequences for public policy. "The flaw in the pluralist heaven [which is said to ignore differences in issue scope] is that the heavenly chorus sings with a strong upper-class accent. Probably about 90 per cent of the people cannot get into the pressure system."[13] In short, the scope of an issue not only goes a long way in deter-mining its authoritative resolution, since scope is associated with the social characteristics and thus the interests of private actors, it also helps to determine whether policies are more or less heavily biased toward the socially privileged within civil society.

Wilson's demonstrably persuasive typology systematically builds upon the extent to which the issues broaden or narrow the incidence of costs and benefits among societal actors. The result is a four-fold classification: issues with distributed benefits and distributed costs; concentrated benefits and con-centrated costs; distributed benefits and concentrated costs;

and concentrated benefits and distributed costs. These patterns are closely associated with and help to determine whether the actors who seek to influence the state are already well organized or have a strong incentive to organize themselves. For instance, with respect to issues whose benefits are narrowly concentrated and costs widely distributed Wilson writes:

> Programs that benefit a well-defined special interest but impose, or appear to impose, no visible costs on any other well-defined interest will attract the support of the organizations representing the benefited group and the opposition of none, or at best the hostility only of purposive associations having no stake in the matter. Of course, *all* programs that help a defined sector impose costs on somebody, but if the costs are widely distributed, usually in the form of generally higher taxes or prices, but the benefiits narrowly concentrated, the beneficiaries will have an incentive to organize and will be able to mobilize effective political support for the policy. Veterans' benefits, agricultural subsidies, oil import quotas, and tariffs on many commodities are all examples of such programs.[14]

Public officials respond to the societal parallelogram as it is weighted by both organization and numbers (public opinion and votes), as in Wilson's most recent application of his typology to the establishment of regulatory agencies and the passage of regulatory legislation.[15]

The most influential typology is Lowi's differentiation among "distributive," "regulative," and "redistributive" issues. It too focuses upon the issues' significance for and impact upon societal actors, which then directly and indirectly account for their authoritative resolution. Whether the issues are aggregative or disaggregative, generalized or narrow, related or unrelated in their significance, it is societal actors who are critical to the derivation of the typology. Where the issue is distributive in nature, the primary societal actors are individuals and firms; where it is regulatory, they are more inclusive groups; and where it is *re*distributive, they approach the scope of social classes and peak associations. Lowi amplifies the typology by linking these characteristics of the private actors who are attempting to influence the issue's resolution to the state arenas in which they are resolved and implemented — legislative committees, the legislature as a whole, the executive, and bureaucratic agencies. Thus, there is a two-step process of policy formation: the nature of the issue helps to determine the structure of the societal parallelogram, and depending upon where and how the involved actors' resources can be most effectively used to constrain the state, the societal parallelogram in turn helps direct the issue's resolution to one state arena or another.

Clearly these typologies rely heavily upon the societal constraint assumptions; they are designed to answer questions about the resource-weighted parallelogram of societal preferences. How many private interests does the issue impinge upon? In what ways do generalized issue differences engender varying societal alignments? How does the issue come to prompt the mobilization of varying numbers of societal actors with differential organizational capacities? How do alternative parallelograms help determine the state arena in which the issue is decided? Which resources are most effective in constraining which kinds of state units?

These are by far the most often cited and applied policy typologies. Neither they nor the others in the literature allow for some significant variation in the explanatory potency of the societal constraint assumptions. None is based upon the different salience that issues have for public and private actors, upon alternative configurations of state-society preferences, or upon the varying importance of public and private actors in shaping the authoritative resolution of issues. The closest approximation to this kind of policy analysis, although still distant from it, is found in Lowi's most recent amplification of his policy typology. Here the societal constraints are set aside, in effect, allowing for the development of hypotheses that relate the policy arena (regulatory, distributive, and redistributive) to the internal characteristics of the American and French bureaucracies that deal with them — the extent to which author-

ity is centralized in headquarters units or delegated to field
units, the different forms of coordination, the level of profes-
sionalism found among the civil servants, and the scope of their
discretionary powers.[16]

Among all the general and specific substantive policies considered in the policy formation literature, none have received
as much attention as the expansion of public expenditures over
time, cross-national differences in the size of the public sector,
and the broad contours of social policy. These overlapping
economic and social policies have been explicated primarily in
a society-centered manner, the societal constraint assumptions
regularly and uncritically applied.

The results of Daniel Tarschys' exhaustive review of some
two dozen explanations for the long- and short-term growth of
public expenditures are ordered according to the "consumer,"
"producer," and "financial perspectives."[17] Propositions that
view "citizens as consumers of public goods . . . who decide on
the scope and substance of government action" are clearly
societal constraint explanations. In contrast, the producer's
perspective at first appears to be decidedly state centered.
"There is no reason to believe that the suppliers of public goods
are idly awaiting the decisions of the consumers," and it is the
civil servants who are the "actual producers of public goods."
But the perspective's state-centered focus is significantly diluted
when Tarschys includes as producers all public employees (for
example, teachers, clerks, nurses), despite their not having formal decisionmaking authority, as well as those "private enterprises who sell most of their production to the government."
This perspective's societal constraint component also becomes
apparent when Tarschys refers to the efforts of producers to
influence governmental expenditures "either through regular
bureaucratic channels or through producer politics in the electoral or parliamentary arena." The financial perspective, which
considers the significance of "new resources" and "expanded
production," could be applied to both state and societal actors.
It is largely limited to the latter. The book by Alan R. Peacock
and Jack Wiseman, which argues that *citizen's* assessments of a

tolerable tax burden is the critical factor in determining the level of public expenditure, is characterized as "the best known representative of the 'financial perspective.' "[18]

In reviewing the extensive writings on social policy forma-tion — "state interventions designed to affect the free play of market forces in the interests of citizens' welfare" — Hugh Heclo identifies four kinds of explanations. These are "socioeconomic variables," "interest-group power," "the internal workings of government itself," and "the electoral process and party com-petition," with the "most pervasive tradition identifying the [lat-ter] as central to policy formation in democratic states."[19] While it may not be remarkable that only one of the four kinds of explanations considers the state's independent impact upon social policy, the studies that fall within this category are few in number, and the independent impact of the state does not ex-tend to the adoption of social policies via Type I or II autonomy. (Heclo's own analysis is discussed in Chapter 4 as one of the very few exceptions.)

David R. Cameron supplies a thoughtful synthesis as well as a sophisticated quantitative analysis of the five commonly cited explanations for the size and growth of the "public economy" — the portion of a country's economic product consumed and distributed by all public authorities.[20] A review of these ex-planations for cross-national and longitudinal differences in public spending again underscores the predominance of societal constraint accounts, and allows for some related obser-vations about this extensive body of writings.

A society's wealth as measured by per capita GNP is the single most oft-cited explanation for the size of the public economy. Although it need not be, it is interpreted exclusively in societal constraint terms. "As elaborated by numerous scholars of public finance, Wagner's 'law' suggests that citizens' demands for services and willingness to pay taxes are income-elastic, and therefore bound to increase with the increase in economic affluence. [Thus] . . . the greater the increment in economic affluence of a nation during a given period, the greater the expansion of the public economy." Those scholars who have doubts about the hypothesis base them solely upon societal preferences as these are shaped by "perceptions of marginal benefits" and the "tolerable burden of taxation." The hypothesis of an inverse relationship between affluence and public expenditures also relies upon and takes for granted the societal constraint assumptions, as in this encapsulation of Aaron Wildavsky's argument: "Where national affluence increases very rapidly, as in Japan, any increased demand for public funds can be met by the added revenues otained by applying a constant public share to a larger economic product. But where economic growth is so modest that it generates insufficient revenues to meet demands for additional public goods, as in Britain, those demands must be met through an expansion of the public share of the product."[21]

What Cameron calls the "political" explanation for variation in public expenditures is equally society centered. Societal preferences as expressed at election time determine public expenditures; public officials not only respond to electoral preferences but also bend over backwards in competing for votes. Political parties "bid up" the scope of expenditure programs to maximize their electoral attractiveness, voters generally act on their preferences for such programs, election outcomes determine the partisan composition of governments, and they in turn regularly translate electoral promises into public policy. In assessing this exclusively societal constraint depiction of public policy formation, Cameron mentions several reasons for thinking that a government's partisan makeup is not regularly translated into expenditure decisions.[22] Some of these—the inexperience of ministers relative to permanent civil servants, the influence of policy professionals among the civil servants, the attractions of incremental decisionmaking, and the restrictive effects of established routines—would be part and parcel of a state-centered interpretation of expenditure decisions.

Moreover, some empirical findings that support the societal

constraint interpretation of the relations between voting behavior and public expenditures could also be used in a partly state-centered scenario. "Empirical studies of the American electorate by Kramer and Tufte have demonstrated that voters have tended to provide short-term electoral rewards to incumbents who can effect, through their tax, fiscal, and monetary policies, increases in real personal income. And as Tufte demonstrates, because incumbents are aware of this relationship, most adopt policies in anticipation of elections which stimulate the economy and increase personal income by pumping funds into the economy."[23] To show that incumbents regularly make public policies that increase real personal income just prior to elections as a way of successfully enhancing their reelection efforts certainly buttresses the persuasiveness of societal constraint accounts generally. Yet neither Cameron nor Tufte even allude to an additional hypothesis that could be drawn from these findings. Might it not be that the incumbents' awareness of the relationship between increases in real personal income and voting behavior just prior to elections, along with their capacity to capitalize upon it, allows, even encourages, them to undertake distinctly unpopular actions in the one to four years before the next electoral contest? Knowing that they can win back much electoral support, it is hardly implausible to suppose that they are willing to act on their divergent preferences between elections — preferences relating to the size of the public economy and to just about any other issue.

The "fiscal explanation" revolves around the nondivisibility of public goods. The costs and benefits of public policies for private actors are not directly linked, benefits are frequently uncertain, and the overall provision of public goods is always suboptimal because all citizens pay for some programs that do not benefit them personally. Private costs or taxes consequently exceed the benefits. "Therefore, it is only when public officials can conceal the costs of policies in a 'fiscal illusion' that they can spend large amounts without incurring the wrath of the electorate."[24] Here is yet another explanation that focuses upon societal preferences. But while commonly interpreted in a societal constraint manner, it is possible to amplify the state-centered component and give it equal prominence. The "fiscal explanation" implicitly assumes that public officials periodically prefer to spend larger amounts than does the electorate as a whole, that they frequently increase the proportion of total revenues raised through indirect forms of taxation so as to "conceal" some of the costs born by the electorate, and that thereby they come to translate their own preferences into public policy. Divergent state preferences and state-devised strategies for acting upon them without suffering societal sanctions thus help account for the growth of the public sector.

A recently developed explanation for the size of the public economy relates it to the "openness" of a country's domestic economy to the international economy, its vulnerability and dependence upon the latter. Cameron's analysis of the data leads him to conclude that "the degree of trade dependence [as the chief measure of openness] is the best predictor" of variations in the growth of the public economy among the advanced industrial democracies during the years 1960-1975. He elucidates two interpretations of the data, a society- and a state-centered account of the strong association between the two variables.[25] With respect to the former, we are treated to an imaginative specification of a complex set of interrelationships by which "openness generates certain structural characteristics in advanced capitalist economies which are conducive to an expansion of the scope of the public economy." The openness of a country's economy is indirectly related to especially large public expenditures by way of the above average concentration of industry, high rates of unionization, strong labor confederations, a wide scope of collective bargaining, frequent emergence of left-dominated governments, and large increases in income supplements. Summarily, economic variations shape certain societal patterns which in turn lead to the election of governments that are given to increasing public expenditures.

The other interpretation of the data has to do with the "force of the exigencies posed by exposure to the international economy that causes government to extract and allocate a

larger share of the economic product." Here is a decidedly
state-centered interpretation of the association between openness to the international economy and the growth of the public
sector. "Just as a high degree of dependence on the international economy for markets for export industries may limit a
government's ability to manage aggregate demand and control
levels of unemployment and capital formation, a high degree of
penetration of the domestic market by external producers also
limits the control by the national government over the
economy." An economic variable is linked to a public policy
variable via its significance for and impact upon state
preferences — preferences for mitigating the effects of the international economy's vagaries upon a vulnerable domestic
economy so as to maintain a substantial measure of state control over employment, production, and consumption levels by
enlarging public expenditures.

Of the five explanations examined by Cameron, only the "institutional explanation" partakes both squarely and exculsively
of the state-centered perspective. "Downs, Niskanen, Wildavsky, and Tarschys argue that government bureaucracies
develop internal pressures for self-aggrandizement and expansion" — pressures whose fulfillment involves increased public
expenditures.[26] Since such goals are presumed to be largely
constant, the critical determinant becomes the "institutional
structure of government." The presence or absence of
numerous independent centers of authority and the degree of
fiscal centralization affects the bureaucratic agencies' opportunities for realizing their expansionary goals. "In nations
where no single authority controls the bulk of public spending
. . . and where the institutional structure guarantees that some
units and levels spend funds that were raised by other units or
levels, the rate of increase in spending should be unusually
high . . . [Federalism most especially] provides considerable
autonomy for subnational and local governments, fragments
the control of public spending, allows some levels or units the
luxury of spending funds which have been raised by other
levels or units, and multiplies the number of self-aggrandizing

bureaucracies." This explanation relies upon the characteristics of certain state units (bureaucracies) as these shape their members' preferences, which are then more or less frequently turned into state preferences depending upon the structured distribution of intrastate resources.

Still, neither this hypothesis nor the state-centered interpretation of the economic openness explanation provide fully state-centered accounts. If the weightiest societal actors prefer an expansion of the public economy, as most writers apparently maintain, then state-society preferences are convergent, irrespective of the differences in the underlying motivations of the relevant public and private actors. Given the nearly unquestioned acceptance of the societal constraint assumptions, it would therefore be argued that the state is able to translate its preferences into public policy *only* because it has the societal support to do so. Both hypotheses then lose most of their state-centered significance. On the other hand, if it is the case that societal preferences do not generally involve increased public expenditures, as maintained by some scholars, then divergent state-society preferences are present. If so, there is a problem: neither explanation for the public economy's expansion says anything at all about *how* public officials manage to act upon their preferences under conditions of divergence. It may be thought unreasonable to expect each hypothesis to be a complete one, but within the extensive body of writings that deals with the issue of public expenditures there is only one assertion that can even begin to fill this gap. Only the part of the previously discussed "fiscal explanation" that refers to the opportunities of public officials for concealing the societal costs of public policy, for creating a "fiscal illusion" via indirect forms of taxation, suggests anything at all about how the state can act upon its preference for greater public expenditures under conditions of divergence.

The heavy reliance upon societal constraint assumptions in the literature on empirical democratic theory and public policy formation is readily understandable: it generates highly plausible explanations. But are they invariably applicable and complete explanations, consistently the most powerful ones? Is their practically uncritical acceptance and near exclusive use justified? The focus upon the state's need for societal support, the great armory of privately controlled resources, and their consistent and effective deployment are clearly warranted, but are they warranted to the extent of practically ignoring the reverse side of the state-society coin?

## The Limits and Limitations
### of Societal Constraint Explanations

Any singularly focused theoretical statement with great explanatory ambitions is likely to have its distinct limits and limitations. When it is as widely accepted and applied as are the societal constraint assumptions, identifying limits and limitations becomes all the more important. The questions to be raised about the applicability and explanatory power of the societal constraint assumptions are important in and of themselves. They can also be read as a set of direct and indirect arguments on behalf of the Type I and Type II state autonomy propositions.

Public officials are unquestionably very much dependent upon the support of private actors. But just how much support are they actually searching for, how much is considered sufficient? If they aim for maximum support, the continuous applicability of societal constraints is not in doubt, at least on this score. But if there are thresholds of desired or needed support, societal constraints begin to lose their potency beyond those points. Several considerations suggest that sufficiency is at least as common as is the maximization of support. Pragmatically, most of the immediate goals of public officials do not necessitate maximum support for their realization. The subjective security of a legislator in his reelection is usually satisfied when a substantial majority (say two-thirds) of the voters are known to be firmly committed to him; a civil servant's goal in having an industry's cooperation in implementing an economic growth strategy is commonly satisfied when he has the backing of the largest firms within it. Also relevant is the microeconomists' central proposition of diminishing marginal utility, which is applicable to most values, not just material ones. Beyond a certain point the value of additional societal support falls off. The social psychologists' negativity proposition is also relevant. The positive subjective utility assigned to a possible or actual increase in a given value tends to be smaller than the negative utility associated with a possible or actual decrease of the same magnitude.[27] A possible loss of societal support tends to have a stronger effect upon the behavior of public officials than does a possible increase of the same magnitude.

The explanatory potency of the state's dependence upon societal support varies not only with the absolute level needed, but also with its importance relative to other interests, in particular, with the realization of the state's preferences. For the societal constraint assumptions to be consistently and fully operative under conditions of divergence, preserving or expanding societal support should outweigh the importance of state preferences. Having seen that the latter are often shaped by such highly valued and salient considerations as the collective interests of state units, a long-standing commitment to a policy mission, closely interdependent relations with other officials, and abiding concerns for the public interest, it is far from certain that maintaining societal support consistently takes precedence over the realization of state preferences. To this there is, of course, the reply found in a central tenet of empirical democratic theory: societal support is necessary for the reelection of incumbents and tenure is their single most important immediate goal, it being a necessary condition for the realization of most of their other important interests.

But consider the following reasons for not overgeneralizing this patently powerful assertion. First, although tenure is commonly the single most important goal, there are others and the value difference between them is not necessarily great.[28] Second, for many elected officials a loss of their positions can be partly if not largely offset by a continued quasi-public if not public career in other positions. Third, the tenet applies only to certain officials, namely, legislators and directly or indirectly elected executives, though they are obviously the most important ones in some respects. Fourth, among these officials the generalization has little applicability to those whose tenure is not primarily determined by the voters, as, for example, in the case of those European legislators elected by proportional representation, where other legislative and executive officials decide the position of an incumbent's name on the party list. Fifth, the tenet loses much of its applicability in the case of legislators who represent "safe" constituencies. Sixth, its applicability is at least somewhat limited in duration, primarily to the year or so before the next election. And seventh, there are a whole host of yet to be discussed possibilities — the state's Type I and Type II autonomy-enhancing capacities and opportunities — that allow incumbents to act contrary to societal preferences without losing, or expecting to lose, societal support.

It is widely recognized that public officials subscribe to substantially different role definitions. Edmund Burke is invariably cited in discussions of representation, at least to raise questions about the possible existence and significance of public officials who are strongly disposed to act according to their own best judgments when these differ from the expressed interests of their constituents, supporters, or society as a whole. Still, it is too often forgotten that some number of officials are disposed to act upon their preferences despite an expectation of ensuing societal sanctions because of their distinctive self-image as public officials and their sense of public responsibility. Certainly the Burkean notion of the independent and independently minded public official has not been incorporated into writings on democratic theory or public policy formation.

In a survey of the members of four American state legislatures, it was found that 63 percent of the total saw themselves as "Burkean Trustees," 14 percent as society instructed "Delegates," with another 23 percent combining or alternating between the two role definitions.[29] This is not to say that the data should be taken literally to mean that two-thirds of American state legislators would actually behave as "free agents," doing what they "consider right or just," acting on their "own judgments based on an assessment of the facts of each case." The open-ended interview item did not stipulate that by acting in such an independent manner the legislators would probably be subject to societal sanctions. The classification of role definitions was based on responses to the question, "How would you describe the job of being a legislator—what are the most important things you should do here?" The data also suffer from the general limitations of using survey studies to draw inferences about actual behavior. However, the numbers are striking, with four times as many of the legislators in California, New Jersey, Ohio, and Tennessee viewing themselves as Trustees than as Delegates.

Further evidence for the presence of Burkean legislators comes from the practically identical findings of three survey studies of the American, French, and Dutch national legislatures. The question wordings differed only slightly in asking the representatives about their likely reaction to a situation in which there is a divergence between their own preferences and those of their constituents, without however saying anything about the likeihood of societal sanctions. Leaving aside those respondents who sidestepped the thrust of the question, it turns out that more than five times as many legislators replied that they would act according to their own preferences. The split was 86-14 in favor of personal judgment or conscience in the United States, 85-15 in France, and 86-14 in the Netherlands.[30] Again, I am not about to infer that fully five times as many national legislators actually behave as they say they would, but surely the data indicate that the behavior of some significant proportion would be of a Burkean variety. These sharply etched findings among three culturally distinct bodies of public officials also raises the possibility that the holding of national responsibilities regularly engenders a role definition featuring considerable independence of societal actors.

Societal constraint assumptions are obviously warranted to

the extent of stressing the reluctance of most public officials to suffer societal sanctions, allowing themselves to be dissuaded from taking actions that are likely to trigger them. But the near exclusive reliance upon the assumption has the effect of leaving aside a critical question: What are the probabilities that the behavior of public officials — both authoritative actions and actions undertaken to enhance their autonomy — will eventuate in a significant loss of societal support? Societal constraint analyses are starkly and decisively based upon a consistently positive answer to this question. But sanctions are not always likely, the risks may even be on the low side, when societal actors do not attribute purposefulness or negative intentions to the state's authoritative actions as these effect their own interests; when only a small proportion of authoritative actions diverge from the societal actors' preferences; when disgruntled societal actors have little choice (they themselves are "constrained") but to continue providing support in order to realize their other preferences. Moreover, in Chapter 5 we will discuss several ways in which .public officials can persuade and dissuade societal actors who are disposed to impose sanctions upon them not to do so.

By focusing so much upon the state's need for societal support it is all too easy to arrive at a particular kind of misinterpretation, one which ignores or denies the independent impact of state preferences upon public policy. Where decisive actions are not forthcoming in circumstances manifestly calling for them, the state's paltry, hesitant policy responses are readily attributed to its unwillingness to sacrifice societal support on the altar of national needs. The absence of patently needed, decisive public policies is explained in terms of the constraining impact of resource-laden groups with incoherent, contradictory, or sharply opposing preferences. This could well be the case, but it could also be that much or most of the explanation relates to the state's own preferences.

Imagine a society confronted with an undeniably serious energy problem, one which public officials define as an energy "crisis." Yet they fail to come up with a coherent, decisive policy for dealing with it, despite some laborious efforts. Imagine further that a good number of weighty societal actors are opposed to any new energy policy, while others favor incompatible policies with respect to overall strategy and the allocation of costs and benefits. A societal constraint explanation for the absence of authoritative action, for a seemingly rudderless state, then becomes highly plausible, if not immediately accepted as patently valid. But there is an alternative explanation, not one which says that a divided society prevents the state from acting, but one which says that a divided state prevents the state from acting. Public officials have very different energy policy preferences; they have little confidence in the efficacy of the currently available options; they themselves are continuing to puzzle through the problem; and the interested officials control sufficient intrastate resources to preclude the emergence of a predominant coalition behind a single, coherent set of preferences. Such an interpretation is almost bound to be overlooked when state preferences generally are given little serious attention. If it is correct, appearances to the contrary notwithstanding, this hypothetical state is indeed acting in accordance with its preferences. Although hardly unimportant, it just so happens that these do not combine into coherent, decisive preferences. The person who cannot decide between a chocolate or vanilla ice cream cone is just as autonomous as the one who has an unswerving commitment to chocolate, assuming that both have fifty cents, that is, the capacity to act on their preferences, whether they are conflicted or crystal clear.

The great debate in empirical democratic theory is, as already seen, about which societal actors control the especially effective resources with which the state is constrained. Its prolonged irresolvability—the conflicting assessments of the relative influence of votes, organization, money, economic resources, and so on—is indirectly suggestive of the overall looseness of the societal constraints. Quite possibly the debate is an ongoing one, with no end in sight, not entirely because it is so difficult to gauge the relative effectiveness of different private resources, but at least partly because each variant of democratic theory makes an eminently plausible case for the special effectiveness of different societal resources. Each set of resources is just about equally weighty, or alternatively, their effectiveness varies in accordance with the diverse, specific circumstances and contextual conditions within which issues are resolved. On either interpretation the state enjoys considerable latitude in choosing which resources or groups it wants to rely upon for its needed support. The state's preferences can go some way in determining which societal actors or combination of actors it turns to, either on a regular basis or in accordance with the (perhaps readily manipulable) specific circumstances surrounding discrete issues. In light of the many diverse and conflicting preferences of the four effective demand groups, the state should have little difficulty in finding a societally predominant group or coalition of groups whose preferences are congruent with its own.

Some empirical support for this point comes from a preeminent public policy study. The broadest conclusion to be drawn from the intensive investigation of American trade and tariff decisions between 1953 and 1962 by Raymond A. Bauer, Ithiel De Sola Pool, and Lewis Anthony Dexter is that both pluralist and antipluralist (or elitist) analyses are wide of the mark. They miss the point "that individual and group interests get grossly redefined by the operation of the social institutions through which they must work. The political outcome [public policy] is something very different from the simple product of a parallelogram of forces input by the conflicting groups. Summing up the conflicting interests at work is only the beginning of political analysis. The heart of political analysis is the discovery of the transformation processes that make the political outputs something very different from what any of the interested parties wanted or sought."[31] Substantively, the principal conclusion of the study is that Congress has markedly more decisionmaking leeway than is widely supposed, and—especially germane at this point—much of the reason for its independence has to do with the numerous, conflicting pressures placed upon it.

> Congressmen feel much freer than most outsiders think. They need not be unduly constrained by demands from constituents, interest groups, or party . . . Among all the conditions that make congressmen free, there is one that deserves special attention; that is the fact that a congressman's own decisions largely determine what pressures will be communicated to him. Paradoxical as it may seem, their "freedom" comes from the excessive demands made on them. The complexity of their environment which seems to congressmen to rob them of initiative thrusts initiative back on them, for, when the demands on a man's resources clearly exceed his capacity to respond, he *must* select the problems and pressures to which to respond.[32]

Other limitations of the societal constraint assumptions become apparent when the state is considered seriously as an autonomy-seeking entity. Is it at all intuitively plausible that the modern democratic state—the elected and appointed officials who populate this large, weighty, resource-laden, institutionalized, highly prized ensemble of authoritative offices—is consistently unable or unwilling to act on its preferences when these diverge from the societal parallelogram of demands and resources? There is no need to deny the state's dependence upon societal actors who control and effectively deploy a great armory of private resources in order to claim that there is most assuredly a reverse (state-centered) side to the proverbial coin. Is the state not also well placed to exploit society's multifaceted dependence upon it and to capitalize upon different societal alignments? Do not public officials also have a diverse array of effective capacities and opportunities with which to deflect, neutralize, negate, ignore, and resist even the weightiest societal demands? Can the state not mitigate the effectiveness with which private resources are deployed and in other ways free itself from societal constraints?

Does not the state have capacities and opportunities to alter the substance of societal demands and the distribution of resources behind them? (These are not rhetorical questions; they receive specific affirmative answers in Chapters 4, 5, and 6.)

After again stressing the plausibility and explanatory power of the societal constraint assumptions, it must also be said that they are just that — assumptions. Not a single study has systematically and empirically demonstrated that the weightiest societal demands regularly prevail under conditions of state-society divergence. Nor has a single study attempted to demonstrate the assumptions' validity by way of a purposeful and determined effort at falsification. This is said in awareness of the plethora of empirical studies whose explicit or implicit reliance upon the assumptions has produced an abundance of apparently confirming evidence in the form of general and specific societal constraint explanations for the public policies of the democratic state.

The evidence is certainly present, but just how persuasive can it be when its presence was almost foreordained? Many societal constraint accounts are partly, if not fully, valid, but nearly all most assuredly tend to be self-validating. In some, the reasoning is circular. In virtually all, the analysis is carried out within a "closed system" that allows only for various societal constraint conclusions. The dependent variable, public policy (sometimes even policy consequences), is used as the primary or sole indicator of the presumed independent variable, the resource-weighted parallelogram of societal preferences. On the *assumption* that the state is consistently responsive to societal preferences, the politically weightiest societal actors are identified as those whose preferences most closely approximate the state's authoritative actions, this correspondence then being recycled as evidence of both their constraining impact upon the state and resource predominance relative to societal actors with different preferences. Closed system analyses are not tautological, but they take for granted what has yet to be demonstrated, the validity of the societal constraint assumptions. The idea of the state acting contrary to the weightiest societal preferences is rejected from the outset or it is not examined as a possibility in the course of the analysis. Prematurely closed and circular analyses can then produce two incorrect conclusions: that the democratic state is consistently and decidedly constrained under conditions of divergence; that societal actors other than those identified as the predominant ones within civil society control most of the especially effective resources.

The societal constraint assumptions must be assessed primarily in the context of divergent state-society preferences. But two points should be made with respect to their significance where state and societal preferences do not diverge. The first is almost axiomatic. When the weightiest societal actors hold preferences that converge or are compatible with the state's, the primacy of the societal constraint assumptions almost necessarily becomes questionable. Just how problematic they become in generating the critical explanations for public policy formation will be addressed in the next chapter; it most certainly becomes hard to deny that the societal constraint assumptions lose a good deal of their applicability in this context. A second point concerning nondivergence is also taken up in the following chapter. There it will be argued that under conditions of nondivergence, public officials can almost freely take advantage of the societal constraints' inapplicability to free themselves from possible *future* constraints. They can purposefully reinforce existing patterns of societal convergence, deference, and indifference so as to forestall the emergence of potentially constraining divergent preferences, and they can do so with little risk of societal sanctions since their behavior does not run contrary to current societal preferences.

### The "Crisis of Democracy": An Alternative Interpretation

The "crisis of democracy" or "crisis of authority" literature offers a widely subscribed societal constraint interpretation that, more than any other, starkly denies the autonomy of several contemporary democratic states. The state in America, Britain, France, and Italy—and, less clearly, in Canada, Belgium, and the Netherlands — is depicted as decidedly weak, as literally overwhelmed by societal demands and besieged by societal groups.[33] Put differently, an overlapping "crisis of authority" and "crisis of democracy" make for a crisis of the democratic state. Since this widely accepted interpretation of democratic politics during the late 1960s and 1970s runs directly counter to my own, it should be considered for this reason alone. The interpretation's accuracy is open to some serious doubts. It might be argued that both in absolute and historically relative terms the societal pressures upon the state have been overdrawn, for instance, by using only the most recent previous political decade of the quiescent, end-of-ideology 1950s as a benchmark — a benchmark that is something other than representative of democratic politics. But pursuing this tack would take us far afield. More germane for present purposes, it can be shown that even if the several claims of the "crisis of democracy" thesis are taken as fully valid, they do not preclude state autonomy; for the interpretation suffers the limits and limitations of an exclusive reliance upon the societal constraint assumptions. Contemporary American and European states may well be autonomous even if there has been a weakening of their legitimacy, governmental instability, and indecisiveness engendered by the absence of solid legislative majorities, an "overloading" of the state with a plethora of powerfully expressed societal demands, with society consequently becoming "ungovernable."

It should be possible to draw some inferences about state autonomy from the incidence of the variables that impinge upon it. The erosion of state legitimacy — the decline in respect and trust accorded high public officials, the popular disaffection prompted by fewer opportunities to participate in complex societal guidance decisions, the more frequent and deeper doubts about the regime's democratic authenticity — is most directly related to a decline in state autonomy when conceptualized as a loss of diffuse support. But given the variety of variables that could affect state autonomy, the weakening of democratic legitimacy alone should not be used to draw any firm conclusions about its decline, and certainly not about its absence. This much goes almost without saying, and does not run contrary to a literature that invokes additional reasons for the decline or absence of state autonomy. But what this society-centered literature does not do is consider other state-centered changes that might have more than offset the loss of legitimacy, the undermining of authority, as it impinges upon state autonomy. One possibility is that public officials responded to the decline in democratic legitimacy by shifting decision-making sites toward state units that are less susceptible to a loss of popular support, such as the bureaucracy, independent agencies, planning commissions, and social and economic councils. This would hardly be surprising given the interest of public officials in the regularized, structural preservation of their autonomy. It could also be that public expenditures in the late 1960s and 1970s increased at a faster rate than did the surge of politicization and participation (the "excess of democracy"); the mobilization of additional societal resources with which to constrain the state's allocation of public expenditures did not keep up with the latter's expansion. Moreover, the heightened interdependence of national economies during these years may have compelled domestically focused labor unions and corporations to become more reliant upon the public officials who handle the levers of international economic policy.

The translation of state preferences into authoritative actions indicates autonomy, but an inability to act because of intrastate divisions does not necessarily entail its absence. It depends on whether the divisions are due primarily to irreconcilable societal demands upon the state, or whether the public officials' own discordant preferences, supported by weighty intrastate resources, prevent decisions from being made. Legislatures that cannot make laws in the absence of issue majorities, as well as unstable, immobilized governments, could well constitute instances of public officials being unable to agree upon what (if any) authoritative actions to take, of irreconcilabilities among the officials' own preferences, rather than instances of societal constraint. Yet the exclusive concern with the latter leads away from, and possibly precludes, the serious examination of the alternative state-centered interpretation—one in which the state is autonomous despite its authoritative inactions.

To say that the state is "overloaded" with heightened societal demands, that the "demand explosion" cannot be dampened with existing public resources, is not necessarily to deny its autonomy. It can easily mean that public officials would like to fulfill these societal demands, but they are unable to do so given the absence of the necessary resources, that they are unwilling to try given their belief that certain societal problems are indeed intractable, or that they are intellectually incapable of doing so because the centralized powers of the state now exceed its "learning capacities." Since the preferences of public officials refer to realistic, potentially realizable goals, the inability, unwillingness, or intellectual incapacity to act upon their ideal preferences does not deny the state's autonomy. Paradoxically, on this interpretation of the "overload" thesis we may even have cases of Type I state autonomy. The state's ideal preferences converge with society's, but being realistic in recognizing that many societal demands cannot be fulfilled—doing so would "bankrupt" the public treasury or require a presently unavailable substitute for a tattered Keynesian economics—public officials prefer not to try to fulfill them. They act accordingly, despite great societal pressures. Again, the societal constraint assumptions directly or indirectly tend to obviate this kind of plausible interpretation, and thereby turn out to be self-validating.

Closely related to the "overloaded" state thesis is the claim that the combination of a demand explosion and stagnant public capacities makes for "ungovernability." If this undefined term refers to certain societal responses prompted by the anger and frustrations of unfulfilled demands, such as riots, demonstrations, and a decline in party identification, whether these detract from state autonomy remains an open question. They certainly do not allow for its denial, even without giving equal consideration to offsetting state-centered developments, such as the further shift of powers to the bureaucracy which is on the whole less constrained than are party dominant legislatures. On the other hand, if "ungovernability" means that public officials cannot act upon their preferences because of the demand explosion, the previous reaction to the "overload" thesis applies: it does not necessarily indicate a decline in autonomy, and even allows for a Type I state autonomy interpretation.

Could it be that the baneful and anxiety-producing predictions that flow from the "crisis of democracy" thesis have not materialized just because the state has, in fact, been far more autonomous than the interpretation allows?

In this chapter the literature on democratic theory and public policy formation has been shown to be pervasively and deeply society-centered; the following three chapters identify the outer state-centered limits of these writings. In this chapter the societal constraint assumptions were seen to have distinct limits and limitations; the next three chapters amplify and specify them in a "positive" fashion in the course of developing the rival state-centered model.

# 3

## Type III State Autonomy

According to Type III state autonomy accounts, public officials translate their preferences into authoritative actions in the absence of divergent state-society preferences. The politically best endowed private actors hold preferences that converge with those of the state and/or defer to the state's preferences, or virtually all significant societal actors are indifferent to state preferences.

Three concerns will occupy us in developing the state-centered model within the context of nondivergent state-society preferences: the frequency with which the state acts on its preferences, the relative explanatory weight assigned to public and private actors in interpreting what the state does and does not do, and the extent to which the state preserves its autonomy by forestalling the emergence of societal preferences that diverge from its own. These link up with the first three of the state-centered model's propositions. The first is at most marginally incompatible with the society-centered model, but the models begin to part company with respect to the second and third propositions. The extent to which they do so depends upon the particular interpretation placed upon the societal constraint assumptions. But even if the incompatibilities are minimal, the foci differ substantially. We will be getting into an area that is not covered in society-centered analyses.

## The Frequency of Type III State Autonomy

Among the panoply of state preferences many converge with, many are compatible with, and many diverge from societal preferences. This first proposition of the state-centered model may seem both unproblematic and not overly significant in and of itself. Its possibly problematic part—the existence of numerous state preferences that diverge from society's—was discussed in Chapter 1. The barely questionable point to be made here is the existence of many state preferences that are convergent and compatible with society's. But while unproblematic, it is indeed significant. With the state invariably acting on its preferences under conditions of nondivergence, the overall frequency of autonomous actions is directly related to the number of nondivergent preferences—an assertion which does not run counter to any society-centered hypothesis or assumption.

Ideally, we would like to estimate the number of nondivergent preferences. But as already noted with respect to divergent preferences, this is neither easily done nor necessary in order to make the point that they are many in number. The abundance of nondivergent preferences can be demonstrated by setting out the range of preferences they encompass, keeping in mind that to say nondivergence is to point to the incidence of Type III state autonomy.

There is surely no gainsaying that nondivergence is exceptionally consequential, and, in a sense, it obtains most often with respect to what are called the "grand issues" of politics. State and societal preferences converge on some fundamental ideas, sometimes so closely that neither set of actors need articulate them, and sometimes to such an extent that they constitute "nonissues." Some public and private actors do take exception to them, but their number and resources are insufficient to turn nonissues into live ones. In most advanced industrial democracies there is a state-society convergence on such grand issues as the desirability of public policies making for economic growth, a full employment economy, substantial corporate profits, the maintenance of the mixed-economy welfare state, the perpetuation of collective bargaining arrangements, and the protection of private property rights as currently defined.

Within democratic theory, each variant identifies certain basic preferences shared by the state and the effective demand groups:[1] the majoritarian decision rule as modified by compromise and bargaining in pluralist theory; the sharing of public powers with the "best organized and most interested" groups and the fulfillment of many of their specialized interests in neopluralism; the direct involvement of private association representatives with one another and public officials, and the application of technical-managerial criteria, in formulating most and adopting many public policies in social corporatism; the preservation of capitalist property and market relations and the realization of most of the bourgeoisie's specific economic interests in Marxist theory. Some of these are mutually exclusive. But with each variant identifying important convergent preferences, they are present whichever variant or combination of variants is thought to be valid.

Nondivergence also obtains during some crisis periods, with the weightiest societal actors wanting the state to act on its preferences. They may or may not have preferences on the issue at hand, and if they do, these may or may not diverge from the state's, but whichever obtains, deference to state preferences is overriding. The weightiest private actors believe that immediate or secretly decided state action is appropriate, obviating the solicitation of societal preferences; that national unity is critical for the effectiveness of any policy option, making for self-restraint in not voicing divergent preferences or expressions of support to permit the state to speak for the country; or that public officials have exclusive information sources, special expertise, and skills that make them best able to select the optimal course of action.

Societal deference is not limited to crisis episodes alone. In the case of some fairly routine decisions, it is especially hard for private actors to know how the selection of one policy option rather than another will actually affect their interests. Public officials are consequently allowed to act as they see fit. This is presumably most often the case when the state is dealing with highly technical issues, those whose consequences will not become apparent for some time, and national security and other international issues. For example, during the Bretton Woods period (1948-1971), America's well-organized grain farmers, exporters, and industrial workers allowed the executive to set international monetary policy; they were not able to predict whether their financial stakes would be favorably or adversely affected by complex policies featuring multiple ramifications and unintended consequences.[2]

Also relevant are those individuals whose attitudes toward the state regularly predispose them to acquiesce in its decisions. They exhibit a subjective willingness to grant independent authority to certain public officials, most commonly those who make up the executive. Such individuals tend to subscribe to procedural norms that legitimize the state's independence so long as it remains within the bounds of constitutional rules or unwritten norms, while others are acquiescent because of the great confidence they have in the capacities of particular public officials. Granted, acquiescent attitudes toward the state are far less in evidence now than they were in the past. But they are by no means absent. For example, in a 1966 survey of Conservative and Labour supporters among English manual workers, the respondents were presented with two situations. In one a Conservative Government and in the other a Labour Government were said to favor a certain policy, "like raising taxes," to which a majority of voters were opposed. They were then asked: "Should the Conservative/Labour Government go ahead with its policies which it believes to be for the good of the country even though the majority of people do not agree with them?" It is not surprising that more than two-thirds of the respondents approved of a Government made up of their own party leaders acting contrary to the preferences of most citizens. But a striking manifestation of acquiescent attitudes is found in the manual workers' reactions to a Government doing so that is staffed by the party to which they are opposed. Fully half of the respondents registered their approval of such an "opposition" Government acting contrary to the majority's preferences. When asked the reasons for their responses, an overwhelming number of those who reacted in an acquiescent manner mentioned some variation on the theme of Government leadership, for instance, saying that "The Government should do what it thinks right"; "We put them in power to get on with the job"; "The Government is there to lead."[3]

Then there are intrastate issues toward which virtually all societal actors are sometimes indifferent, including possible changes in the state units' formal powers relative to one another, policy implementation responsibilities, budgetary allotments, staffing, organization, and standard operating procedures. Many such issues do impinge, and impinge differentially, upon private interests, which is one reason for the appearance of opposing coalitions made up of both public and private actors. But others are of no concern to any politically significant private actors. The issue has no discernible relevance for them: its alternative resolutions do not have varying consequences for their interests; the possibly concerned actors do not have differentially hospitable or advantageous relations with the disputatious public officials; the intrastate issue is well embedded in a broader substantive one on which state-society preferences converge. Two exceptionally consequential intrastate issues that have evoked only societal indifference are the enlargement of governmental powers vis-à-vis the legislature, and the bureaucracy's powers relative to both the government and legislature. In post-1945 Britain, Germany, Sweden, Norway, and Austria (though not America, France, or Italy), few societal actors have apparently viewed these changes as salient issues.

Societal indifference is also found within some areas of convergence. It almost goes without saying that convergent preferences do not regularly include entirely identical, precisely shared preferences, and certainly not with respect to broadly defined issues. Societal preferences do not cover all questions of substance, procedure, application, and implementation.

Where societal actors are not totally indifferent, where their preferences are barely lukewarm or articulated, it should not be forgotten that public officials have their hands directly on the policy levers. With this kind of "hands on power" they readily pull them in accordance with their preferences when society evinces barely marginal interest.

Nor is it just that society is sometimes indifferent. The state is never indifferent, never neutral. At least some public officials hold distinct preferences on every possible authoritative action and inaction, including their most detailed, though not necessarily insignificant, aspects. Preferences are not only derived from the issue's substantive content. There are other reasons why every issue generates policy preferences on the part of some officials. The issue bears upon career interests and relations with other officials, involves greater or lesser convenience and predictability in policy formulation, adoption, and application, and has material or symbolic consequences for the state units' collective interests.

The range of nondivergent preferences thus encompasses authoritative actions whose targets are intrastate relations, state-society relations, and the collective and noncollective values of societal actors and their interactions with one another. Nondivergent preferences encompass broad and narrow, routine and crisis, domestic and international issues. The frequency with which nondivergent preferences appear is in fact greater than indicated by this discussion of their range for two reasons. First, only the most common areas of nondivergence were mentioned.[4] There are also other instances of nondivergence that appear sporadically and thus do not allow for generalizations to be made about them. Second, nondivergent preferences are by no means limited to instances in which practically *all* significant societal actors hold convergent or compatible preferences, nor to those instances in which the nondivergence is based *solely* upon convergence, deference, or indifference. There are all sorts of combinations that entail nondivergence. For example, in the purely hypothetical case in which all societal actors have equally weighty resources, nondivergence obtains when 30 percent of them hold divergent preferences, 20 percent subscribe to convergent preferences, 20 percent defer to the state's preferences, and 30 percent are indifferent. The societal parallelogram of resource-weighted preferences is then a nondivergent one in which the state has the support of 28 percent and is opposed by 21 percent of the interested actors, each of whom controls equal resources.

To repeat the point which serves as the primary rationale for this discussion, to say that state-society preferences are often nondivergent is to say that the state frequently engages in Type III autonomy actions and inactions.

### The Relative Explanatory Importance
### of Public and Private Actors

When state and societal preferences are nondivergent, public officials invariably translate their own preferences into authoritative actions, and their preferences have at least as much explanatory importance as societal preferences. It is the latter part of this second state-centered proposition — the claim that state preferences are at least as important as society's in interpreting instances of nondivergence — that is more or less forcefully denied by the societal constraint assumptions. To rely upon them is to place a society-centered interpretation upon Type III state autonomy, one which says or implicitly assumes that the state was able to act upon its preferences *because* of societal support or the absence of societal opposition. Were preferences divergent rather than nondivergent the state would not have been willing or able to act on its own.

When preferences converge we encounter the slippery problem of estimating the relative importance, power, or influence of two actors who more or less jointly succeed in realizing their shared preference. The easy and partly arbitrary way out is to assign equal weights or joint determinancy to the two actors. I would have no problem accepting such a "solution," but given the firm and pervasive grip of the societal constraint assumptions, this option may well be rejected. Another way to handle the problem is to estimate the relative strengths of the actors in those instances in which their preferences are divergent and then apply that assessment in probabilistic form to instances of convergence. This is, of course, the justification for placing society-centered interpretations upon authoritative actions in the context of convergent preferences. But what if the societal constraint assumptions do not have nearly as much explanatory power as claimed? If, as already suggested, they are subject to distinct limits and limitations, and if, as will be suggested in the following chapters, the state periodically acts on its preferences when these diverge from society's, then state preferences should be assigned a good measure of explanatory importance under conditions of convergence.

Take as an example the differential public benefits and advantages enjoyed by French economic interest groups. Some of them enjoy regular access and close relations with high-ranking civil servants, as well as being the consistent beneficiaries of public policy. Othes are without either. The patterned differentiation is readily explicable in society-centered terms, for the favored groups are decidedly more cohesive, organized, and technically proficient and they control greater economic resources. On the other hand, a state-centered interpretation is also persuasive. Ezra Suleiman's subtle analysis of the relations between high-ranking civil servants and interest groups does not report any instances in which the politically better endowed groups had to deploy their resources. Rather, the civil servants have a decided preference for these groups; they alone are "considered legitimate." Their political resources *per se* (cohesiveness, organization, technical proficiency, and concentrated economic controls) serve the bureaucracy's economic modernization strategy, and their "demands accord with government policy." State and societal preferences converge on an economic growth strategy featuring the concentration and modernization of French industry, and the state's promotion of exports. The dynamic economic groups with abundant political resources are thus the beneficiaries of public policy partly, if not primarily, because they are the preferred groups, while the "Malthusian" groups are generally disdained for reasons having little to do with their relatively weaker political endowments.[5]

This illustration is used not just to emphasize the problematics of a society-centered interpretation — something it does only too well, since Suleiman's analysis is carried out from the vantage point of the state. And this is exactly the other point to be made. Instances of convergence can be interpreted in state- or society-centered terms depending almost entirely upon the perspective from which the analyst chooses to view them. But these might be no more than appearances; they should not be allowed to affect the conclusion. Suleiman's analysis could easily be used to argue that state preferences have greater explanatory importance than society's, yet this should be resisted and is resisted here.

There is another approach to the problem. It involves moving back the link between public policy on the one hand and state and societal preferences on the other. The issue becomes one of accounting for the occupation of public offices by individuals who hold certain values and policy views. When addressed from this perspective, there is, of course, a powerful argument for placing a societal constraint interpretation upon cases of convergence: public officials are elected by private individuals and selected by other officials with societal preferences very much in mind. The argument is undeniably powerful, yet it is not a determining one with respect to the interpretive issue at hand. The presence of public officials whose preferences are congruent with society's is also explicable in state-centered terms. Public officials play a critical role in perpetuating themselves and recruiting others with similar preferences. Among others, their special opportunities and prerogatives for reproducing themselves include the self-assigned advantages of incumbency and the establishment of particular criteria for the recruitment of appointed officials. The limits and limitations of the societal constraint assumptions also have some relevance here. Their weaknesses in accounting for the adoption of public policies also pertain to the selection, assignments, promotion, and dismissal of nonelected officials. Moreover, to the extent that the state purposefully reinforces societal preferences that match its own—an argument developed in the following sections of this chapter—private actors come to prefer incumbents and challengers whose policy views are congruent with the state's.

This is not to argue that the slippery problem of counterfactuals, of estimating the relative influence of two actors upon a mutually desired outcome, can or cannot be circumvented. However, if it is thought possible to do so, on balance there is little justification for putting forward a societal constraint interpretation; one-sided interpretations of public policies adopted under conditions of convergence are usually just that—one-sided. In short, private actors must share the actual or hypothetical explanatory honors with the state when their preferences converge.

Whatever the exact distribution of honors in those instances, it shifts toward the state when compatible preferences are involved. Where society defers or is indifferent to state preferences, the latter enjoy at least some explanatory priority. The limits and limitations of the societal constraint assumptions call into doubt a one-sided interpretation which says that the state acted on its preferences because societal actors wanted or allowed it to do so. In terms of the substantive cast given to authoritative actions, the state's preferences have patent priority. All of the narrow crevices and many of the broad substantive contours of public policy are primarily explicable in terms of state preferences when these are consonant with society's. This is not to exclude the significance of societal preferences, but to point out that they stand somewhere in the explanatory background.

In the case of American decisions during the Cuban missile crisis, for example, the convergence of state and societal preferences on the need for a forceful response to the emplacement of Soviet missiles does not allow us to say whether public or private preferences were of greater explanatory importance. But beyond this area of convergence, beyond President Kennedy's "Excom" rejecting the nonforceful options, there still remained the critical selection of one forceful option from among several. On this question, by far the weightiest societal actors deferred to the state. As such, they stood in the explanatory background when the "Excom" rejected the invasion and air strike options in favor of a blockade of Cuba.

Taking convergent and compatible preferences together, it should then be evident that state preferences have at least as much explanatory importance as societal preferences under conditions of nondivergence. Moreover, the following pages offer additional support for this claim. When public officials purposefully forestall the emergence of divergent societal preferences so as to continue to act on their own, state-centered explanations must surely be assigned additional importance in interpreting the adoption of public policies under conditions of nondivergence.

### The State's Reinforcement of Nondivergent Societal Preferences in Empirical Democratic Theory and Public Policy Studies

There are all sorts of reasons why societal preferences are congruent or consonant with the state's over time and at any one time. But it is far beyond the scope of this book to explore those aspects of the socialization process, the continuing elaboration of historical traditions and memories, the contours of the social and economic structure, the distribution of political resources, the structural dimensions of state and regime, and the patterns of past and present public policy as they help make for societal convergence, deference, and indifference. On the other hand, it is most certainly within the bounds of a state-centered study to ask whether public officials undertake successful efforts to *reinforce* convergent and compatible preferences as a way of maintaining or increasing the extent to which they can act autonomously.

When state and societal preferences do not diverge, public officials periodically capitalize upon their autonomy-enhancing capacities and opportunities to reinforce societal convergence, deference, and indifference to forestall the emergence of preferences that diverge from the state's. Before developing this, the third proposition of the state-centered model, a few words of clarification. In contrast to Type II autonomy accounts, which involve a state-engineered shift of a divergent societal parallelogram via an alteration of preferences and/or resource distributions, Type III autonomy-enhancing efforts refer to instances of nondivergence and are limited to the reinforcement of societal preferences per se. The proposition is further delimited by its exclusive concern with purposeful state efforts, even though other behavioral and structural patterns may have similar consequences. For example, the complex structure of the modern democratic state tends to discourage societal attempts to influence public policy because it is often exceptionally difficult to identify the responsible public officials. But while structural complexity helps reinforce societal indifference, public officials have not knowingly fostered complexity with this goal in mind. The outer limits of the proposition's meaning may be gauged from the claim that the repetition of stale, outworn, largely meaningless ideas and phrases on the part of public officials has the effect of "dulling the critical faculties" of private actors.[6] Such rhetoric is sometimes used with the intent of reinforcing convergent preferences by relating authoritative actions to widely shared, largely unquestioned values and symbols, but it is not thought to be employed with the intent of dulling societal capacities to think critically, to assess the pros and cons of public policies.

The societal constraint assumptions do not present any problems for our proposition. Even if they are thought to be operative under conditions of nondivergence, they do not question the possibility of the state purposefully reinforcing nondivergent preferences. In fact, the proposition lends credence to the constraining consequences of divergent societal preferences. The state would not undertake efforts to forestall their emergence did they not have a potentially inhibiting impact upon it. Even so, empirical democratic theory and public policy studies are so firmly and extensively society-centered that they have little to say about the state's purposeful efforts to solidify convergent and compatible preferences.

In contrast to the pluralist, neopluralist, and social corporatist variants, which are silent on this score, Marxism includes numerous references to the purposeful "mystification" of the working class, to the cultural hegemony of the bourgeoisie achieved by getting the dominated class's "active consent" to its own domination. But the state itself is only marginally responsible for hindering the formation of a powerful sense of working-class consciousness by instilling certain beliefs and values, such as the identification of capitalist interests with the public interest. Nicos Poulantzas takes Antonio Gramsci sharply to task for assigning even a minimal role to the state in this regard.[7] The purposeful mystification of the working class — the reinforcement of its convergent preferences, indifference, and deference — is primarily attributed to societal actors — the mass media, corporations, conservative political parties, intellectuals ("bourgeois idealists"), and churches. Marxist writings that offer nonpurposeful, structural accounts of how false consciousness is instilled and reinforced are further removed from our state-centered concerns.

Public policy studies broadly conceived have more to contribute, although certainly not by virtue of their number. In fact, it may be only a marginal exaggeration to say that what they do contribute does not extend much beyond Murray Edelman's singularly important study of politics as "symbolic form," in which he elucidates the subjective impact of political actions over and above their "objective consequences."

> In all countries and cultures men dwell on lore about the state; what it is and does and should be. The lore includes much that is vague, yet comes to have a powerful emotional pull. It includes much that is plainly contrary to what we see happen, yet the myth is all the more firmly believed and the more dogmatically passed on to others because men want to believe it and it holds them together. Sometimes politics is not myth or emotion at all, but a cool and successful effort to get money from others or power over them. Perhaps it can be cool and successful for some only because it is obsessional, mythical, and emotional for some or for all . . . A man's relationship to the state is

complicated. The state benefits and it threatens. Now it is
"us" and often it is "them." It is an abstraction, but in its
name men are jailed or made rich on oil depletion allow-
ances and defense contracts, or killed in wars. For each individual the political constitution condenses all these
things, in all their ambivalence and ambiguity. In doing
so it symbolizes the complication that the individual is
himself . . . Political forms thus come to symbolize what
large masses of men need to believe about the state to reas-
sure themselves. It is the needs, hopes, and the anxieties of
men that determine their meanings.[8]

Here then is a fundamental assertion about the power and effectiveness of political forms in conveying benefits, as means of
expression, and as psychologically salient references.

It needs to be stressed that the potency of political actions as
evocative symbols is largely premised upon the remoteness of
the state. It is difficult, sometimes impossible, for private actors
to know whether authoritative actions are hurtful or helpful to
themselves; there are great obstacles in the way of determining
how public officials behave as well as imponderables in assessing their performance. When individuals are not aware of the
actual meaning of political acts "the meaning can only come
from [their] psychological needs." It is then that important or
controversial actions evoke a "quiescent or an aroused response," depending upon whether they are symbolically reassuring or threatening.[9]

I do not go all the way with Edelman in saying that it is "political actions that *chiefly* shape men's political wants and 'knowledge,' not the other way around."[10] But clearly something other
than the authoritative actions themselves, namely the impressions projected by public officials, serve as cues and reference
points which shape societal reactions to public policy, more
specifically for us, which reinforce societal convergence,
deference, and indifference. Impressions are most often con-
veyed by "the gestures and speeches that make up the drama of
the state." The importance of language in reinforcing nondivergent preferences is difficult to overemphasize.

> If politics is concerned with who gets what, or with the authoritative allocation of values, one may be pardoned for wondering why it need involve so much talk . . . The employment of language to sanctify action is exactly what makes politics different from other methods of allocating values. Through language a group can not only achieve an immediate result but also win the acquiescence of those whose lasting support is needed . . . It is fair enough to complain that the politician is not deft in his talk, but to complain that he talks is to miss the point. That talk is powerful is not due to any potency in words but to needs and emotions in men.[11]

Beyond these analytic guidelines, several of Edelman's specific generalizations bear upon particular Type III autonomy-enhancing capacities and opportunities for reinforcing nondivergent preferences.

His recurring reference to the great potency of widely shared, largely unquestioned values and symbols means that public officials can deepen the confidence and affect with which convergent preferences are held by wrapping up authoritative actions with these values and symbols. Given the well-established psychological proposition that people tend to read their own preferences into ambiguous statements and actions, by adopting a "passive" style — avoiding firm and specific positions — public officials can reinforce societal perceptions of a state-society convergence.[12] They can also reinforce deference to themselves by giving the impression of being in command of the situation; those who dramatize their competence tend to be "eagerly accepted" on their own terms. "The clue to what is politically effective is to be found not so much in verifiable good or bad effects flowing from political acts as in whether the incumbent can continue indefinitely to convey an impression of knowing what is to be done."[13]

The conceptual and empirical work of Peter Bachrach and Morton Baratz is especially relevant in thinking about how the state reinforces societal preferences that converge with its own. They argue persuasively that power has "two faces." Power is not only exercised when one actor participates in making decisions that affect another. "Power is also exercised when A devotes his energies to creating or enforcing social and political values and institutional practices that limit the scope of the political process to public consideration of only those issues which are comparatively innocuous to A. To the extent that A succeeds in doing this, B is prevented, for all practical purposes, from bringing to the fore any issues that might in their resolution be seriously detrimental to A's set of preferences."[14] It is from this two-fold view of power that Bachrach and Baratz derive their concept of a "nondecision"—"a decision that results in suppression or thwarting of a latent or manifest challenge to the values or interests of the decision-maker." Some forms of nondecisionmaking lie outside the purview of Type III autonomy-enhancing efforts. The one which speaks directly to the latter involves the purposeful invocation of "an existing bias of the political system—a norm, precedent, rule or procedure—to squelch a threatening demand or incipient issue. For example, a demand for change may be denied legitimacy by being branded socialistic, unpatriotic, immoral, or in violation of an established rule or procedure."[15] As nondecisionmakers public officials can forestall the transformation of some convergent preferences into divergent ones by discouraging their public consideration, keeping nonissues off the public agenda by labeling as extremist or irresponsible those who raise them.

It is within this framework that one small part of Charles E. Lindblom's multifaceted case for the "privileged position of business" in democratic regimes becomes relevant for present purposes. Among the several kinds of arguments presented, the chapter called "Circularity in Polyarchy" elucidates the corporations' actions in reinforcing the "consensus on what we have called the grand issues of politico-economic organization: private enterprise, a high degree of corporate autonomy, protection of the status quo on distribution of income and wealth, close consultation between business and government, and restriction of union demands to those consistent with business profitability, among others. [The corporations] try, through indoctrination, to keep all these issues from coming to the agenda of government." Over and above their own efforts in reinforcing the popular legitimization of the privileged position of business, "on the grand issues, corporate voice is joined by the voice of many government officials." Public officials want to shore up these popular preferences because "they are caught in a potential crossfire between privileged controls and polyarchal [that is, popular] controls. Hence they would like to remove from politics those highly divisive issues on which businessmen would be loath to yield. Since theirs is the task of seeing to it that business performs [its economic functions], they do not want the fundamentals of private enterprise to become lively political issues."[16]

There are other policy related studies that examine the behavior of public officials in shaping societal preferences.[17] But it is Edelman's seminal work that has provided the major impetus for this line of inquiry and delineated its theoretical contours; other studies do not seem to me to go much beyond it, including Edelman's most recent work, in which he develops the narrower argument that language is such an important political resource that it can very much determine how policies are enacted and how society reacts to them.[18]

### Type III Autonomy-Enhancing Strategies and Options

With these analytical leads and generalizations in mind, I want to come as close as possible to identifying all those capacities and opportunities that are available to the democratic state for reinforcing nondivergent preferences. Here, and with respect to their Type I and II autonomy-enhancing counterparts as well, this will be done by first setting out the three or four broad strategies that relate to each type of state autonomy. These refer to some combination of the societal actors at whom state efforts are directed (those with convergent, compatible, and divergent preferences) and what they are intended to accomplish (reinforcing existing preferences, altering preferences, changing the distribution of resources, or minimizing the extent and effectiveness with which resources are deployed). The strategies are used to generate and order the specific autonomy-enhancing capacities and opportunities that are available to the state. Once having identified them, I will refer to them as autonomy-enhancing options. Besides being a convenient shorthand alternative, the term "options" highlights the point that officials have real, diverse, and meaningful choices. They are more or less free to avail themselves of the options, choose from among them, and combine them for maximum effectiveness.

Type III autonomy-enhancing strategies are quite straightforward, for the way in which nondivergent preferences have been differentiated immediately points to the three sets of societal actors whose preferences are to be reinforced. Public officials can maintain or strengthen the degree of commitment of those societal actors whose preference converge with the state's. One option for doing so is to limit the dissemination of information that casts doubt on the advisability of the mutually preferred policy, for example, by legally restricting public knowledge of intrastate policy disputes. Another option involves publicizing and inflating the success of ongoing programs by crediting them with desirable outcomes upon which they did not in fact have much impact. According to the second strategy, public officials can maintain or solidify deference to the state on the part of those societal actors who want the state to act on its own preferences. They have the option of doing so by recruiting well-known experts for high official positions, as in the appointment of a professional economist to head the finance ministry. Public officials can also make it known that they are actively grappling with societal problems, looking for and developing remedies, for example, by reorganizing the state units in ways that seem to promise budgetary savings or the more effective use of existing personnel. Third, public officials can maintain or foster the indifference of those societal actors who do not hold preferences that relate to the state's. One option is to stress their impartiality among societal groups regardless of their more or less weighty resources, which could be done by creating a prestigous, nonpartisan fact-finding or advisory commission to consider a highly visible issue. Another is to claim that decisionmaking responsibility resides with "nonpolitical" state units that are beyond their control, for example, by pointing to the formal powers of city managers, judges, or managers of nationalized industries to explain or justify inaction.

These strategies yield the fifteen Type III autonomy-enhancing options set out in table I. Considering the number and diversity of options, it is no exaggeration to say that the means for forestalling the emergence of divergent preferences are hardly in short supply. This allows for considerable choice in identifying one or more appropriate options for the particular uses to which they are to be put. Almost all of these options are regularly available. Admittedly, public officials do not regularly have the chance to play up the exigencies of a situation or societal problem; nor are statist traditions and deferential attitudes toward authority which public officials can capitalize upon all that common. But except for these, it can be said that the appearance and usability of the options are not dependent upon unusual circumstances. Furthermore, none of the options requires any exceptional, and thus uncommon, qualities or skills on the part of public officials for their employment or effectiveness. This is not to suggest that just about every public official can effectively use any of the options, but rather, that they are not beyond the abilities and skills of the typical official, they are not restricted to a minority. We can then say that at least one to three Type III autonomy-enhancing options are regularly available as "live" options — ones that are appropriate for the issue at hand, there to be used, and relatively undemanding of their users.

Table I
Type III Autonomy-Enhancing Strategies and Options

Public officials can maintain or strengthen the degree of commitment of those societal actors whose preferences converge with the state's by:
  1. Limiting the dissemination of information that casts doubt on the advisability of the mutually preferred policy (for example, by le-

gally restricting public knowledge of intrastate policy disputes);

2. Making ambiguous statements and taking contradictory actions to allow societal actors to read their own preferences into them (for example, by not taking publicly firm and specific issue positions);

3. Publicizing and inflating the success of ongoing programs (for example, by crediting the programs with desirable outcomes upon which they did not in fact have much impact);

4. Discouraging serious consideration of divergent preferences, keeping "nonissues" off the public agenda (for example, by depicting those who raise them as extremist, irresponsible, or unpatriotic);

5. Relating authoritative actions to widely shared, largely unquestioned values and symbols (for example, by asserting that they are in the service of efficient administration, international stability, "the French people").

Public officials can maintain or solidify deference to the state on the part of those societal actors who want the state to act on its own preferences by:

6. Recruiting well-known experts for high official positions (for example, by selecting a professional economist to head the finance ministry);

7. Making it known that they are grappling with societal problems, actively looking for and developing remedies (for example, by reorganizing state units in ways that seem to promise budgetary savings or the more effective use of existing personnel);

8. Playing up the exigencies of a situation or societal problem, the need for prompt and decisive action (for example, by exaggerating a national security threat or its immediacy);

9. Capitalizing upon existing statist traditions and deferential attitudes toward authority (for example, by figuratively wrapping themselves up in the official garments of the state, placing themselves within its imposing settings, or taking part in its formal rituals);

10. Encouraging the belief that they are highly capable in dealing with the problem, that they know precisely what needs to be done (for example, by giving the impression of self-confidence, of being in command of the situation).

Public officials can maintain or foster the indifference of those societal actors who do not hold preferences that relate to the state's by:

11. Underscoring their impartiality among societal groups regardless of their more or less weighty resources (for example, by creating a prestigious, nonpartisan fact-finding or advisory commission to consider a highly visible issue);

12. Declaring that decisionmaking responsibility resides with "nonpolitical" state units that are beyond their control (for example, by pointing to the formal powers of city managers, judges, or managers of nationalized industries to explain and justify inaction);

13. Giving the impression that they evaluate policy alternatives in a highly rational, apolitical manner (for example, by adopting a technical-managerial style of decisionmaking);

14. Stressing their responsiveness to societal expectations and demands (for example, by recounting recent and forthcoming decisions on noncontroversial, consensual issues);

15. Highlighting the adherence to formal-legal procedures in the consideration and adoption of public policies (for example, by citing the formal powers of the state units within which they were made or announcing decisions amidst imposing formal settings).

Each option in our inventory is thought to be potentially effective in reinforcing nondivergent preferences. But this is not to say that they are applicable with respect to all kinds of issues or societal actors, nor that where applicable they are equally effective. At least a roughly discriminating analysis is then called for to indicate when and where the options are applicable and more or less effective. There is another, equally important rationale for such a discussion — that of showing these options to be applicable and effective over a wide rather than a narrow political landscape.

Two aspects of the political landscape are certainly among the most prominent ones in assessing the applicability of any autonomy-enhancing options. First, there are the characteristics of the issues to which state and societal preferences refer. Issue complexity serves as an encompassing, commonly used dimension with which to distinguish among the entire range of policy preferences. Complexity refers to the number of facets or components making up an issue, the degree to which these are interrelated, and the extent to which their specific interdependencies and policy consequences are difficult to predict. Second, there is the literal and figurative distance between the state and the relevant societal actors—the ease with which public and private actors can communicate with one another. The inclusive notion of distance captures the societal actors' levels of political involvement and participation and their direct and mediated relations with the state, with both being closely linked to the organizational variable. Much political activity occurs within, is channeled through, and is undertaken by organizations, and it is organization leaders, representatives, and staff who constitute many or most of the actors who enjoy close, direct connections with the state.

The Type III autonomy-enhancing options are applicable along the entire issue complexity continuum, although on the whole with somewhat greater effectiveness toward the more complex end. In the case of especially complex issues it becomes all the easier to shore up convergent preferences by making ambiguous statements and taking contradictory actions, and all the more likely that societal actors will read their own preferences into them. When the issues are highly complex, societal deference can be more effectively promoted insofar as the recruitment of well-known experts for high positions takes on special significance for societal actors, and public officials can more plausibly assert that they are grappling with stubborn societal problems. Public officials attempting to foster societal indifference by stressing their impartiality among societal groups and by giving the impression that they evaluate policy alternatives in a highly rational manner can do so more readily, and their efforts are more believable, when the issue at hand is especially complex. All other options apply about equally along the entire length of the continuum, with issue complexity neither adding to nor detracting from their effectiveness.

As may already have been surmised, the options are especially effective in reinforcing the preferences of private actors who literally and figuratively stand at a good distance from the state. Since the options involve rhetoric, posturing, appearances, and gestures in making different kinds of impressions, their applicability is very much contingent upon the inability of societal actors to compare the state's messages with actual policies, policy impact, and the policy consequential behavior of public officials. They are thus most effective when used to reinforce the preferences of societal actors who stand on the lower rungs of the various political participation and involvement ladders. These actors have no first-hand knowledge of the workings of the state and little reliable information about public policy and its actual effects. Indeed, these actors very much depend upon the visible behavior and pronouncements of public officials themselves, at least as mediated by the mass media, for what information they do have.

On the other hand, several options (1, 5, 6, 7, 8, and 13) involve behaviors that could very well be meaningful and materially consequential in and of themselves, over and above the impressions they make. And most of the intended impressions are far from being demonstrably false. Since they are not patently at variance with political realities, more or less irrelevant and misleading inferences can readily be drawn from them. As such, the options also have some applicability to private actors who are not very far removed from the state, those who stand on the middle rungs of the political participation and involvement ladders, for example, moderately active association members. Moreover, it is not just mass publics who sometimes defer to public officials in specific instances. Many among the politically engaged also evidence mild deferential tendencies which may be reinforced by the recruitment of well-known experts for high positions, by perceptions of public officials actively grappling with societal problems, by the exigencies of a situation or societal problem, by the activation of existing statist traditions, or by a belief in the decisionmaking capacities of public officials. These considerations are, of course, especially applicable to national security and international issues. On these issues not only is there a distinct tendency to defer to state preferences, in addition, the secrecy surrounding intended state actions, the relative absence of information sources other than the state itself, and the oftentimes great gap between authoritative actions and consequences constitute advantageous contextual conditions that extend the applicability and heighten the effectiveness of the state's options for reinforcing societal deference.

To a considerable degree the overall effectiveness of any set of options also depends upon the possibility of using several of them simultaneously. The larger the number that can be employed at any one time, their separate impacts being additive or even mutually reinforcing, the more likely it is that they will have their intended effects. On this score there are two reasons for according a good measure of effectiveness to the Type III autonomy-enhancing options. First, only a few are incompatible in and of themselves. Most obviously, public officials cannot easily claim that decisionmaking responsibility resides with "nonpolitical" state units beyond their control or make ambiguous statements and take contradictory actions, while pursuing the several activist options (3, 6, 7, 8, 9, 10, 13, and 14). But for the rest, public officials can put together a handful of options to maximize the extent to which nondivergent preferences are reinforced, such as the mutually reinforcing combinations of numbers 5, 7, 8, 9, and 10 and of 1, 4, 5, 6, 11, and 13. Second, there are few problems standing in the way of the simultaneous use of several options because there are no apparent conflicts among those societal actors whose preferences converge with the state's, who defer to the state's preferences, and who are indifferent to the state's preferences. All three autonomy-enhancing strategies can thus be pursued simultaneously even though they are directed at different societal actors.

Having discussed their regular availability as "live" options, their applicability, and their effectiveness, there is still a critical question to be asked of these options: How likely is it that they will actually be used? The single most important and encompassing factor determining whether or not public officials avail themselves of the opportunity to do so is their expectation of society's reaction. Is their use more or less likely to result in a loss of societal support, in the application of societal sanctions against the public officials who capitalize upon the state's autonomy-enhancing capacities and opportunities?

The probability of sanctions is definitely on the low side, even approaching zero. Public officials who avail themselves of the options for reinforcing current societal preferences are not taking authoritative actions that run counter to societal preferences, nor behaving in ways that appear to be leading up to such actions. Moreover, neither the behavior of public officials nor the intentions attributable to them are seen to involve purposeful efforts to forestall the emergence of divergent preferences. Public officials who avail themselves of any one of the fifteen options are likely to be seen as furthering societal preferences and/or as attempting to maximize societal support, which hardly calls for societal sanctions, as might visibly purposeful actions designed to shape societal preferences. Even in those few instances in which the officials' manipulative efforts are recognized as such, the probabilities of societal sanctions are still on the low side, for the options do not detract from the societal actors' "targeted" preferences or significantly jeopardize their others. With so little, if any, risk involved, and a good deal to be gained in avoiding the potentially constraining effects of divergent societal preferences, public officials are wont to make frequent use of the numerous Type III autonomy-enhancing options.

The three state-centered propositions discussed in this chapter are the least problematic ones, for they tend less to challenge than to complement the societal constraint assumptions by focusing upon the state. The following chapter constitutes far more of a challenge to them, although not a totally direct one.

# 4

## Type II State Autonomy

TYPE II STATE AUTONOMY accounts are those in which state and societal preferences diverge and public officials purposefully bring about a shift in the societal parallelogram of resource-weighted preferences, then translating their now nondivergent preferences into authoritative actions. The periodic occurrence of Type II autonomy constitutes our fourth state-centered proposition. If taken to their extremes, or by imputing something to them that is only there implicitly, the societal constraint assumptions deny the possibility of Type II state autonomy. The democratic state is said to be so highly constrained that it is regularly dissuaded from trying to shift the societal parallelogram; the attempt would trigger unacceptable societal sanctions and would probably not succeed. This interpretation is part of an occasionally exaggerated pluralism in which the state is no more than a "cash register" totaling up societal resource credits and debits, and part of a "vulgar" Marxism according to which public policy is a direct, undistorted "reflection" of underlying economic forces. But as they are most commonly interpreted, neither the societal constraint assumptions nor the writings on empirical democratic theory and public policy formation to which they are central deny outright the possibility of Type II autonomy. For the state does not translate its preferences into public policy unless and until the divergence in state-society preferences is turned into nondivergence.

What is denied, downplayed, or ignored in all but a few of these writings is, first, the regular availability of state capacities and opportunities for shifting the societal parallelogram; second, the willingness of public officials to make use of those autonomy-enhancing capacities and opportunities that are available; and third, the reasonable likelihood of success when the attempt is made, with respect to both the least and best politically endowed actors. Type II state autonomy is seen as no more than an unusual occurrence. When it does obtain it is due to the confluence of uncommon and uncommonly propitious circumstances, such as an exceptional measure of unity within the state on the need for an immediate response to a national security threat. When the circumstances are not exceptionally advantageous, public officials are deemed fully cognizant of the societal constraints as they severely circumscribe the possibilities of Type II autonomy-enhancing efforts and very much jeopardize the interests of public officials who might attempt to undertake them. Much caution, little or no temerity, initiatives limited to the floating of trial balloons, leadership attempts restricted to instances in which a *society*-generated shift in preferences is foreseen — these make up the conventional portrait of democratic officials responding to the possibility of Type II autonomy-enhancing efforts.

The societal constraint assumptions have succeeded only too well in doing what they are supposed to do, drawing attention away from the democratic state as an autonomous entity capable of shaping societal preferences in accordance with its own. It is one thing to emphasize the state's dependence upon privately controlled, effectively deployed resources. It is quite another to draw attention away from the state on that basis alone, without giving extended consideration to the possibilities of Type II state autonomy. The societal constraint assumptions have apparently had such a inhibiting effect upon political scientists themselves, even those who study political leadership, that not one has identified and drawn together the capacities and opportunities that public officials can capitalize upon in shifting the parallelogram of preferences and resources. In the absence of such an inquiry, any assumptions about the scarcity of these capacities and opportunities are problematic, any judgments about their putative ineffectiveness, high risks, and unacceptable costs are overly presumptive.

### Type II State Autonomy Accounts in Empirical Democratic Theory and Public Policy Studies

In a literature on empirical democratic theory that has little to say about political leadership in general, and is practically devoid of Type II state autonomy analyses, one study stands out in lending our proposition considerable support. Yet even here the Type II autonomy implications have not been fully appreciated, nor have the findings been incorporated into the theoretical variant that informed the study and was said to be substantiated by it.

In his pluralist classic, Dahl asks *Who Governs?* in New Haven. To find out he gets into a detailed and systematic analysis of three kinds of issues: the nomination of political party candidates, public education, and urban renewal. The first does not involve authoritative actions, the second does not buttress our proposition, the third very much does so. Mayor Lee translated his own preferences for a major urban renewal program into public policy, taking the initiative in enlisting other relevant officials and generating and orchestrating widespread support for his preferences among societal actors who were decidedly indifferent, somewhat negatively disposed, or vaguely supportive. None of any significance held policy views that converged with Lee's at the outset; at most, he had some "latent" support.

> Neither in 1950 nor in later years was there anything like a discernible popular demand for measures to reverse the physical and economic decay of New Haven, though citizens were evidently discontented with the city in various ways . . . Politicians were [not] pressed into action by public demand. On the contrary, they had to sniff out the faint smell of distant political success, generate the

demands, and activate the latent consensus . . . Although
the organized interest groups were too weak and divided
to carry on the task of initiating and coordinating
redevelopment, they were strong enough so that their
vigorous opposition might easily have blocked a proposal
. . . [They] had to be persuaded by Lee and Logue [the
man hired by Lee to serve as Development Administrator]
to back redevelopment . . . What Lee did as Mayor was to
push redevelopment and renewal to the center of focus
and to hold it there year after year . . . The Mayor sought
support for his redevelopment proposals from as strange a
coalition as had ever existed in New Haven . . . The
elaborate structure of citizen participation . . . was de-
liberately *created* by Mayor Lee . . . [The Citizens Action
Commission] gave legitimacy and acceptability to the
decisions of the leaders, [and] created a corps of loyal auxiliaries who helped engender public support for the program and . . . forestall disputes . . . Indeed, by creating
the CAC the Mayor virtually decapitated the opposition
. . . The appointment of over four hundred people to the
various action committees [of the CAC] gave urban
redevelopment a broad and heterogenous set of subleaders
. . . [who] initiated no key decisions; they were auxiliaries
. . . who would help enlist a community following.[1]

Dahl does stress that the mayor and his closest associates did
not press specific proposals upon the CAC, the organized interests, or the voters that would have engendered significant
opposition. But these self-imposed restraints in no way com-
promised their basic redevelopment goals or the programmatic
strategies for their implementation.

Single cases are widely thought to be incapable of proving a
proposition. Perhaps. But a single case that is analytically
strategic, constituting a least likely case in several regards, can
lend much plausibility to a proposition. On Harry Eckstein's
argument some can even validate a generalization.[2] Whatever
one's estimate of the overall frequency of Type II autonomy attempts and successes, they are markedly more problematic in
societies with a decidedly weak statist tradition (for example,

the United States) than in those in which the state is expected to undertake major initiatives (for example, France). Type II autonomy is significantly more problematic with respect to purely domestic issues, which regularly preclude public officials from capitalizing upon national loyalties. It is also more problematic on the part of local as opposed to national officials, who have special engineering advantages; elected as opposed to bureaucratic officials, almost all of whom are securely tenured; elected officials subject to frequent reelection as opposed to those with four- to six-year terms of office; and officials who must depend largely on their own skills as opposed to those with secure, independent power bases. And Type II autonomy is more problematic when state and societal preferences are at a considerable substantive distance from one another on issues that impinge sharply upon the interests of private actors who control the entire range of effective resources for constraining the state.

Yet here we have an American case, involving a domestic issue, in which a local official, subject to reelection every two years, without an independent power base, chose to initiate and successfully acted upon his preferences, which at first diverged substantially from societal preferences in their direction and ambitiousness, and which impinged sharply upon the interests of a plenitude of private actors with control over all the especially effective political resources. It is also relevant that this case appears in a landmark pluralist study, for pluralism is the most society-centered of the four democratic variants. There is then good reason to treat this case as something far more than an ordinary one — as one that supplies only limited evidence for the proposition. As a least likely case within a landmark pluralist study, the generalized support it lends our proposition should not be underestimated.

Public policy studies also have very little to say about Type II autonomy. Equally important, almost all of those that do speak to the proposition are not readily generalizable; they do not allow us to infer more than the occasional occurrence of Type II autonomy. The policies studied approximate most likely cases for the proposition's confirmation, they are explicable in terms of less than common circumstances, or both, as in the case of the Marshall Plan. The issue was of a national security, near crisis variety, arising from the perceived communist threat to a severely weakened Western Europe and thus to American security as well. There was no more than minimal opposition to the executive's initiatives on the part of other national officials. With the deteriorating situation in Europe calling for urgent measures and with European recovery impinging sharply upon all American interests — humanitarian, economic, political, and strategic — the state was basically unified in supporting a massive aid program.[3] The circumstances surrounding the Marshall Plan's adoption consequently turn it into something approximating a most likely case for the Type II autonomy proposition, and taken together, or even singly, they are far from being commonly present ones.

In a public policy literature that has little to say about Type II autonomy, the several analyses of French economic policy-making not only stand out. They also appear to offer impressive evidence for the proposition. After economic recovery had been completed in the early 1950s, the higher civil service was able to alter the policy preferences, even the general outlook, of the "big business community" and gain acceptance for indicative planning and a several-pronged strategy of economic growth and modernization. The Planning Commission served as a forum and means of "adult education." The state's influence over the credit markets was used to induce private investment, while tax rebates, subsidies, guaranteed markets, and other financial carrots were overtly held out to companies that agreed to make their investment, product development, and export pricing decisions in accordance with the state's economic plans and targets.[4] "Since the Government had a substantial part of the nation's economic activity under its direct control and exerted an indirect, though powerful, influence on a great deal more, it was not too difficult to convince private business that its decisions would be more intelligently made, over a wider range of industry, if they were made in

unison with the public authorities."[5] These observations eluci-
date the success of the higher bureaucracy in shaping societal
preferences and then translating its own into public policy.

Still, this case provides less than telling evidence for the
proposition. Its generalizability is limited. Over and above the
state's many policy levers for influencing the business sector,
there are other aspects of French economic policymaking that
turn it into an approximation of a most likely case for the proposition, tending toward the opposite pole of urban renewal in
New Haven. The French state was much advantaged, featuring a highly cohesive, intellectually well-endowed, and well-
trained civil service, and benefited from society's strong statist
tradition and a long-standing dependence upon the state. Since
this combination is not commonly found in other countries or
as applicable to other kinds of public policies, I do not want to
make too much of this case as support for the proposition. It
does, however, indicate that the state can shape the preferences
of even remarkably well-endowed private actors, in this instance, the "big business community."

There are three studies in the public policy literature, though
they may be the only three, that do lend the proposition a good
deal of generalized support. We are very much given to thinking that leadership is not possible on the part of legislative
assemblies, especially highly fragmented, institutionally cum-
bersome legislatures such as the American congress. But this
reasoned presumption should not, as it does all too often, lead
us to ignore or rule out the possibility that the discrete individuals who constitute the legislature engage in Type II
autonomous actions in relation to their particular constituents,
supporters, and clients. It is within this analytical context that
Raymond A. Bauer, Ithiel De Sola Pool, and Lewis Anthony
Dexter's investigation of trade and tariff policy under the
Eisenhower and Kennedy administrations takes on some
special significance. In a summary of the chapter entitled
"Some Areas of Initiative," they write:

> [The congressman] is freed from a slavish dependence on
> the elements in his coalition, not only because he can

change it, but, even more important, because once he has built a coalition, he tends to lead it. His closest supporters, who may have originally rallied around him because they wanted him to take certain stands, come to be his men. Within very broad limits, when he shifts, they shift. They gain prestige by being close to a congressman, and they fear to break a relationship which may some day be useful for important purposes. Once the leader has committed himself, his supporters are inclined to go along.[6]

With American congressmen undertaking successful policy initiatives, it becomes all the more likely that officials in very different kinds of institutional settings also engage in Type II autonomous actions.

Hugh Heclo's detailed analysis of income maintenance policies in twentieth-century Britain and Sweden examines the relative explanatory significance of socioeconomic variables, interparty competition, interest group pressures, and bureaucratic learning and behavior. While reluctant to make a forced choice, Heclo concludes that bureaucratic explanations are decidedly the most important ones—civil servants reacting to what they see as the deficiencies of existing policies, taking the initiative in formulating remedial changes, and promoting and orchestrating support for their preferred policy corrections.

Our evidence suggests the activist civil service role is a pervasive policy phenomenon rather than the exception. It is a phenomenom unmistakable even in the home of the ideal of administrative neutrality. British administrative consultations with outsiders have seemed more often aimed at persuading interest groups than reconciling their positive pressures.[7]

Heclo's evidence takes on special significance not only because it "even" comes from what is supposedly the architypically neutral British civil service. In addition, Swedish and British bureaucrats are not known to have uncommon advantages or capacities, and perhaps less so with respect to income maintenance policies relative to several others. Moreover, the evidence is suggestive of the wide range of Type

II autonomy actions because we do not usually think of bureaucrats as engaging in leadership efforts to shift societal preferences *away* from the status quo, and this despite their direction of economic moderization in France and the initiation of the Great Society programs in America.

Given his ambitious claims for what amounts to both Type II and Type I state autonomy explanations, Stephen D. Krasner's study of American foreign raw materials investment policies represents a major departure in the policy formation literature. He uses some two dozen cases to test these explanations against "the governing liberal paradigm [which] does not view the state as an independent entity" and against a Marxism in which public policies "reflect either the preferences of the bourgeoisie or the structural needs of a capitalist system." In contrast to "both the liberal and Marxist perspective [which] explain the action of public officials in terms of private pressures or needs," the evidence shows the state to be an "autonomous actor" in a good number of instances.[8] This is said even of the "weak," fragmented American state confronting the managers of the largest oil, rubber, copper, aluminum, steel, and food corporations.

Krasner does not distinguish among different types of autonomous actions, but his two major explanations link up closely with our Type II and Type I state autonomy. When state-society preferences diverge, "the state can exercise political leadership," this leadership variable partly overlapping with our notion of state-engineered autonomy. "In the area of international raw materials investments the most important manifestations of leadership have involved altering private preferences and exploiting divisions among societal groups."[9]

One way in which public officials can alter private preferences "is by offering a compelling interpretation of events that corporate managers are unable to make sense of on their own. By providing a coherent frame of reference the state can alter the way in which private managers define their own interest." Public officials sometimes have a clearer notion of their own preferences and a more sophisticated or at least broader sense of how public policy affects private interests, which, along with better information about the issue at hand, makes private actors susceptible to public persuasion. In addition, public officials can play up and play upon societal interests other than the currently salient ones. When the financial interests of corporate managers on foreign raw materials investment issues diverge from state preferences, public officials can capitalize upon their "non-pecuniary" interests by appealing to "the notion that managers are trustees of social resources, or to their (latent national) loyalties as citizens, or to their private desires for status and privilege." Krasner specifies his generalizations in arguing that public officials can more readily exercise political leadership when they confront big "oligopolistic, diversified corporations than when (they) must deal with sectors composed of large numbers of small owner-operated producing units."[10] It is easier for public officials both to alter the perceptions of the managers of large complex corporations and to make good use of public recognition in rewarding those who accede to their entreaties.

The other part of the leadership proposition is left undeveloped. Krasner does not identify the ways in which officials can purposefully "exploit divisions among societal groups" to enhance their autonomy. Nor does he estimate the relative weights of the political resources behind the conflicting private preferences, for instance, those of the differentially affected oil companies or those of the corporations that reacted differently to the likelihood of a foreign state nationalizing their properties. Insofar as those with the weightier resources have preferences that converge or are compatible with the state's, public officials need not exploit societal divisions in order to act on their preferences. The data may thus also include cases of Type III state autonomy.

These few studies do not add up to a mountain of supportive evidence for the periodic incidence of Type II state autonomy, but they surely provide more than a mole hill of generalizable evidence. It may also be surmised that were scholars as open to the possibilities of Type II autonomy as Dahl and Bauer, Pool, and Dexter, were they as self-conscious in estimating the contributions of state-centered explanations relative to the society-centered alternatives as Heclo, and were they to begin their analyses with the goal of making as strong an empirically documented case for the autonomy of the state as Krasner apparently did—if the work on empirical democratic theory and public policy formation were undertaken along these lines, it would probably substantiate many more instances of Type II autonomy. Since this has been done only on occasion, it is hardly surprising to find something other than an abundance of evidence supporting the Type II autonomy proposition. The existence of only a limited amount of supportive evidence should therefore not be overemphasized as a reason to doubt the periodic incidence of Type II autonomy—a point which is equally applicable to Type I autonomy.

### Type II Autonomy-Enhancing Strategies and Options

How can the state go about transforming a divergent into a nondivergent resource-weighted parallelogram of societal preferences? What constitutes the autonomy-enhancing capacities and opportunities upon which our proposition is based? A few of them have just been noted in discussing the relevant literature. What may be a comprehensive inventory is generated by beginning with four distinct Type II autonomy-enhancing strategies. Two of them are directed at those societal actors whose preferences diverge from the state's, one toward those who are indifferent to the state's preferences, and another toward those whose preferences converge with the state's and who want the state to act on its own preferences. (See table 2.)

The first strategy revolves exclusively around persuasion. Public officials can persuade societal actors who hold divergent preferences to alter them, or at least instill enough uncertainty about their desirability to get them to withdraw to the political sidelines. One option is to play up and play upon shared interests and values, for example, by appealing to loyalties to, or identification with, political and societal entities to which both public and private actors belong, such as the nation, a class, or a political party. Another option is to make the case that state and societal goals are actually the same, but that the state's policy preferences are more likely to promote their realization, putting forward a powerful intellectual argument or one based on privileged information, for example. The second strategy is intended to minimize the extent to which societal actors who hold divergent preferences choose to deploy the resources they control. This can be accomplished by pointing out that the adoption of state preferences will also result in their societal rivals or reference groups experiencing value losses, for instance, by marshaling statistical evidence to indicate thay they too will be shouldering a good part of the policy's financial costs. Public officials also have the option of heightening the visibility of the preferred policy's advantages and benefits relative to its disadvantages and costs, as when they rely upon hidden forms of taxation to finance a new program.

Public officials can mobilize and gain the support of currently indifferent actors. One option within this third strategy is to change the way in which the issue is defined or perceived, for example, by bringing to light its less immediately apparent and indirect consequences as they impinge on the interests of the indifferent actors. Public officials can also superimpose the issue upon existing class, ethnic, or regional divisions, perhaps by revealing or publicizing that the societal actors with divergent preferences are clustered within one societal segment. Following the fourth strategy, public officials can increase the level and weight of the political resources deployed by those societal actors who hold convergent preferences and those who want the state to act on its own preferences. Public officials can induce them to mobilize and deploy a level of political resources greater than that dictated by their interest in the issue at hand, for instance, by proposing to press ahead with other policies that both they and the public officials favor (an exchange that is nearly costless to the latter). Public officials can also provide their supporters with special advantages for mobilizing additional resources, possibly by lending them prestige or visibility to facilitate their organizing efforts.

## Table 2
### Type II Autonomy-Enhancing Strategies and Options

Public officials can persuade societal actors who hold divergent preferences to alter them, or at least instill enough uncertainty about their desirability to make for a withdrawal to the political sidelines by:

1. Playing up and playing upon shared interests and values (for example, by appealing to loyalties to, or identification with, political and social entities to which both state and societal actors belong, such as the nation, a class, or a political party);

2. Making the case that state and societal goals are actually the same, but that the state's policy preferences are more likely to promote their realization (for example, by putting forward a powerful intellectual argument or one based on privileged information);

3. Convincing them that their real or genuine interests are not what they believe them to be (for example, by offering an alternative interpretation of reality or one focused on a moderate to long-term view of expected developments and likely scenarios).

Public officials can minimize the extent to which societal actors who hold divergent preferences choose to deploy the resources they control by:

4. Pointing out that the adoption of state preferences will also result in their societal rivals or reference groups experiencing value losses (for example, by marshaling statistical evidence that indicates that they too will be shouldering a good part of the policy's financial costs);

5. Heightening the visibility of the preferred policy's advantages and benefits relative to its disadvantages and costs (for example, by relying upon hidden forms of taxation to finance a new program);

6. Asserting that, divergent preferences notwithstanding, they are not motivated by the wish to negate the societal actors' interests (for example, by professing that state preferences are genuinely, even if mistakenly, thought to serve their interests);

7. Offering them every opportunity to alter the public officials' preferences (for example, by inviting them into private discussions to allow for the most forceful, open, and least embarrassing presentation of their views);

8. Capitalizing upon the ways in which they continue to promote and fulfill the societal actors' other interests (for example, by recounting their efforts and accomplishments in distributing defense contracts and irrigation projects to their districts);

9. Proferring a mutually advantageous exchange, although one that is practically costless to the public officials (for example, by offering to promote other policies that they and the public officials both favor).

Public officials can mobilize and gain the support of indifferent societal actors by:

10. Changing the way in which the issue is defined or perceived (for example, by bringing to light its less immediately apparent and indirect consequences);

11. Superimposing the issue upon existing class, ethnic, or regional divisions (for example, by revealing or publicizing that the societal actors with divergent preferences are clustered within one societal segment);

12. Generating an emotionally charged response to the issue (for example, by playing upon societal fears, prejudices, or stereotypes);

13. Making them feel that their support is important and much needed (for example, by appealing to national or community loyalties and responsibilities).

Public officials can increase the level and weight of the political resources deployed by those societal actors who hold convergent preferences and those who want the state to act on its own by:

14. Inducing them to mobilize and deploy a level of political resources greater than that dictated by their interest in the issue at hand (for example, by offering to place an issue of mutual concern on the formal agenda and/or to deal with it expeditiously);

15. Providing them with special advantages for the mobilization of additional resources (for example, by lending them prestige or visibility to facilitate their organizing efforts);

16. Facilitating the most effective use of their resources by helping to build an issue coalition among them (for example, establishing quasi-public advisory committees and populating them with representatives of otherwise disparate interests).

Table 2 makes it clear that the democratic state is well endowed with Type II autonomy-enhancing options. It would not do to describe them as an embarrassment of riches, but they are surely not in short supply. The four strategies yield sixteen options of marked diversity. They range from assertions about state intentions, to offers of mutually advantageous exchanges, to a reworking of the issues with respect to content, significance, and affective meaning, to changes in the distribution of societal resources. Moreover, not a single one depends upon unusual circumstances for its appearance; they are all more or less regularly available to the state. Except for options 2 and 3, which usually require a high level of expertise and intellectual and/or persuasive abilities, none requires public officials with exceptional and thus fairly scarce skills and characteristics for their effectiveness. At least a handful are therefore regularly available as "live" options.

The Type II autonomy-enhancing options can be used along the entire issue complexity continuum, and some can be applied in an especially effective manner at both ends. When the issue at hand is highly complex, with several components interrelated in difficult to predict ways, it becomes all the easier for public officials to persuade societal actors to alter their preferences with intellectual arguments and privileged information. Complex issues are conducive to the emergence of contradictory (and mistaken) policy views on the part of similarly motivated individuals, thereby allowing for a more convincing case that they do not intend to negate the societal actors' interests. Issues that feature several facets or components give public officials more of an opportunity to point out that the adoption of state preferences will also result in value losses for the societal actors' rivals or reference groups, heighten the visibility of the preferred policy's advantages and benefits relative to its disadvantages and costs, change the way in which the issue is defined or perceived, and help build a diverse supportive coalition. Simple issues, on the other hand, increase the possibilities of appealing to shared loyalties, calling upon felt responsibilities, generating an emotionally charged response, and superimposing the issue upon existing societal divisions. The effectiveness of the remaining options is neither heightened nor lowered by issue complexity; they can be applied equally well to issues found at any point along the continuum.

Most of the options grouped under the two strategies that are directed toward societal actors with divergent preferences are most effective, often only effective, with those who stand fairly close to the state. Their effectiveness depends largely upon high levels of political involvement, participation, and organization and regularized contacts with the state. Public officials can then most effectively use intellectual persuasion, communicate information about other societal actors, give assurances about their own motivations, offer societal actors opportunities to meet with them, emphasize the various ways in which they fulfill the societal actors' other interests, and offer mutually advantageous exchanges. Only options 1, 5, and 6 among those relating to societal actors with divergent preferences can be pursued regardless of their distance from the state. On the other hand, all the options that are directed toward societal actors who are indifferent to the state's preferences and those who are supportive of them are applicable along the entire length of this broadly conceptualized continuum, and are perhaps somewhat more effective with those standing at some distance from the state. The options grouped under the third and fourth strategies can be used to win the support and enhance the political resources of all sorts of groups, from the best to the least organized.

Unlike the Type III autonomy-enhancing options, the effectiveness of their Type II autonomy counterparts is limited insofar as public officials are not entirely free to put together any combination that seems most advantageous with respect to the issue at hand. This is possible among the options making up the first and second strategies, and among those grouped under the third and fourth strategies, but options from the former and latter can rarely be combined. Whereas the first and second strategies involve persuasion, positive assertions, and inducements to win over or minimize the opposition of societal actors with divergent preferences, the third and fourth strategies, while not involving threats or sticks, are decidedly conflictual. For public officials to mobilize additional support for themselves among indifferent actors and those who already support the state is also to generate greater societal opposition to those who hold divergent preferences. Sometimes it is possible simultaneously to talk and to oppose, to negotiate and to fight, occasionally with mutually reinforcing effects, but this is not a generalized prescription for political effectiveness.

What can public officials expect in the way of societal sanctions that would prompt them to reject or take up these regularly available, widely applicable, and in some ways especially effective autonomy-enhancing options? Certainly the likelihood of societal sanctions being directed at the public officials who use these options is significantly greater than in the case of the Type III autonomy-enhancing options. The latter comprise actions whose motivations are barely visible while the former depend upon such visibility if they are to be at all effective, and clearly the reinforcement of nondivergent preferences engenders far less societal opposition than does the shift from a divergent to a nondivergent parallelogram of resource-weighted preferences. However, and this is the point to be emphasized, the chances of societal sanctions following in the wake of Type II autonomy-enhancing efforts is not nearly as high as suggested by the societal constraint assumptions.

To begin with, Type II autonomy does not entail authoritative actions that run counter to societal preferences. Public officials do not translate their own preferences into public policy until they have succeeded in changing societal preferences to make them congruent or consonant with their own. In fact, public officials who engage in Type II autonomy actions may wind up enjoying greater societal support than had they acted in accordance with existing societal preferences. There is the example of Mayor Lee, who gained enormous support by engineering a shift on the urban renewal issue. Without the benefit of the popular approval he generated on that issue even his reelection would apparently have been doubtful. There may then be a positive incentive for public officials to risk the possibility of societal sanctions.

A reliance upon any of the options making up the first and second strategies entails only a low to moderate risk of societal sanctions. Where intellectual persuasion, appeals to shared interests and values, carrotlike inducements, and other nonantagonistic means are used, where public officials are attempting to work with rather than against societal actors who hold divergent preferences, public officials have little reason to expect a withdrawal of significant support. Moreover, the first and second strategies do not involve any overt manipulation, behind-the-scenes scheming, or a difficult-to-justify exploitation of the state's authority and resources. Even when such attempts at political engineering prove unsuccessful, the public officials' losses are likely to be limited to the unrecompensed expenditure of political capital, which is hardly unimportant, but which does not compare with the often telling consequences exacted by societal sanctions.

The situation is quite different when public officials attempt to mobilize indifferent actors and heighten the level of resources deployed by those with convergent preferences and those who want the state to act on its own preferences. The third and fourth strategies involve a decided risk of societal sanctions, for the state is visibly, purposefully, and actively attempting to transform today's resource-predominant winners into tomorrow's losers. Such conflictual, sometimes antagonistic, behavior is probably sufficient to generate a disposition to sanction the state. The disposition can only be strengthened when those who hold divergent preferences are compelled to undertake additional mobilization efforts to counter those of the state, these being more or less costly depending upon, among other factors, whether most of the slack in their resources has already been taken up. In addition, there is the danger that the state will succeed only too well, its strategies not only shifting the distribution of private resources with regard to the issue at hand, but also altering them for the near future, with the societal actors who hold divergent preferences losing their resource-predominant position on other issues as well. The generalized level of politicization among the indifferent actors could be raised significantly as a result of the scope of a single issue being broadened; the additional resources mobilized by those who support the state on a current issue might carry over into the near future. These would indeed be distinctly unhappy eventualities for the resource-predominant actors, making societal sanctions all the more probable.

There are, however, some important mitigating considerations. There are reasons why even those actors with strong dispositions to sanction the state do not regularly act upon them, and the state itself can further reduce the likelihood of their doing so. Since these are even more extensively applicable to Type I autonomy-enhancing efforts and authoritative actions, they are taken up in the following chapter.

# 5

## Type I State Autonomy

TYPE I STATE AUTONOMY accounts are those in which public officials translate their preferences into authoritative actions when state-society preferences are divergent. Such accounts run up squarely against the societal constraint assumptions, and are explicitly or implicitly denied in practically all writings on empirical democratic theory and public policy formation. Type I state autonomy accounts do not merely say—as do neopluralism, Marxism, and a good number of policy formation studies—that the state acts contrary to the preferences of *certain* societal actors (large publics, the working class, ethnic minorities, voters, the poorly organized and financed, and so on), none of whom are said to control especially weighty political resources. According to the two propositions developed in this chapter, the democratic state acts contrary to the demands of *any* private actors, including the best endowed actors who predominate consistently within civil society, and it does so with some frequency. They consequently constitute the most ambitious of our state-centered propositions.

The denial of Type I state autonomy is so deeply embedded in the conventional widsom that citizens, journalists, and scholars alike rarely consider even the possibility that the state can act contrary to the demands of the politically weightiest actors. The state's Type I autonomy-enhancing capacities and opportunities for freeing itself from societal constraints have been given even less attention than their Type II autonomy counterparts, for Type I autonomy is directly at odds with the societal constraint assumptions. To be sure, there are references to various political strategems — who is unfamiliar with "divide and rule"? — that could be employed under conditions of divergence. But these have not been brought together, not discussed with the aim of generating an inclusive inventory with the democratic state in mind, not examined with respect to their range of applicability and differential effectiveness — in sum, not used to build a sturdy analytical platform upon which to consider when, how, and why the democratic state is able to translate its preferences into public policy under conditions of divergence. While the inherent, defining powers of the state can hardly be questioned, their use is most certainly denied on the premise that public officials do not act contrary to the resource-weighted parallelogram of preferences because of the societal sanctions that would regularly, if not almost surely, follow. Little attention (and thus credence) has been given to the ways in which public officials can avoid societal sanctions when taking authoritative actions that diverge from the demands of the politically best endowed actors.

When state and societal preferences diverge, public officials periodically capitalize upon their autonomy-enhancing capacities and opportunities to free themselves from societal constraints and then translate their preferences into authoritative actions. This, the fifth state-centered proposition, is developed first.

### Type I State Autonomy Accounts
### in Empirical Democratic Theory and Public Policy Studies

Marxism constitutes the outer limits of the state-centered model as found in empirical democratic theory. It is the only variant that allows for, indeed clearly insists, that the state is able to act on its preferences when these diverge from those of the politically weightiest actors, the effective demand groups as we have called them. But even so, Marxism, whose recent revitalization is partly connected with the "relative autonomy of the state" proposition, only claims that it does so intermittently. The liberal capitalist state does not act contrary to the demands of the bourgeoisie or capital more than sporadically at the very most. The "relative autonomy" proposition only supplements the three core explanations for unswervingly class-biased public policies, explicating why the democratic state, like any state in a class-structured society, invariably serves the interests of the class that controls the means of production.

The first of these explanations is probably the most frequently applied one in Marxist theory as a whole. Reiterating the societal constraint assumptions shared by the other variants, and identifying the bourgeoisie as the effective demand group, the state is viewed as an instrument of that class, compelled to act as its "agent." The second explanation derives from the "social character" of the state. With basic beliefs and norms shaped by their bourgeois family backgrounds, education, professional and social relations, and other socialization experiences, the overwhelming number of public officials prefer to serve bourgeois interests. The third is a "structural" explanation, based on objective, impersonal "constraints." With the viability of the capitalist state and the preservation of capitalist relations of production being dependent upon a reasonably healthy economy, public officials are constrained to respond in ways that fulfill the economy's structural requisites. They alone are capable of overcoming capitalism's inherent economic and political contradictions. The state necessarily serves capitalist interests because it is solidly embedded, structurally and functionally, within capitalist relations of production, no matter what the social character of its personnel and the extent of the bourgeoisie's political resources.

This tripartite core is supplemented by the now "conventional Marxist notion of 'relative autonomy' "[1] — a double-barreled proposition that points to certain distinctive state preferences and their translation into public policies that diverge from the preferences of most, even virtually all, members of the economically and politically dominant class. Wedded to what

Marx called its "narrowest and most sordid private interests," the bourgeoisie is shortsighted, unaware of its common, long-term political advantages in staving off the threat from below, and if aware, unwilling to bear the necessary material costs. Public officials recognize these and other policy requisites, resulting in certain distinctive state preferences — those that public officials "conceive to be the 'national interest,' and which in fact involve the service of the interests of the ruling class."[2] Neither that class nor any other societal actor subscribes to the preferences of Engels' "ideal collective capitalist."

The second part of the proposition asserts that the state acts upon its distinctive preferences despite their divergence from those of the economically and politically dominant class. "It takes charge, as it were, of the bourgeoisie's political interests and realizes the function of political hegemony which the bourgeoisie is unable to achieve. But *in order to do this, the capitalist state assumes a relative autonomy with regard to the bourgeoisie.*"[3] Nicos Poulantzas's words are paralleled by Claus Offe's. The state "presents itself to the particular and narrow interests of individual capitalists and their political organizations as a supervisory, tutelary force — at all events one which is an alien and sovereign authority — since it is only through the State's becoming relatively autonomous in this way that the multiplicity of particular and situation-bound special interests can be integrated into a class-interest."[4]

Despite the proposition's theoretical centrality — Ralph Miliband claims that at certain times public officials "absolutely need" to be autonomous[5] — the question of just how often it obtains has not been given any consideration. In asserting that at times the state must be free from the control of the politically dominant class in order to promote its long-run, collective interests (the preservation of its privileged economic position and capitalist relations of production), the incidence of Type I autonomy is simply and implicitly assumed to be an invariant function of the state's perceived needs for it. Not a single study explores these needs and draws them together. To suggest that relative autonomy obtains with some frequency runs up against

Marx's and Engel's assertions that the state is autonomous only "by way of exception," dilute the theory's class specific character, and sharply downgrade the state's instrumental responsiveness to bourgeois demands. On the other hand, Poulantzas, Offe, and other structural Marxists would not necessarily find a recurring relative autonomy incompatible with their understanding of the capitalist state. (In the next chapter it is shown that a straightforward reading of Marxist theory and analyses clearly points to the frequent occurrence of Type I autonomy among the advanced industrial democracies.)

Marxist theory provides two explanations for the occurrence of relative autonomy, two ways in which the state frees itself from the bourgeoisie's control. If and when the political resources of the opposing classes are nearly balanced, the state has the opportunity to act upon its preferences under conditions of divergence. In *The Eighteenth Brumaire of Louis Bonaparte*, Marx writes that "the state seem[s] to have made itself completely independent. As against bourgeois society, the state machine has consolidated its position so thoroughly that [the second Bonaparte] suffices for its head."[6] Here, and in *The Civil War in France*, it is the opposing classes' near equal strength that allows for the state's autonomy, as summarily captured in the statement that the Second Empire "was the only form of government possible at a time when the bourgeoisie had already lost, and the working class had not yet acquired, the faculty of ruling the nation."[7]

In addition, Marx and Engels note the state's capacity for manipulating the opposing classes, purposefully playing them off against each other to enhance its autonomy, as in this passage from Engels:

> By way of exception, periods occur in which the warring classes balance each other so nearly that the state power, as ostensible mediator, acquires for the moment, a certain degree of independence of both . . . Such was the Bonapartism of the First, and still more of the Second French Empire, which played off the proletariat against the bourgeoisie and the bourgeoisie against the proletariat. The

latest performance of this kind . . . is now the New German Empire of the Bismarck nation: the capitalists and workers are balanced against each other and equally cheated for the benefit of the impoverished Prussian cabbage Junkers.[8]

In more abstract language, Poulantzas reiterates and extends Marx's and Engels' reasoning:

> In order concretely to take on this relative autonomy . . . the state is supported by certain dominated classes of the society, in that it presents itself, through a complex ideological process, as their representative: it encourages them in various ways, to work against the dominant class or classes, but to the political advantage of the latter. In this way it succeeds precisely in making the dominated classes accept a whole series of compromises which appear to be in their political interests . . . Thus, in fulfilling its political function, the capitalist state comes to rely on dominated classes and sometimes to play them off against the dominant classes.[9]

In this account the state's manipulative capacities do not depend upon the opportunity afforded by a near balance of class strengths.

Without questioning their validity, how well can these autonomy-enhancing capacities and opportunities account for Type I autonomy? While two partly interrelated variables — the near equilibrium between opposing classes and the state's capacity for manipulating the class conflict — can certainly explain some instances of relative autonomy, it is far from certain that they are regularly available when required, and when available, that they are effective in all kinds of situations calling for Type I autonomy. Moreover, Marx's and Engels' analyses do not refer to any democratic regimes, while the claims of Poulantzas and others apply to both democratic and authoritarian regimes. There is then the possibility that democratic states, unlike many authoritarian ones, are not sufficiently unified, are without the sometimes necessary single locus of power, for effectively formulating and executing manipulative strategies involving the exploitation of enormously wide-ranging, multifacted class conflicts.

Among policy formation studies, Krasner's alone presents a Type I state autonomy assertion, and like Marxism, claims that some preferences are distinctive to the state. Certain officials have "aims of their own that are separate and distinct from the interests of any particular societal group. These goals are associated either with general material objectives or with ambitious ideologies related to beliefs about how societies should be ordered. They can be labeled the national interest."[10] Three criteria are used to identify these national interest preferences: they must relate to "general societal goals, persist over time, and have a consistent ranking of importance."[11] Krasner persuasively defends an inductive approach for identifying their substantive content, and demonstrates that American "central decision-makers" have held preferences relating to foreign raw materials investment issues that satisfy the concept's definitional requirements.

However, Krasner's cases cannot immediately be used as evidence for Type I autonomy because his "state" and ours are not identical. Krasner defines the state solely in terms of those officials who hold national interest preferences, and these turn out to be only the "central decision-makers." This conceptualization thus entails a rather curious change in the state's identity, both cross nationally due to differing institutional arrangements and intranationally when the issues involve different "central decision-makers." On foreign policy issues "the American state" is made up almost exclusively of the White House and the State Department, which leads to such assertions as: "In trying to promote the national interest, the American state often confronts dissident *bureaus*, a recalcitrant *Congress*, and powerful private actors."[12] The state could have been defined in any one of several ways to include officials who do and do not hold national interest preferences, leaving ample room to analyze how they are sometimes translated into public policy. In choosing not to do so, Krasner removes most bureaucrats and legislators from the state, leaving them in a conceptual no-man's-land, since they are also distinguished from private actors.

The solution to our problem in interpreting Krasner's findings consequently hinges on being able to identify the state parallelogram of resource-weighted preferences in terms of *both* the "central decision-makers" and those whom we must refer to as noncentral public officials. Fortunately, the cases need not be subjected to a strained interpretation in getting them to speak to the possibility of Type I state autonomy. The "central actors" are shown to hold national interest preferences on foreign raw materials investment issues that diverge from societal preferences, those of large American corporations whose enormous resources provide "direct access to Congressional committees, executive departments, and often the White House itself."[13] Krasner does not identify the specific preferences of the noncentral legislative and bureaucratic officials, but they are said to have opposed the "central actors" preferences because of *pressures* placed upon them by societal actors—by the managers of the large and largest oil, copper, rubber, aluminum, steel, and food corporations. Thus they may very well have held preferences which, though they did not fulfill all three national interest criteria, were in specific instances substantively similar to those of the "central actors." If so, state preferences as defined here clearly diverged from societal preferences, and in several instances these were translated into public policy. On the other hand, if the noncentral officials did not hold specific preferences that coincided with those of the "central actors," Type I autonomy still obtained if (as may reasonably be supposed) the latter's intrastate resources and strategic positioning with respect to the international issues at hand made for their predominance vis-à-vis the noncentral actors. On either interpretation state and societal preferences diverge, and Krasner's data show that certain state preferences were translated into public policy.

Krasner's explanations for Type I ("state" or state) autonomy revolve around the "concentration of policy-making in arenas that are relatively insulated from societal interest groups . . . [and] relatively impervious to private pressures."[14] Given marked variations along this dimension, the critical variables are those that determine whether policy is made in more or less insulated arenas. "The arena in which an issue is decided is partly a function of its inherent nature and partly a function of the way in which it is defined."[15]

There are apparently two respects in which an issue's "inherent nature," its substantive content, helps determine the decision arena. The first is quite simply that different state units handle the policy levers that impinge upon different substantive issues. International raw materials investments, when they involve the pricing and ownership of foreign raw materials, are foreign policy issues. As such, they are decided in the (well-insulated) White House and State Department, whose occupants handle the policy levers that "can lead to the use of force or diplomatic confrontation." Secondly, using the previously discussed classifications of policy issues developed by Shattschneider, Lowi, and Wilson, issue content is said to affect the societal parallelogram of preferences and resources, which in turn helps determine the decision arena. When they constitute domestic economic issues, international raw materials investment policies are narrow in scope and distributive in their impact, and involve either concentrated costs and diffuse benefits or concentrated benefits and diffuse costs. As such, all three typologies "suggest that the government will confront well organized and powerful political interest groups. Decisions are likely to be taken in arenas that maximize the power of these groups, most notably Congressional committees or executive departments like Agriculture and Interior that are responsive to a narrow range of societal groups."[16]

Over and above the issue's substantive content, "the way in which it is defined" also determines where it is decided. Here we return to Krasner's "leadership" explanation discussed with respect to Type II autonomy. Public officials "can themselves redefine a dispute and change both its scope and the arena in which it is decided." As an international issue, foreign raw materials pricing and ownership can affect "the nation's ability to make war, the general health of its economy, the stability of its political system, [and] its influence over other states . . . By playing upon these broader themes [public officials] can increase competitiveness and [issue] visibility, the two primary means by which the scope of the conflict is increased. By increasing the scope of conflict they can change the arena in which the issue is decided."[17] Public officials have helped move issues into state arenas where they are able to resist societal pressures.

As with the Marxist accounts of Type I state autonomy, there is some serious doubt about the range and frequency with which Krasner's are applicable. He appears to be offering several explanations. But the two involving the issue's "inherent nature" are beyond the control of the state, and these two, plus the ways in which public officials can shape the definition of an issue, are all made to relate to a single proximate explanation — whether the decisions are taken in well-insulated units that allow for resistance to societal pressures or permeable units that facilitate societal constraint. This is hardly an unimportant variable, but it is only one variable, and as such, it may not be able to account for more than a limited number of Type I autonomy actions. Moreover, public officials may not have the opportunity to shift decision sites; the sites that are available to particular officials or within any one state may be *similarly* impervious or permeable. Although the dispersal of decision sites per se does not make for overall variations in their imperviousness, the larger the number of sites the greater the likelihood of pronounced variations among some of them. The American state with which Krasner is primarily, but not exclusively, concerned is the polar case of dispersed sites, while the modal pattern among the advanced industrial democracies is substantially closer to the concentration of decision sites.

There is a way in which this limitation could be largely remedied. The permeability or insulation of state units could be given a broad interpretative cast, conceptualizing it as something like the state's capacities to resist societal pressures. In fact, since Krasner does not define his terms here, he may actually have something like this in mind. But such a conceptualization would only be warranted if we knew how and why state units vary in their resistance capacities. Otherwise the concept would remain broad but vacuous. Krasner's analytical discussion and empirical inquiry allow for the identification of the critical variables that make for greater or lesser resistance (or insulation/permeability), but he chose to focus exclusively upon the just mentioned factors that determine whether policy is made in one unit or another. An extended analytical and/or empirical examination of the reasons for the better insulation, or greater resistance capacities, of some state units than others is surely missing. Not only would we then know much more about how and why the democratic state is able to act contrary to the weightiest societal demands, the explanations would have a substantially wider range of applicability as well.

These then are the outer limits of empirical democratic theory and public policy studies as they depart from the societal constraint assumptions in claiming autonomy for the state under conditions of divergence. Yet even these writings do not claim that Type I autonomy occurs with some frequency, and were that claim to be read into them (as might fairly be done with Krasner's book) it would remain largely unsupported. For they identify only a minimal number of Type I autonomy-enhancing capacities and opportunities, each of which is restricted in its applicability. To be able to say that the state periodically acts contrary to societal preferences it must be shown that there are in fact more than a few effective Type I autonomy-enhancing capacities and opportunities, and that they are regularly available and widely applicable. We need also take up the question that these writings barely touch upon: Can the state use its autonomy-enhancing capacities and opportunities to free itself from societal constraints and take authoritative actions that run counter to societal demands without suffering a significant loss of societal support?

### Type I Autonomy-Enhancing Strategies and Options
The Type I autonomy-enhancing strategies are intended to free the state from the constraints of the predominant societal actors

who hold divergent preferences. As such, each strategy is directed at these actors and each speaks directly to one of the three societal constraint assumptions—assumptions that should hardly be ignored in arguing for the state's ability to counter their effects. The aim is not, as with the Type II autonomy-enhancing strategies, to alter societal preferences or the distribution of resources, but rather, accepting them as they are, to free public officials from their constraining impact and allow for the translation of state preferences into public policy.

The first strategy does not seek to deny the critical import-ance of privately controlled resources, but says that public officials can neutralize or markedly diminish the constraining *effects* of the political resources deployed by those societal actors who hold divergent preferences. One option here is for the state to employ its own resources or those controlled by it to neutral-ize the effects of similar private resources. For example, public officials can use state-generated data to offset the information resources of private associations, or state-owned or -controlled banks to counter the threat of an "investment strike" by private capital. The constraining effects of private resources can also be markedly diminished by using a decisionmaking style that is difficult to decipher and permeate, for example, by taking au-thoritative actions in an informally nuanced, largely hidden, or secretive manner.

Without questioning the ability of societal actors to deploy their resources in maximally effective ways, the second strategy allows public officials to mitigate the extent and effectiveness with which societal actors who hold divergent preferences are *able* to deploy their resources. Public officials can disengage or co-opt some of the leaders or other visible group members, for example, by the judicious distribution of honors, appoint-ments, jobs, or contracts. Another option involves actions that fracture the unity of the societal actors with divergent prefer-ences, for example, by disaggregating the issue so as to isolate coalition members who have different reasons for joining it.

The third strategy does not ignore the state's dependence upon societal support, but says that public officials can *dissuade* those societal actors who hold divergent preferences from deploying most of their resources and exerting implacable pressure upon the state. One option is to threaten the realization of their other policy preferences, more or less overtly reminding them of their dependence upon the state, for example, by slowing down the implementation of a program they favor. Public officials can also jeopardize the societal actors' position or predominance vis-à-vis rival societal groups. One way of doing so is to raise the possibility of extending equally privileged quasi-public representation to the latter.

Neutralizing or markedly diminishing the constraining effects of private resources, mitigating the extent and effectiveness with which societal actors are able to deploy them, and dissuading societal actors from fully deploying them — these are the three strategies that public officials can use to free themselves from societal constraints. As seen in table 3, they help generate and order sixteen options for enhancing state autonomy. The existence of this many options begins to turn the denial of Type I state autonomy into a problematic assertion. As with the Type II and Type III autonomy-enhancing options, few if any of them depend upon unusual circumstances for their appearance. Nor do they require exceptionally skilled and thus fairly scarce officials for their effective use. Thus, when taken together with the great diversity of the options — options relating to state resources, decision sites, manipulation of issues and groups, relations within and between societal groups, and societal dependence upon the state, among others — at least a small handful is almost sure to be regularly available as "live" options.

## TABLE 3
### TYPE I AUTONOMY-ENHANCING STRATEGIES AND OPTIONS

Public officials can neutralize or markedly diminish the constraining effects of the political resources deployed by those societal actors who hold divergent preferences by:

1. Employing state resources or those controlled by it to neutralize similar private resources (for example, by using state-generated

data to offset those of private associations, or state-owned or -controlled banks to counter the threat of an "investment strike" by capital);

2. Using a decisionmaking style that is difficult to decipher and permeate (for example, by taking authoritative actions in an informally nuanced, largely hidden, or secretive manner);

3. Selecting decision sites whose occupants are relatively insulated from societal pressures (for example, by assigning the authoritative resolution of the issue to a state unit made up of securely tenured civil servants);

4. Taking visible, formal authoritative actions that conform to societal preferences, while negating these publicly proclaimed goals in less visible ways (for example, by establishing a new program without authorizing adequate funds for the achievement of its publicly stated goals, or assigning the implementation of vaguely worded legislation to an agency that can be expected to interpret it in ways that run counter to the legislation's manifest goals);

5. Serving as the ostensible mediator between opposing societal groups (for example, by manipulatively negotiating compromises that favor those groups whose preferences converge with the state's);

6. Turning to those actors with convergent preferences for substitute support (for example, by taking full advantage of situations in which rival societal groups control almost equally weighty resources).

Public officials can mitigate the extent and effectiveness with which societal actors who hold divergent preferences are able to deploy their resources by:

7. Disengaging or co-opting some of the leaders or other visible group members (for example, by judiciously distributing honors, appointments, jobs, or contracts);

8. Fracturing their unity (for example, by disaggregating the issue so as to isolate coalition members who have different reasons for joining it);

9. Exacerbating divisions and mistrust among them (for example, by "consulting" with association leaders and claiming to have accepted their demands, concomitantly deflecting unwanted responsibility);

10. Getting them to direct at least some of their resources toward

other nondivergent issues or rival societal groups (for example, by heightening the salience of other societal divisions);

11. Prolonging the policy information process so as to make the continuing deployment of resources more problematic (for example, by establishing fact-finding commissions whose reports finally appear after the societal coalition has lost its cohesiveness or ad hoc organizations have run out of financial resources).

Public officials can dissuade those societal actors who hold divergent preferences from deploying most of their resources and from exerting implacable pressure upon the state by:

12. Threatening the realization of their other policy preferences, more or less overtly reminding them of their dependence upon the state (for example, by slowing down the implementation of a program they favor);

13. Being less forthcoming in providing services and "particularized" benefits (for example, interceding with other officials who are processing their requests, claims, applications, or proposals only after repeated promptings and with minimal effort);

14. Jeopardizing their position or predominance vis-à-vis rival societal groups (for example, by raising the possibility of extending equally privileged quasi-public representation to the latter);

15. Putting their advantageous relations with the state at risk (for example, by cutting back on the regularity or openness of their consultations);

16. Endangering their organizational cohesiveness (for example, by proposing to place another, cross-cutting issue on the immediate agenda).

The regular availability, applicability, and effectiveness of the options is given additional credence by noting that nearly half of them are closely related to the mixed economy welfare-state. Given its enormous size and structural complexity, public officials can more readily employ decisionmaking channels that are difficult to decipher and permeate, assign issues to relatively insulated decision sites, negate formal authoritative actions in not easily visible ways, and prolong the policy formation process. Due to the panoply of societal guidance, regulatory, and distributional activities, public officials have numerous opportunities to employ state-owned or -controlled resources to offset similar private ones, disengage or co-opt group leaders, threaten the realization of the societal actors' other preferences, and be less than forthcoming in providing services and "particularized" benefits. Partly because of this panoply of activities, at any one time numerous and variegated demands are made upon the executive, legislature, and less specialized bureaucratic units, which allows them a measure of leeway in choosing which groups to respond to; they have some opportunity to substitute the support of one for another on different kinds of issues.[18]

The first and second strategies enjoy an enormously wide range of applicability. Almost all of the options grouped under them can be employed effectively where the issues are both complex and simple and to societal actors who are both close to and distant from the state. Only option 4—public officials taking visible, formal authoritative actions that conform to societal preferences while negating their publicly proclaimed goals in less visible ways—is limited in its effectiveness to societal actors who stand at some distance from the state. Only option 11—public officials prolonging the policy formation process so as to make the continuing deployment of resources more problematic—is limited in its effectiveness to unorganized or poorly organized groups whose cohesiveness is likely to be dissipated over time.

The applicability of the third strategy is not restricted by the issue's complexity, but it is limited to societal actors who stand at least fairly close to the state. Each of the options for dissuading societal actors from fully deploying their resources requires direct, and for maximum effectiveness, private communications. On occasion, carrots can be dangled openly, but sticks, which is what these options are, must usually be brandished informally. The last two options are applicable only to societal actors who are at least moderately well organized. They commonly have advantageous relations with the state, which enables public officials to put these at risk. It is the value they place upon existing organizational capacities that allows public officials to endanger them, for example, by proposing to place another, cross-cutting issue on the immediate agenda.

The options' effectiveness is partly related to the possible incompatibilities among them, since these would detract from the simultaneous employment of many and obviate the selection of a particularly effective combination for the situation at hand. Unlike the Type II autonomy options, of which half involve working with and the other half working against the societal actors who hold divergent preferences, here there is hardly any incompatibility on this score or any other, such as the style with which the options are employed or the circumstances allowing for their use. With two exceptions (4 and 5), all involve visible, direct, oppositional efforts to free the state from the constraints of the politically weightiest actors. Public officials are consequently able to employ just about as many Type I autonomy-enhancing options as they see fit in whatever combinations strike them as most advantageous.

With respect to societal sanctions following in the wake of the Type I autonomy options, the probabilities are far greater than in the case of Type II autonomy-enhancing efforts. However, there are some significant differences among the three Type I autonomy strategies, the first being considerably safer for public officials to pursue than the others. Two of the options (4 and 5) are barely visible to the private actors with divergent preferences. They are unlikely to be aware that the state is taking authoritative actions that conform to societal preferences while taking less visible actions to negate their publicly proclaimed goals, and similarly, that the state is serving as the ostensible mediator between groups with conflicting preferences. The effects of options 2 and 3 are known to the relevant societal actors, but they need not be aware of the purposefulness or intent with which they are employed. What can remain hidden when selecting relatively well-insulated decision sites and employing a decisionmaking style that is difficult to decipher and permeate are the purposeful intentions in doing just that. Their use may be seen as givens, as characteristics of the state rather than as variables that public officials chose to capitalize upon. The other options with which public officials can neutralize or markedly diminish the constraining effects of private resources are visible in terms of both their use and purposefulness. Still, in employing state resources to offset similar private ones and in turning to those actors with convergent preferences for substitute support, the state is not detracting from the societal actors' interests other than those which relate to the issue at hand — a point which also applies to the other options making up the first strategy were they to become visible as purposeful autonomy-enhancing efforts.

There is no hiding the actions of public officials in mitigating the extent and effectiveness with which societal actors holding divergent preferences are able to deploy their resources. Of the options making up the second strategy, only two (7 and 11) allow for the possibility of public officials disguising their intentions. Moreover, the societal actors' dispositions to apply sanctions are likely to be strengthened insofar as each of the options impinges upon their interests over and above those relating to the immediate issue, jeopardizing or actually weakening their political resources. Even if their leadership capacities, cohesiveness, overall size, and other resources are not adversely affected, directed elsewhere, or spent, strenuous efforts may be needed to maintain them. Were they adversely affected, substantial rebuilding costs would have to be incurred, if indeed the losses can be recouped. Private actors are strongly disposed to inflict sanctions upon public officials who rely upon the second strategy.

The third strategy, that of dissuading societal actors from deploying most of their resources, has similar implications. The options are all necessarily visible and there is certainly no disguising the intent behind them. In addition, public officials may generate antagonistic feelings by using more or less subtle threats to exploit the state's special advantages and the societal actors' dependence upon it. The threats pertain to the actors' interests beyond those which are immediately at stake — those involving the realization of other policy preferences, their predominance relative to other societal groups, their advantageous relations with the state, and organizational capacities — each of which constitutes a critical interest. There is one reason for supposing that the disposition to sanction the state is somewhat mitigated, at least in comparison with the second strategy. Here the societal actors have a choice. If they attach less importance to the immediate issue than they do to the preservation of their other interests, they can avoid jeopardizing the latter by agreeing not to exert implacable pressure upon the state.

Private actors are undoubtedly much disposed to apply sanctions against public officials who seek to capitalize upon their Type I autonomy-enhancing capacities and opportunities. That disposition is further strengthened when public officials are sufficiently successful in freeing themselves from societal constraints to translate their preferences into authoritative actions under conditions of divergence. But despite their strength or intensity, these are dispositions; there is still the question of whether or not they will be acted upon. The answers to this question—the reasons for thinking that they are not translated into behavior with any regularity—also apply to the likelihood of societal sanctions being directed at public officials who successfully or unsuccessfully rely upon the Type II autonomy-enhancing options.

The disposition to sanction public officials, even an especially strong one, may be formed by any one action on the part of the state. But the likelihood of its being translated into behavior is to a significant extent a function of the total number or proportion of authoritative actions that run counter to the societal actors' preferences. Officials whose authoritative actions have regularly conformed to the preferences of their constituents, clients, and supporters can usually act contrary to them without being much concerned about the withdrawal of support. "Particularized" benefits are also relevant here. These include some authoritative actions but extend beyond them to all sorts of services public officials provide for their constituents, clients, and supporters. The more such benefits provided, the less probable that public officials will lose societal support when acting contrary to societal preferences.

Two studies of the American Congress highlight the importance of this consideration.[19] Between 1948 and 1972 the number

of marginal congressional districts — those in which the successful candidates received between 50 and 55 percent of the vote —
decreased steadily from 25 percent to 10 percent of the total.
The point here is not that congressmen have less reason to fear
for their reelection and can thus more readily act contrary to
constituent preferences. (Besides, this pattern is not widely rep-
licated in other legislatures, within the United States or in Europe.) It is the explanation for the "vanishing marginals" that is
germane. "Over the past quarter of a century expanded constituency service and pork-barrel opportunities have given the
marginal congressman the opportunity to switch 3-5 percent of
those who would otherwise oppose him on policy grounds to his
supporting coalition. Considering the magnitude of the growth
of the federal role during that same period, such a shift seems
eminently plausible."[20] In a survey study that asks "What
Makes Legislators in Great Britain and the United States Popular?" it is also found that legislators can protect themselves
against incumbent challengers and national party swings by at-
tending to district activities, diligently doing casework, and
serving the special interests of the constituency.[21] The point
then is simply this: with the mixed-economy welfare state providing all sorts of opportunities for servicing and interceding on
behalf of societal actors, and these activities having a substantial impact upon their interests and behaviors, they are
significantly less likely to withdraw their support from public
officials who provide "particularized" benefits, despite the
disposition to do so.

There is also the question of whether it is in the overall interests of presumptively rational societal actors to act upon their
dispositions. Can they afford to withdraw their support and apply other sanctions? There is no readily generalizable answer.
But that is just the point. Sometimes societal actors can afford to
apply sanctions, even with the expectation of enhancing their
overall interests, and sometimes they cannot — a "generalization"
of which public officials are hardly unaware. The simple
withdrawal of support from elected incumbents could lead to the
installation of challengers who are less sympathetic to their

preferences as a whole, less effective in promoting them within the state, or less susceptible to the particular blandishments they have to offer. To this extent it is the societal actors who are "constrained' in their choices; it is sometimes unreasonable, even self-defeating, for them to translate their dispositions into behaviors when public officials act contrary to their preferences.

Public officials need not sit passively by, only hoping that societal retribution will not be exacted for their autonomy-enhancing efforts and authoritative actions. Public officials who are confronted with the very real possibility of societal sanctions are not all of a sudden denuded of their positions, formal powers, or the special advantages and opportunities that go along with them. If they were able and willing to act as autonomy-seeking officials under conditions of divergence, they are probably capable of threatening to impose some significant costs upon societal actors strongly disposed toward retribution. Except for those that might have already been fully used, the options grouped under the third Type I autonomy-enhancing strategy continue to be available, applicable, and effective. At this point, they are used not to dissuade societal actors from exerting implacable pressures upon the state, but to deter them from imposing sanctions upon the state.

There is also the reverse side of the deterrence coin. Public officials can buy off disgruntled societal actors by taking authoritative actions that they prefer—doing so with dispatch after acting contrary to their preferences or at some other relevant moment, most obviously just prior to the next election. Knowing that they have the authority to take actions that will pacify many of those who are disposed to apply societal sanctions, public officials need not be as wary of acting contrary to societal preferences. From a state-centered perspective this is where Edward Tufte's *Political Control of the Economy* takes on its greatest significance. With Congress and the president fully aware of the strong relationship between short-term electoral behavior and increases in real personal income, they regularly adopt tax, fiscal, and monetary policies to increase the voters' income prior to elections. "In election years, unemployment drops, social welfare programs expand, and beneficiary payments to millions of people increase. The months before the election are the 'liberal hour,' replacing the administration's efforts earlier in the term to build 'business confidence.' There appears to be a tendency for an administration to broaden the scope of its economic patronage as the course of its term in office moves closer toward the upcoming election."[22] Knowing that they can win back electoral support, probably most effectively by increasing personal income, we may infer that public officials are less reluctant to act upon their unpopular preferences on economic and other issues during the calendar years prior to elections. However, this point is limited in its applicability. If the pacification policies run contrary to the state's preferences, then the state is only partially autonomous, acting on its own preferences in one instance and on society's in another.

## The Inherent Powers of the State

The possibilities for Type I state autonomy do not stop here. Over and above the autonomy-enhancing capacities and opportunities for freeing themselves from societal constraints and then translating their preferences into public policy, there is another tack available to public officials. They can simply and directly act upon their preferences, with or without first attempting to make good use of the Type I autonomy-enhancing options. Public officials have the exclusive authority—a monopoly of legislative, executive, and administrative powers—to take any and all actions other than those which violate the constitutional format and other legitimized procedural principles. Surely these basic, undeniable features of the state itself should not be overlooked. This brings us to the last of our state-centered propositions. When state and societal preferences diverge, public officials periodically rely upon the inherent powers of the state, its plenary authority, to translate their preferences into authoritative actions.

These powers are not contingent upon societal support or indifference; they inhere to the democratic state regardless of divergent societal preferences and opposition. Private actors may well be able to induce the state to take authoritative actions when it prefers inaction, but they cannot compel it to do so; they may well be able to dissuade the state from adopting particular public policies, without however being able to prevent it from doing so. Only by voting in (if an election is imminent) a different set of incumbents could society overcome the state's plenary powers. This much — and it is surely no small matter — is probably not subject to dispute. But will public officials avail themselves of the state's inherent powers, under conditions of divergence?

Granted, many authoritative actions require the active cooperation of private actors for their implementation, and such assistance might not be forthcoming were public officials to rely exclusively upon their inherent powers — a point which also has some applicability to authoritative actions taken after employing the Type I autonomy-enhancing options. Where societal cooperation is required and unlikely to be forthcoming, public officials have little incentive to translate their preferences into public policy. Private actors can dissuade them from acting on their preferences. Yet this form of societal constraint is sharply limited. There are many authoritative actions, quite possibly the vast majority, that do not depend upon societal cooperation for their implementation; they can be executed despite societal opposition and noncooperation. These include authoritative actions relating to the structure, standard operating procedures, and budgets of state units; virtually the entire range of authoritative *in*actions; public policies that involve little contact between public and private actors, such as national security and monetary policy; as well as those authoritative actions requiring only simple compliance rather than active cooperation, such as the setting of taxation and income supplement levels.

Even where the state is dependent upon private assistance, divergent preferences do not regularly eventuate in noncooperation. The policies are seen as objectionable, yet considerations of legitimacy and legality predominate, the costs of noncooperation are prohibitive, or some of the Type I autonomy-enhancing options are used to "enlist" the cooperation of distinctly unhappy private actors. Only when the policy's implementation requires societal cooperation, societal actors are disposed to withhold it, and they cannot be dissuaded from doing just that — only when all three conditions obtain do the state's inherent powers lose their applicability.

Although societal actors obviously do not care for the idea of the state using its inherent powers to make public policies that run counter to their preferences, public officials can reasonably expect not to lose societal support in a significant number of such instances. In relying exclusively upon its inherent powers the state does not endanger or detract from the private actors' interests other than those immediately involved in the issue at hand. It does not, for instance, reduce the effectiveness of their resources for pressuring the state on other issues, jeopardize their predominance relative to societal rivals, or fracture their cohesiveness. Nor do public officials rely upon oppositional strategies, manipulative tactics, or the exploitation of the private actors' dependence upon the state, which would probably generate an affective hostility. The dispositions to sanction the state are, at least on this score, not likely to be exceptionally intense. Being largely, if not entirely, shaped by the importance attributed to the substance of public policy, the overall disposition to sanction the state is substantially weaker than in the case of comparably significant policies being adopted via most of the Type I autonomy-enhancing options.

The state can also make some purposeful efforts to further dampen these dispositions. The dispositions to exact retribution on the part of disappointed, dissatisfied, disgruntled, and even angry societal actors can be weakened by various kinds of open and private messages. Public officials can claim that the policy intent is not that of harming the societal actors' interests; that they were under enormous, unyielding pressure from those groups whose preferences were enacted; that they had little decisional latitude, for example, because in the current international context a different decision would probably have brought on an international trade war; that they acted according to their own Burkean lights in judging how best to promote the public interest or the "real" interests of the dissatisfied actors; and so on. Such claims are all the more plausible since an exclusive reliance upon the state's inherent powers does not detract from the societal actors' other interests and does not involve actions of an oppositional cast.

The previously mentioned costs that would have to be borne by societal actors who are disposed to exact sanctions are also relevant here. It may not be in their interest to act upon their dispositions — something which is unlikely to escape the notice of public officials in deciding whether to rely upon the state's inherent powers. Finally, if the probabilities of societal sanctions being applied are not minimized because of these "passive" and "soft" possibilities, the "hard" and "active" ones remain available to the state, those comprising the third Type I autonomy-enhancing strategy. These sticks can be more or less overtly brandished after acting contrary to societal demands as a way of deterring the imposition of sanctions.

In short, societal sanctions actually being triggered by the use of the state's inherent powers or autonomy-enhancing options under conditions of divergence are by no means as consistently probable as the societal constraint assumptions would suggest. In several different kinds of circumstances they are unlikely to begin with, and where likely, public officials can sometimes prevent the translation of dispositions into behaviors. Both kinds of Type I autonomy actions are thus often politically viable ones — in terms of the regular availability of autonomy-enhancing options and the state's inherent powers, the wide and diverse circumstances within which and to which they can be effectively applied, and the considerable opportunities for public officials to act upon their preferences without expecting significant societal sanctions to follow. At this point it is also worth recalling the limits and limitations of the societal constraint assumptions, in particular, the conditions under which the likely loss of societal support does not have a determining significance for public officials, and the willingness of some to undertake autonomy-enhancing efforts and act on their preferences despite expectations of societal retribution.

# 6

## Type I State Autonomy and Empirical Democratic Theory

THE ASSERTIONS AND ARGUMENTS made on behalf on Type I, Type II, and Type III state autonomy may or may not vary in their persuasiveness, but even if each set were thought to be equally and decidedly plausible, there is good reason to extend and amplify the case for Type I autonomy. For unlike Type II and Type III state autonomy accounts, which extend beyond, depart from, and are more or less incompatible with society-centered analyses, Type I autonomy accounts run up squarely against the powerful societal constraint assumptions. Some special attention is called for to provide added sustenance for the claim that the democratic state periodically makes public policies that run counter to the resource-weighted parallelogram of societal preferences.

Ideally, I should marshall a bevy of empirical cases or a few least likely cases to demonstrate that the democratic state frequently acts upon its preferences under conditions of divergence. But the available cases were all too quickly exhausted in the previous chapter in delineating the outer limits of the society-centered literature on empirical democratic theory and public policy formation. Existing studies that do not address the salient question directly, can sometimes be reinterpreted, carrying out a secondary analysis to get them to speak to the issue at hand. But this is not possible here either. For the literature has not been conceptualized along lines that sufficiently approximate the concept of Type I state autonomy; even among those studies that do differentiate clearly between state and society none offers estimates or a clear basis for estimating the state and societal parallelograms of resource-weighted preferences. The focus is commonly upon the societal parallelogram on the assumption that the state is constrained by it under conditions of divergence. A secondary analysis might also very well turn out to suffer from a serious complication. With the great debate in empirical democratic theory leaving unresolved the identification of the especially effective private resources and thus the politically weightiest societal demands and demand groups, a reinterpretation of the literature would have to deal with *each* variant's assertions on this score, or somehow manage to circumvent the issue.

In light of these presently insurmountable difficulties I take a different tack, extending and amplifying the case for Type I state autonomy within the context of empirical democratic theory. At the level of generality used in this study, there may not be any additional way in which to make a persuasive case for the realization of Type I autonomy via a reliance upon the state's inherent powers. But a good deal more can be said about the proposition that the state has a sizable number of diverse, widely applicable, effective, and regularly available Type I autonomy-enhancing capacities and opportunities which it uses periodically to translate its preferences into public policy.

In effect, we will place the fifth state-centered proposition within the context of empirical democratic theory and then watch to see what happens to it. The primary purpose in doing so is to lend the proposition additional credence. If it can be established that the society-centered variants of democratic theory do not, in fact, preclude a good number of Type I autonomy-enhancing capacities and opportunities, then we can at least say that these variants are not incompatible with the most ambitious of the state-centered propositions. Type I autonomy becomes all the more possible. If it is seen that the society-centered variants actually provide for such capacities and opportunities, that the former can be joined together, even partly incorporated with the latter, then the persuasiveness of the most ambitious state-centered proposition will be significantly enhanced. Type I autonomy becomes all the more likely. In short, Type I autonomous actions will be seen as possible and likely despite and because of the characteristic society-centered depictions of the state and state-society relations found in empirical democratic theory; a good measure of the plausibility attaching to the variants of empirical democratic theory is consequently conferred upon the Type I autonomy proposition.

Just how much more persuasiveness is to be attibuted to the proposition very much depends upon the extent to which our approach serves to stack the cards against it. A case study that bears out a proposition is all the more telling to the extent that it is a least likely case; it can thus be claimed that it is borne out even under conditions or in circumstances that are decidedly inhospitable for its confirmation, as in our reinterpretation of urban renewal policy in New Haven under Mayor Lee. In fact, it has been argued that a suitably selected single case can do as much to validate a generalization as can a study based on many cases.[1]

What I propose to do here is to pursue an approach that may be viewed as a "theoretical" equivalent to a systematically constructed least likely case study. The Type I autonomy proposition will be considered in the inhospitable context of society-centered democratic theory in such a way as to set up some high hurdles for it to clear, concomitantly placing some fairly onerous requirements upon it. If the state is seen to have autonomy-enhancing capacities and opportunities even when figuratively clearing high hurdles, in rough terrain, while carrying heavy weights, then the proposition is surely deserving of a hardy dose of plausibility. Just how much plausibility depends upon the extent and thoroughness with which the cards have been stacked against its theoretical demonstration.

Granted, this approach is hardly a familiar one; it may well raise the eyebrows of those who are especially skeptical of any theoretical argument made on behalf of a proposition's plausibility. Over and above the reasons for thinking that this approach is indeed a viable one, I want to stress that the near absence of usable empirical studies helps justify our assessing the proposition's plausibility in a theoretical manner. Empirical studies have not demonstrated — as opposed to presenting foreordained, though not necessarily invalid, evidence — that societal preferences consistently prevail when they diverge from the state's. The assertion therefore very much hinges upon the plausibility of the underlying societal constraint assumptions. Since neither society-centered explanations nor the assumptions upon which they are premised have been systematically demonstrated with empirical evidence — or subjected to determined efforts at falsification — the rival Type I autonomy proposition should be granted equal empirical latitude.

Still, for those who might not be fully persuaded there is a secondary rationale which will almost certainly be thought acceptable — that of putting some additional empirical flesh upon the Type I autonomy proposition. The previous discussion of Type I autonomy-enhancing capacities and opportunities did not make more than occasional references to particular state, societal, or state-society patterns. It did not, in other words, place the proposition in one or another distinctive empirical setting. Since the four variants of empirical democratic theory provide a nearly complete portrayal of the differing contexts, placing the proposition within these generalized settings serves to illustrate and specify how the state manages to act autonomously under conditions of divergence. Up to now the theoretical variants have been discussed only with respect to their identification of the especially weighty private resources and the effective demand groups. They also offer distinctive portrayals of the contours of civil society, state-society relations, and the structure of the state. This chapter sets out the many ways in which the state's autonomy-enhancing capacities and opportunities relate to and emerge from several different state and societal constellations.

### Five Guidelines for a Least Likely Theoretical Analysis

Carrying out this least likely theoretical analysis revolves around five methodological guidelines, loosely construed. The more demanding these are thought to be, the greater the plausibility attaching to the proposition — assuming of course that it survives, that it is not disconfirmed along the way. In positing a divergence between state and societal preferences, the first guideline stipulates that the divergence involves the effective demand groups. Public officials acting contrary to the demands of societal actors *outside* the effective demand group universe is hardly without significance. But demonstrating Type I autonomy vis-à-vis the effective demand groups is clearly far more telling given their disproportionate control over those resources that are especially effective in constraining the state. Moreover, authoritative actions that run counter to the expressed interests of noneffective demand groups may be explicable in terms of the support accorded the state by the effective demand groups, rather than being due to its own autonomy-enhancing capacities and opportunities.

The second guideline takes the first a step further in positing divergent preferences with respect to each of the four effective demand groups identified by the major variants of empirical democratic theory. To argue that certain societal actors constitute *the* effective demand group in the advanced industrial democracies, and then limit ourselves to them alone, would not generate the most persuasive case for the proposition. Not only are four efforts at falsification more convincing than one, given the great variations in demand group interests, resources, and structures, doing so also obviates the possible objection that the "chosen" demand group does not help stack the cards against the proposition as much as some other might. In addition, those scholars who believe that societal actors other than the chosen ones constitute the effective demand group, who find the proposition premised upon an inaccurate depiction of civil society, would surely remain unpersuaded. Similarly, scholars who hold that different societal actors constitute the effective demand groups in different societies would find the argument to be limited in its applicability.

The third guideline stipulates the generalized empirical setting within which the proposition is to be demonstrated, namely, the inhospitable context provided by the four decidedly society-centered variants of democratic theory. The proposition must be seen to hold despite and/or because of their descriptive and explanatory generalizations. These are taken as given, except of course for the denial of Type I autonomy itself. All other assertions about civil society, the state, and their interrelationships are taken as presumptively valid, subjected to no criticisms whatsoever. For example, pluralist theory is not weakened by neopluralist or Marxist counterassertions, followed by a demonstration of autonomy founded upon some amended pluralist generalizations. The argument must be premised upon and limited by the complete, unmodified generalizations of four diverse, inhospitable society-centered constructs.

Taking the last a step further, the fourth guideline requires that nothing be added to the society-centered generalizations found in each variant. The argument for state autonomy must be based exclusively upon and limited by the descriptive and explanatory assertions of each variant. They cannot even be expanded to include patterns of public policy, state structure, state-society relations, or societal features that are indisputably present. For example, pluralism does not focus upon the mixed-economy welfare state as such, but according to this guideline we cannot point to this partial oversight and then present an argument for Type I autonomy, based upon the characteristics of the positive state. This does, of course, restrict the case to be made on behalf of the proposition, but the more important consideration here is that of coming as close as possible to a theoretical equivalent of the least likely case method.

Fifth, the state must be shown to have Type I autonomy-enhancing capacities and opportunities that are general and regularly applicable, rather than particular and intermittent. To argue that it can act contrary to the expressed interests of the effective demand groups with respect to specific issues (for example, national security), in particular situational contexts (for example, economic crisis), or when certain public officials are heavily involved (for example, well-entrenched bureaucrats) would surely be significant. Yet it would leave open the question of just how much autonomy the state enjoys. To tie autonomy to particular issues, situational contexts, or state actors would only demonstrate that it obtains under especially favorable circumstances; any inferences about state autonomy under other less propitious and more common conditions would be most problematic. Public officials must therefore be seen to have general and commonly applicable autonomy-enhancing capacities and opportunities.

The following three sections each summarize a variant of democratic theory—the theory of the liberal state, the distorted liberal state, and the liberal corporatist state—and their society-centered answers to the question with which we began this book: How account for the authoritative actions and inactions of the democratic state? After positing divergent preferences between the state and the effective demand groups identified by each variant, it is argued that despite and/or because of the empirical conditions and propositions found within each variant, the state enjoys several kinds of general and regularized autonomy-enhancing capacities and opportunities. In the final section dealing with the liberal capitalist state the argument takes a somewhat different form. For as already seen, the Marxist variant does claim, and is the only one to do so, that on occasion the state acts contrary to the expressed interests of the effective demand group. Consequently, the liberal capitalist state must be shown to act contrary to the demands of the bourgeoisie far more *often* than acknowledged in Marxist writings, and this has, of course, to be done while remaining within the methodological guidelines.

## The Autonomy of the Liberal State

Until around 1960 pluralism[2] was practically unchallenged as the reigning variant of empirical democratic theory in American political science. Even after being dethroned by methodological and substantive critiques and rival theories, it may still remain "first among equals." More than any other variant it unabashedly says look to civil society and the political process to understand what the state does and why it does so. The possibility of the liberal state acting contrary to the societal parallelogram of demands and resources is strenuously denied. Not one of the dozens of state units in David B. Truman's compendious study[3] adopted legislation or regulations that were opposed by the weightiest, or even the potentially strongest, of the interested groups.

As portrayed by pluralism, civil society is made up of a plethora of diverse, fluctuating, competing groups of individuals with shared interests. Many effective political resources are available to them: numbers, votes, organization, money, expertise, information, social status, a positive public image, access to the mass media, and control over economic resources. Even an intensity of feeling may be an effective resource, able to transform "potential groups" into actual groups and slack resources into usable resources. In Robert A. Dahl's unusually emphatic words, "Virtually no one, and certainly no group of more than a few individuals, is entirely lacking in some influence resources."[4] Most groups control a disproportionate share of some resources, but the diversity and widespread distribution of resources makes for a noncumulative pattern of "dispersed inequalities." The effective demand group universe is almost totally inclusive, encompassing all politically active groups. The political marketplace in which so many diverse resources serve as effective political coin is almost coterminus with civil society.

Bounded by a fairly broad procedural and substantive consensus, and with existing divisions tempered by cross-cutting interests and overlapping group memberships, societal actors usually pursue their interests with moderation. Given the many effective resources, the great number and diversity of societal interests, and the low barriers to access, groups tend to form quickly and easily, even spontaneously, in defending and pressing their interests upon societal rivals and public officials. Groups with conflicting interests also tend toward a shifting equilibrium of resources; the resource strengths of long-standing rival groups are regularly balanced. For when existing interests and groups are weak relative to their rivals, they can, at least over time, generate additional resources, turn to the ones that have some slack, and mobilize "potential groups." Where nearly all groups are effective demand groups, no one group predominates within civil society; within any one issue area, a single group can predominate temporarily at most before it and the liberal state are confronted with countervailing resources.

The liberal state is guided and constrained by the resource-weighted parallelogram of societal preferences; its authoritative actions are the "resultant of effective access by various interests." With voters choosing the elected officials they prefer, elected officials competing for popular support and tailoring their public actions to calculations of electoral advantage, elected and appointed officials being lobbied at numerous access points and pressured at permeable decision sites, and public officials relying upon group support in adopting public policies and group cooperation in implementing them—under these conditions the state consistently responds to societal demands. Public officials are even wary of acting contrary to the interests of "potential groups."

The liberal state has been depicted as a mere "cash register" that totals up the resource credits of competing groups, more often by pluralist critics than pluralists. But public policy is not by any means simply a direct, undiluted, unmediated response to the political marketplace. The liberal state plays a critically important role in aggregating, balancing, and reconciling conflicting demands; it is continuously active as a broker and mediator, working out and facilitating the acceptance of policy compromises on the part of competing groups. With public officials serving as advocates for their geographical, demographic, and specialized constituencies, pressing the interests of rival constituencies upon one another in a forthright but conciliatory fashion, the state regularly succeeds in mediating disputes and finding mutually acceptable compromises.

In a pluralist work that focuses upon the bureaucracy, the "policy maker" is depicted as "travelling on three parallel tracks — often in alternation, or with retractable wheels resting with uneven weight on two or all three tracks. He moves his vehicle as far as he can on the smooth track of consensus; he changes as necessary to the rough track of reconciliation of conflict; he rides farther with a wheel on each, seeking reconciliation by compromise and further development of consensus; and he rides occasionally on the majoritarian track, either by gauging the interests affected or by sharing the decision power with others, and hopes that he finally may travel again on the smooth track of a newly developed consensus."[5] The liberal state is able to operate in this manner — responding to, reconciling, absorbing, and adjusting demands — largely because of the broad consensus within which rival groups differ and the moderation with which they pursue their interests, with state successes having a feedback effect in reinforcing societal consensus and moderation.

Accepting all these pluralist assertions about state and society without emendations or additions, and then positing a divergence between the preferences of any set of public officials and any set of private actors within the effective demand group universe, how can the liberal state free itself from these imposing societal constraints? Where are its autonomy-enhancing capacities and opportunities to be found that can neutralize the constraining effects of the groups' resources, mitigate the extent and effectiveness with which they are able to deploy their resources, and dissuade the groups from fully deploying them?

From James Madison on, cross-cutting group interests and overlapping group memberships have been used to account for the moderation with which groups pursue their demands. Yet pluralists have not seen, or at least not acknowledged, that these patterns can be exploited by the state to fracture group cohesiveness and reduce group size, thereby diminishing the resources with which they can pressure the state. By redefining issues more broadly, by linking them to other currently salient issues, or by placing other issues on the immediate agenda, public officials can place group members in a conflicted and/or psychologically cross-pressured situation, thereby reducing group cohesiveness, mobilization efforts, and perhaps the size of the group. This point is especially applicable to large groups with diverse memberships. It also applies to smaller, more cohesive groups given the leaders' sensitivity to a possible decline in group cohesiveness. Truman identifies the "maximization of cohesion" in the face of the members' other group attachments and interests as "the continuing and primary task of leadership in the internal politics of interest groups."[6] Because group cohesion affects the leaders' authority as well as serving as a critical resource, it is possible for public officials to dissuade the leaders from actively pressing group demands upon the state, or at least from doing so in an implacable manner, by threatening to restructure the issue in a way that endangers the much-valued group cohesion. The state's options for exploiting the many cross-cutting interests and overlapping group memberships can be used both to deter and defend it against demand group pressures.

Pluralists do not maintain that most groups control approximately equivalent resources, but they do state that this is true for those who are regularly opposed to one another. On long-standing issues, such as labor-management relations, rival groups are usually balanced in strength; pressure begets counterpressure, and if imbalances do appear, these are soon rectified by the weaker groups' mobilization of slack resources. Here then is a common and easily grasped opportunity for autonomous action on the part of the state. Given an approximately balanced bimodal distribution of preferences and resources, the state need not be constrained by the societal parallelogram to adopt a policy position that is midway between the rival groups, which is how a societally constrained state would respond. It can tip the scales in favor of its own preferences, doing so without even an overall loss of support, by substituting the support of one group for the loss of another's. Moreover, with a panoply of diverse groups making demands upon them at any one time, many public officials can choose which group's demands to satisfy on different issues—doing so according to their own preferences and without suffering an overall loss of support.

While the demand groups have a great armory of diverse resources with which to gain access to and control over the state, these are far from decisive if they cannot be brought fully to bear upon the state. The societal context affords the liberal state numerous opportunities to neutralize or diminish their constraining effects. To say that civil society is composed of a plethora of groups and potential groups, fluctuating in size, with diverse, cross-cutting and oft-changing interests, is to underscore the weak structure of the demand group universe, one lacking in clarity, coherence, and stability. It is a societal context that offers public officials many chances to maneuver among and between groups, evading, deflecting, and impeding the effective deployment of their resources by highlighting group differences or shared interests, broadening or narrowing group conflicts, playing off rival groups against one another, or encouraging or discouraging the activation of potential groups. Nor is it the societal context alone that generates these advantageous opportunities. The liberal state, with its numerous access points and decision sites, also makes a signal contribution. Public officials can thus deflect pressures toward other officials, misrepresent their positions, exaggerate their opposition, shift decisional responsibilities and decision sites. If they choose to, they can at the same time claim to be actively pressing constituent demands within the state. Both state and societal structure do much to facilitate the maneuverability of public officials.

There are two respects in which the liberal state's mediating activities serve to enhance its autonomy. First, public officials have the leeway not only to insert but also to press for their own policy preferences. Mediation occurs in an informal manner, negotiations are worked out more or less quietly, brokerage is a complex, nuanced activity. Thus despite the great access of societal actors, the actual decisionmaking processes are not readily decipherable. The constraining effects of private resources are diminished to the extent that societal actors are unable to determine just how accurately public officials represent their preferences and how forcefully they press for them. Not only is it possible for public officials simply to go through the motions, they also have opportunities that are not readily visible to act in ways that actually run counter to the demands of societal actors, including their constituents, clients, and supporters. Neither real estate brokers nor public officials are all "honest brokers."

Second, without forgetting the liberal state's many-faceted dependence upon the demand groups, there is the latter's dependence upon the state in its mediating role. Private actors may not be concerned with the advantages of mediation as a process, but they are certainly interested in particular policy compromises that are relatively advantageous for themselves, and thus dependent upon the good offices and services of public officials for working them out. If societal groups pressure public officials in an unyielding fashion, bringing their resources fully to bear upon them, they risk losing the officials' determined efforts to mediate immediate and other group disputes in ways that will produce relatively favorable compromises. If societal groups are not already aware of this possibility, public officials can more or less gently remind them of it so as to dissuade them for exerting implacable pressures upon the state.

A final consideration is a limiting one, constituting a case for partial state autonomy. The liberal state can act upon one set of its preferences, while giving up another, by engaging in a profitable exchange with the demand groups. Given the great number and diversity of demand groups and the weakly structured demand group universe, there is no reason to suppose that public and private actors consistently regard the same issue divergences as the most important ones. Public officials are likely to attach a higher priority or value to one currently salient issue and the weightiest demand groups to another. Public officials can link two issues by agreeing to fulfill group demands on the issue of greater importance to them, societal actors in turn agreeing not to deploy their resources fully with respect to the one that has a higher priority for the public actors. The liberal state can readily arrange for this kind of profitable exchange because of its mediating activities per se and what accompanies them: a storehouse of detailed information about group preferences to rely upon in formulating exchange possibilities, frequent contacts with the demand groups to allow for the terms of the exchange to be explored, and sufficiently good mutual access to facilitate successful negotiations.

## The Autonomy of the Distorted Liberal State

Neopluralism[7] grew out of a two-pronged critique of pluralist theory. Pluralism is said to offer a flawed interpretation of civil society and to downplay the extent and significance of the state's exceptionally close relations with certain kinds of groups. It has consequently failed to recognize the systematic biases of the political process and the public policies it produces. From this critique, and the empirical studies informed by it, comes what can be called the theory of the distorted liberal state.

Pluralism and neopluralism place great store upon the identification and distribution of political resources within civil society and agree that they come in numerous shapes and sizes. But neopluralists contend that only a few are especially effective in influencing the state and that the effectiveness of the others is further diluted because they are underutilized. The effective resources are strictly limited to organization, specialized policy concerns, and money. Neopluralism also differs from pluralism in claiming that these resources are distributed cumulatively rather than dispersed throughout civil society. They are regularly found among, and commonly limited to, relatively small groups with politically homogeneous memberships. Largely because of their well-developed organizational structures, the internal relations of these groups are decidedly oligarchical; the leaders are able to pursue interests that conflict with those of the members. The effective demand group universe is composed of relatively small, hierarchically organized, financially well-endowed groups with primary interests in narrow bands of public policy. It does not include large participant publics, and certainly not "potential groups."

The liberal state is in frequent contact with private actors who have easy access to, yet remain separate from, the state. Not so the distorted liberal state, whose distinctive feature is the frequent merging of public and private power. The distorted liberal state invites private actors into "the interior processes of government" and recognizes private associations as the exclusive representatives of particular interests. "The most interested and best organized" business, labor, agricultural, trade, and professional groups of teachers, lawyers, accountants, doctors, and so on nominate and place private individuals on quasi-public boards, commissions, agencies, and advisory councils, whose decisions and advice are rarely rejected. Some associations have even been largely "called into being by actions of government officials," concomitantly being accorded "the power to exert great influence over policy and administration."[8]

The public-private distinction is further blurred as the distorted liberal state goes about its business of making, applying, and implementing public policy in a characteristically informal manner. Legislation is neither universalistic in its applicability nor specific with regard to objectives and the means for realizing them. The great legislative powers of the state, the lawmaking powers, are knowingly delegated downwards to administrative departments, regulatory commissions, and other kinds of public agencies where private interests are well represented. It is they who interpret vague laws and exercise large grants of discretionary authority, notably unconstrained by the procedures or substance of legal formalism. In the absence of rigidly, clearly, and extensively articulated formal rules, informality becomes the rule. It is then no accident that separate legislative and administrative units maintain close, informal connections with specialized clienteles. State-society relations are highly compartmentalized. Public officials consult with, take the advice of, accord public powers to, and serve the interests of their clients—those demand groups whose narrow interests relate directly to the separate state unit's authoritative responsibilities. Neopluralism therefore also rejects pluralism's assertions about countervailing societal patterns and state mediation of societal conflicts.

The distorted liberal state is then doubly biased toward the effective demand groups: public powers are shared with them and specific public policies consistently conform to their demands. This double bias is explicable in terms of the state's dependence upon and preference for these advantaged groups. Their organizational capacities, sizeable treasuries, and the technical expertise and information that go along with specialized interests, make the state heavily dependent upon them for direct and indirect electoral support, assistance in policy formulation, and cooperation in its implementation. With issues being compartmentalized, the separate state units remain "beholden" to their specialized constituencies; there are no others that they can easily turn to for support. When issues cut across compartmentalized lines of state-society relations, and when the demand groups are engaged in issue conflicts among themselves, the state responds to those with the weightiest resources.

The effective demand groups also turn out to be the preferred groups. Public officials believe that the merging of the public and private spheres is a pragmatically warranted and normatively justified formula for the governing of complex societies. Where the state has facilitated the formation of private associations and endowed them with public powers the impulse has been a pragmatic one. "The potential gain in support for the officials is a clear incentive. There is also a strong desire to avoid conflict and to gain a 'voluntary' settlement of disputes in the making of policy."[9] Normatively, what Theodore J. Lowi calls the ideology of "interest-group liberalism" holds it to be "both necessary and good that the policy agenda and the public interest be defined in terms of the organized interests in society."[10] Public officials believe that they should be responsive to "the most interested and best organized" groups, since they represent all significant societal interests and their leaders speak for the membership. Enfranchising them as the exclusive representatives of particular interests and inviting the leaders into the "interior process of government" maximizes representation, responsiveness, decisional effectiveness, and political stability. The preferred groups then also turn out to be the advantaged groups — advantaged in being endowed with public powers.

Expressed in our terms, the distorted liberal state is portrayed as both autonomous and constrained. The state has acted on its preferences with respect to the merging of the public and private spheres and numerous substantive policy decisions. On the other hand, there is "the conquest of segments of formal state power by private groups and associations." The separate state units are exclusively dependent upon, "beholden" to, and "captives" of the specialized groups that constitute their narrow geographical and functional constituencies.[11] Yet there need not be, and neopluralism does not imply, an incompatibility between these generalizations. For while the state has been able to act on many or most of its preferences, it has only been said to do so in the absence of state-society divergences. That nondivergence rather than the state's Type I autonomy-enhancing capacities and opportunities allowed for the merging of the public and private spheres and the satisfaction of demand group preferences is further emphasized by the societal constraint assertions — as "captives" of their client groups public officials surely could not act contrary to their preferences — and by the absence of any neopluralist references to the state's autonomy-enhancing options with regard to the effective demand groups.

Before positing a divergence between state and demand group policy preferences, a few admittedly speculative ideas are worth pursuing with regard to the relative importance of state- and society-centered explanations for the merging of the public and private spheres under conditions of nondivergence. Estimating the relative importance of two actors upon an outcome when their preferences do not diverge is usually problematic. Yet state preferences may be assigned greater explanatory weight when authoritative actions that conform to group interests are undertaken without any pressures being placed upon the state, all the more so if public officials are not even asked to undertake them. (Public officials might have acted in anticipation of such pressures, but this is always a possibility under conditions of nondivergence and neopluralists do not offer any evidence or reasons for supposing that they did so.) Moreover, in the absence of group pressures and requests, the resource-weighted parallelogram of societal preferences can hardly be estimated with great confidence. It could be that public officials did not in fact act with societal support behind them. These points are applicable to the distorted liberal state's efforts in helping to form some associations and its sharing of public powers with others; to that extent it is less subject to societal constraints than neopluralism generally allows. We can be more precise.

There is no indication, or reason to suppose, that any objections were expressed by those groups that were assisted by public officials in forming associations and then recognized as the exclusive representatives of particular interests. Neither is there any indication that they pressured the state or even made any demands upon it. They obviously did not possess any organizational capability, the critical resource in neopluralist theory, prior to their formation. This merging of public and private power probably occurred as Grant McConnell says it occurred: public officials acted on their own initiative and for their own reasons.[12] Moreover, in the absence of pressures upon the state, especially considering that the relevant groups' organizational resources had not yet been developed, it is by no means clear whether state and societal preferences did or did not diverge with respect to selective enfranchisements.

In discussing why private associations were brought into the "interior process of government" Lowi contrasts the motivations of American public officials in the 1930s and 1960s. In the 1930s the state accorded official recognition to private associations out of weakness; it was "forced to share its sovereignty in return for support." In the 1960s, however, similar actions were undertaken "voluntarily"; by then public officials had become strongly imbued with the ideology of "interest-group liberalism." Rather than being "forced upon the national leaders" in this later period, the formal delegation and informal relegation of public powers to the advantaged groups was "voluntarily pursued as the highest expression of [the public officials'] ideology."[13] Here then is the distorted liberal state acting on its preferences without being pressured by the effective demand groups. Moreover, with the latter not flexing their muscles it is possible that state preferences did not have societal support behind them. Lowi's brief assessment in another part of the book allows for such an interpretation. The actions of public officials in the 1960s are explained in terms of their belief in the "virtue" of delegating public authority to private associations, but the amount and degree of delegation extended *beyond* that called for by "the realities of power."[14]

To be sure, these are speculative comments which do not constitute a strong case for the Type I autonomy of the distorted liberal state. But they do warn against attributing unwarranted importance to societal constraint explanations in interpreting the formation and actions of the distorted liberal state. We now turn to its autonomy under conditions of issue specific divergences.

The neopluralist version of societal constraint analysis attributes great importance to the state's decisive dependence upon the effective demand groups. Given the compartmentalization of state-society relations — certain state units and specialized clienteles constantly and often exclusively interacting with one another — public officials rely upon the support of their client groups, and no others, leaving them little choice but to fulfill their demands. Yet there is also the reverse side of the coin. To the extent that public officials have nowhere else to turn for societal suport than to the specialized groups whose interests fall within the scope of their authoritative responsibilities, the advantaged groups are also exclusively dependent upon particular public officials. For the demand groups to turn to other, presumably less recalcitrant state units is not likely to be helpful. Other state units do not always have the authority to act within the narrow bands of policy with which the demand groups are concerned. With respect to those units that do, the groups' specialized resources may have little effect upon them, especially in the case of those whose authority is sufficiently inclusive to have large constituencies, thereby placing smaller groups on relatively weak ground. Compartmentalization — decisionmaking within what have been called "cozy little triangles," "policy whirlpools," and "subgovernments" — makes for both state and societal dependence. And to say interdependence means that public officials can exploit the groups' dependence to dissuade them from exerting implacable pressures upon the state.

Compartmentalized state-society relations are also relevant when two state units with the authority to resolve an issue hold conflicting preferences that match those of their respective clienteles. The issue divides two coalitions each made up of public and private actors. State-society preferences diverge insofar as the relative resource position of the state units differs from that of the two societal groups relative to one another. One coalition includes the state unit that is predominant vis-à-vis its public counterpart; the other coalition includes the societally predominant group. In these hardly uncommon situations the state's preferences determine the resultant public policy far more than societal preferences. With the separate state units preferences matching their clients' preferences, private resources lose most of their constraining impact. Policy is then affected far more by the relative resources, hierarchical standing, and strategic positioning of the state units involved than by the distribution resources. The issue is largely resolved within the state.

The effective demand groups benefit enormously from their enfranchisement and the sharing of public powers, turning them into especially advantaged groups. But having derived these benefits from the state, the advantaged groups are dependent upon it for their continuation. What has once been given by the state probably cannot be taken away, but it can be given to others as well, thereby diluting its value considerably for the current beneficiaries. The distorted liberal state that assisted in forming some private associations, enfranchised many as the exclusive representatives of particular interests, and inducted many of these into the "interior processes of government" can do as much for other groups and associations. State units can enlarge their constituencies, make them more diverse, and break the oligopolies and monopolies of official representation by enfranchising additional groups and sharing public powers with them. Under conditions of divergence, public officials might readily be tempted to do so by the pragmatic calculation that somewhat greater support may be derived from the enfranchisement of additional associations. The newly privileged associations are likely to be supportive of their public patrons, at least initially; their resources would help counter those of the already enfranchised associations, and their newly acquired advantaged position would probably attract more societal resources to them. In this situational context of dependency, the advantaged groups can ill afford to deploy their resources in an implacable fashion, fully applying them against the state. Public officials can dissuade them from doing so by exploiting their dependence upon the state for the continued enjoyment of critically important public benefits; if acted upon, such a threat could jeopardize the groups' predominance vis-à-vis their rivals.

Given the neopluralist emphasis upon organizational capacity and membership homogeneity, there is no doubting that intragroup divisions would detract sharply from the full mobilization and effective deployment of demand group resources, all the more so if internal divisions separate leaders and members and turn the former toward the state. The neopluralist use of Roberto Michels' "iron law of oligarchy" to depict the associations' internal relations allows for the actualization of this possibility. "Leaders tend to identify their own interests with those of the organization and seek to preserve the foundations of their own positions, thus laying the foundation for conflict of interests between leaders and led . . . And in contests between [them], the former have virtually all the advantages."[15] Public officials can exploit this situation, dividing the two strata by drawing the leadership toward themselves. In order to head off or mitigate confrontations with the advantaged groups, the state can try to co-opt the leaders, offering them public recognition, appointments to (more important) public agencies, assistance in maintaining the organization, and varied noncollective rewards in return for their willingness to engage in "responsible" behavior—that is, a willingness to support public officials by not acting upon the membership's "unreasonable" demands and by turning aside the "excessive" pressures that would otherwise be directed at the state. Although neopluralism does not say so explicitly, given the close relations between public officials and association leaders and staff, the latter may be all the more disposed to go along with the former than with the more distant group members whom they represent. The distorted liberal state is thus advantaged in being able to mitigate the extent and effectiveness with which the demand groups are able to deploy their resources, even turning them toward its own purposes.

The constraining effect of private resources is partly vitiated by the signal importance of civil servants for the advantaged groups. With the legislature of the distorted liberal state choosing not to write laws that are clearly specified and rigidly and uniformly applicable, the bureaucracy enjoys great decisional latitude in interpreting legislation, revising regulations, and using its authority to make new rules. Private actors interested in effecting or preventing incremental changes within narrow policy areas—which is exactly what the demand groups aim for—turn first and foremost to administrative officials. When dealing with, and certainly when confronting, such a bureaucratically weighted state under conditions of divergence, the groups' resources lose much of their potency. The effectiveness of expertise and technical information is at least partly vitiated when dealing with civil servants who possess similar resources. The other two especially effective resources — organization and financing — lose a good deal of their effectiveness when confronting securely tenured civil servants. The bureaucracy's dependence upon the demand groups for cooperation in implementing policies and for shoring up support among its legislative overseers and appropriating units is not to be forgotten, yet its overall importance is significantly offset by the relative ineffectiveness of demand group resources for constraining the bureaucracy.

### The Autonomy of the Liberal Corporatist State

Social or liberal corporatism's[16] recent emergence has been inspired not so much by direct critiques of the other variants,[17] as by the empirical observation that certain European democracies have come to exhibit a distinctive pattern of interest intermediation — that of functional representation broadly conceived. Social corporatism's singular feature is the direct, continuous, regularized involvement of associational leaders with both *one another* and the state in the formulation, adoption, and administration of most public policies. All organized groups have not only access to the state, but also virtually guaranteed rights of consultation and participation in the making of authoritative decisions. Sweden, Norway, Denmark, Finland, Austria, and the Netherlands clearly exhibit this defining feature of social corporatism; in Germany, Britain, Belgium, and Switzerland it appears to a recognizable degree, especially in the making of economic policy. What will be referred to as the theory of the liberal corporatist state is said to provide a decidedly accurate acount of public policy formation in the first group of countries and to have considerable applicability within the second.

The other descriptive feature of the social corporatist variant, though not entirely distinctive to it, is the structuring of civil society along organized functional lines, especially those that differentiate the economic activities and associations of the business, labor, and agricultural sectors. It is these associations and their interactions that delimit and structure the effective demand group universe. Although not invariably present, where they exist the most important ones are the nationally organized, densely populated peak associations enjoying monopolies of representation within each major economic sector. Their especially effective resources include a large membership comprising the overwhelming majority of sectorally situated individuals, enterprises, and groups, centralized organization, control over critical economic resources, and technical expertise and information. In a less concentrated and abundant form, these same resources constitute the especially effective ones for the smaller, more functionally specialized associations. It is not altogether clear whether the votes of association members constitute an especially effective resource; they may have far more impact upon the choice of governing officials than upon their authoritative actions.

Whereas the effective demand groups remain separate from one another in their efforts to influence the liberal and distorted liberal states, even when sharing the latter's public powers, in the liberal corporatist state they deal with one another directly. Public officials and association representatives at high and middle levels meet regularly in influential advisory committees, in national social and economic councils, and in ad hoc groups to work out and adopt authoritative decisions ranging from the detailed administration of social services to the annual setting of price and wage levels.

> The crucial decisions on economic policy [in Norway] are rarely taken in the parties or in Parliament: the central area is the bargaining table where the government authorities meet directly with the trade union leaders, the representatives of the farmers, the small holders, and the fishermen, and the delegates of the Employer's Association. These yearly rounds of negotiations have in fact come to mean more in the lives of rank-and-file citizens than the formal elections. In these processes of intensive interaction . . . decisions are not made through the counting of heads

but through complex considerations of short-term and long-term advantages in alternative lines of compromise.[18]

Although occasional breakdowns occur, the negotiations commonly take the form of more or less cooperative bargaining sessions in which technical and managerial criteria are used in helping to decide among policy options. "To challenge the technocratic governmental process by politicizing an issue is generally regarded as counterproductive."[19]

Public policies are primarily explicable in terms of the associations' demands upon one another and the state as weighted by their resources. The state depends upon the associations for expert advice in the making of policy, for their agreement to abide by and administer public policies, and for their legitimation of public policy. Being heavily involved in societal guidance and economic management, the state is also constrained by the association's control over critical economic resources. The state consequently responds to associational demands largely in accordance with the resources they are able to bring to bear upon one another and the state. However, considerations of mutual advantage and technical and managerial criteria also have a place in policy formation. Public policy does not consistently correspond to resource-weighted preferences in a one-to-one manner, but the possibility of the liberal corporatist state acting on its own preferences when these diverge from those of the demand groups is denied, ignored, or at most only hinted at.

As is also true of neopluralism, the possibility of Type I autonomous actions is considered only with respect to the enfranchising of certain societal groups, the selective granting of representational monopolies. And as with neopluralism, empirically it is unclear whether the national peak associations were granted their representational monopolies under conditions of divergence or nondivergence.

Phillippe Schmitter is the only writer who has addressed this question. Socioeconomic explanations are important for understanding the "initial associational responses," the growth of nationally organized sectoral associations. Beyond that point, however, state preferences become critical in accounting for the spatial and longitudinal variations in the emergence of social corporatism.

> Once the new collective actors begin to acquire resource and organizational properties of their own and once the state has expanded the scope and volume of its policy interventions, the mode of interest intermediation may be molded "from within" and "from above," so to speak, in relative independence from the conditions of civil society and even in disregard for the preferences and interests of the individuals, firms, sectors, classes, and so on whose interests are supposedly being represented.[20]

Public officials act upon their preferences in recognizing, licensing, and granting representational monopolies to the national associations. The implication to be drawn from this passage is that they did so under conditions of state-society divergence. Yet it is most likely that the national associations were short on political resources prior to their incorporation, or that they had reason to oppose it. In another essay, Schmitter in fact refers to the "osmotic process whereby the modern state and modern interest association seek each other out."[21]

When we ask why the public officials granted the representational monopolies, three different but not incompatible answers are offered.

> The more the modern state comes to serve as the indispensable and authoritative guarantor of capitalism by expanding its regulative and integrative tasks, the more it finds that it needs the professional expertise, specialized information, prior aggregation of opinion, contractual capability and deferred participatory legitimacy which only singular, hierarchically ordered, consensually led representative monopolies can provide. To obtain these, the state will agree to devolve upon or share with these associations much of its newly acquired decisional authority.[22]

In a later essay, the state's preferences are said to derive from certain "organizational affinities" and concerns for particular private interests.

> The preferences of discrete and/or autonomous agencies of the state for correspondingly organized functional "partners" in the issue arenas they are mandated to regulate legally, subsidize materially, or placate symbolically . . . plus the deliberate attempt to create encapsulated segments of associational privilege and policy protection especially for groups, sectors, and classes threatened by the secular trends of industrialization and capitalist development, go a long way in explaining persistent differences in mode of intermediation across Western European societies of otherwise similar economic and social structures.[23]

These depictions of state preferences begin to address, but do not clearly answer, the question of whether the liberal corporatist state emerged via Type I autonomy actions. In any case, they indirectly underscore the significance of state preferences in interpreting instances of state-society divergence after the emergence of the liberal corporatist state.

Turning to the liberal corporatist state's relations with the effective demand groups, and positing a divergence between them, one argument for Type I autonomy derives from the manner in which the social corporatist pattern emerged. The national peak associations were "recognized or licensed (if not created) by the state and granted a deliberate representational monopoly within their respective sectors in exchange for observing certain controls on their selection of leaders and articulation of demands and supports."[24] In return for the granting of representational privileges, the state is able to maintain some control over the associations. The application of demand group resources occurs within definite limits—limits on the ambitiousness of the demands advanced and the pressures exerted on their behalf. Public officials are able to define demands that diverge overly far from their own preferences as unacceptable and attempts to bring overbearing pressures upon them as unallowable. It appears that the peak association leaders have generally abided by these limitations over time, while central-ized organization has enabled them to mediate and control membership attempts to overstep the limits. On a more specu-lative level, it may well be that the explicit and implicit limita-tions that the liberal corporatist state has placed upon the na-tional peak associations have also filtered down, that they have become established as norms applicable to the smaller, special-ized associations as well.

It is a well-known proposition that process very much helps shape decisional outcomes. The liberal corporatist state exer-cises markedly greater control over the process than do the pri-vate associations, thereby neutralizing some of the impact and mitigating the effective deployment of societal resources. Con-sultation and participation are guaranteed the associations, but the allocation of seats, the overall and more precise formulation of the agenda, and the direction of the deliberations are far more influenced by public than private officials. In Sweden, some seventy-five Royal Commissions are established each year to make (regularly accepted) policy recommendations to the government based on their comprehensive reports of condi-tions and collections of facts. About 80 percent of the commis-sion members are drawn from the civil service, legislators and associational representatives sharing the remaining 20 percent. Upwards of 80 percent of the commissions are chaired by civil servants, and as a rule, the chairman has a "dominating influ-ence."[25] In Norway, over a thousand permanent and tempo-rary public-private committees are at work at any given time, and the government and legislature accept nearly all their rec-ommendations without dissent. More than half of the chairmen and the secretaries who usually formulate the proposals are civil servants.[26] The state is also predominant among the well over 400 public-private committees found in Finland at any one time. The secretary or secretariat plays the key role of col-lecting relevant materials and preparing drafts of committee re-ports. Association representatives hold only 10 percent of the total and civil servants occupy almost all the other secretariat positions.[27]

There is no questioning the abundance of resources controlled by the private associations, but to the extent that the
state is not heavily dependent upon them, they lose a good deal
of their impact on public policy formation. The ubiquitous involvement of civil servants — not just their disproportionate
presence as members and heads of the public-private commit-
tes, but also their role in the formulation, adoption, and application of nearly all public policies[28] — is especially important in
this regard. A bureaucratically weighted state can neutralize or
diminish the constraining effects of societal resources. These
bureaucratic officials are at least as well endowed with information and expertise as are the private associations, allowing
them to formulate and press for their preferences without having to rely upon the latter. To a significant extent they can use
their resources to offset the associations' similar ones. With civil
servants securely tenured and promotions determined by se-
niority and professional competence, the constraining impact
of the associations' membership and organizational resources is
sharply mitigated.

The likelihood of public officials translating their preferences
into authoritative actions is also buttressed by "the technocratic
governmental process." Over and above the relative weights of
the resources standing behind them, alternative policy options
are selected to the degree that they are supported by persuasive
analyses of shared information and positively evaluated on the
basis of technical and managerial criteria. "The behavior of
Norwegian interest groups on [public-private] committees is
characterized by an emphasis on technical argumentation realized by sending technocrats as representatives and by presenting statements in a well-researched technical format. How
much [compelling] technical information can be presented in a
technical format by a well-known and respected specialist is the
key to success." When a sample of Norwegian committee members were asked to identify the factors that determine whether
Parliament accepted their reports, the technical skills of the
committee members was mentioned far more often than any
other factor.[29] What might be referred to as the technocratic

decision-rule then allows for the inference that state preferences prevail at least as often as associational demands, for the expertise and analytical skills with which shared information is scrutinized and policy positions evaluated are abundantly and about equally present among both private and public officials.

The degree to which the state is constrained in negotiating public policies by the associations' resources is reduced if these approximate a bimodal balance. When conflicting societal demands are backed by similarly weighted resources, the state can afford to ignore such a self-neutralizing parallelogram without loss of support. It is not constrained to adopt a compromise position midway between them. By lending additional weight to their own policy preferences public officials can increase the likelihood of their adoption. If resource imbalances do exist among the national peak associations, they are less than pronounced, given exceptionally, if not uniformly, high levels of membership inclusiveness and organizational capacities, themselves partly the product of identical representational monopolies. With these associations each controlling major economic resources and activities within the context of a highly interdependent economy, those of each sector having decided consequences for the others, their leverage over one another is also likely to be balanced along this resource dimension. A balance is also fostered insofar as the negotiations share the characteristics of a competitive bargaining game. When the same set of three to five players take part in a regular game, each experienced and skilled at the game, each holding at least a good hand, each aware of what the others have in their hands and often their game strategies as well, each playing in accordance with known and agreed upon rules — when associational resources are applied in this fashion, a balanced opposition on discrete issues is quite likely.

The public-private negotiation of public policy dilutes the constraints of numbers and organizational resources because the association membership knows full well that their representatives are heavily involved in making public policies; when policies are found wanting and when negotiations are stalemated, it is the association leaders rather than public officials who are held responsible. With the rank-and-file membership directing blame and displeasure first and foremost at their own leaders, the state need not be overly mindful of the societal constraints. Norwegian associations are represented on some 1,000 committees that are directly attached to all administrative departments, independent agencies, and public corporations, with responsibilities for overseeing their activities, proferring advice, and formulating public policy. There is then no doubting the publicly visible sharing of responsibility, which in turn "guarantees the government little adverse reaction to legislation once effected; that reaction, if it comes, would be directed not toward the government, but at the participants — the interest groups and their representatives — who accept legislation on behalf of the organization membership."[30] In the annual setting of wage and price levels and other economic guidelines, public officials may very well be less concerned than the associational leaders about a breakdown in the negotiations, since the rank-and-file assigns primary responsibility to the association(s) whose recalcitrance is seen to have brought on the collapse. Public officials can thus be at least as firm as the association leaders in holding out for their policy preferences. The structure of the liberal corporatist state in effect constrains the full application of private resources.

## The Autonomy of the Liberal Capitalist State

What is now the "conventional Marxist notion of relative autonomy" has already been discussed in terms of its double-barreled assertion — why the liberal capitalist state's preferences sometimes diverge from those of the bourgeoisie and how the state manages to free itself from the latter's constraints to act upon its own preferences. We also saw that the applicability of the relative autonomy proposition is exceptionally restricted; Type I autonomy actions occur intermittently at most, although the state is assumed to have sufficiently effective autonomy-enhancing capacities and opportunities at its disposal whenever these are needed.

To demonstrate that our proposition holds in the context of this fourth variant of democratic theory it therefore has to be shown that the liberal capitalist state acts contrary to the demands of the bourgeoisie far more *often* than acknowledged in Marxist writings. This has to be done while remaining within our methodological guidelines, taking each of Marxism's generalizations as given, without amending, subtracting from, or adding to them. It then turns out that on a straightforward reading, without any tortuous textual interpretations, Marxist theory itself points to the frequent occurrence of Type I state autonomy. We will be doing what Marxist scholars have not done, identifying and pulling together those aspects of the theory that indicate when and why the capitalist state acts contrary to bourgeois demands, concomitantly pointing out that the Marxist-specified conditions that call for Type I autonomy actions are decidedly common ones among the advanced industrial democracies.

One condition calling for relative autonomy derives from *The Communist Manifesto*'s most oft-quoted assertion: "The executive of the modern state is but a committee for managing the common affairs of the whole bourgeoisie." Here Marx appears to conceive of the state as no more than an instrument controlled by the bourgeoisie. But Ralph Miliband points out that a quite different interpretation is also warranted. "The reference to 'the common affairs of the whole bourgeoisie' clearly implies that the bourgeoisie is a social totality made up of different and therefore potentially or actually conflicting elements . . . while 'common affairs' implies the existence of particular ones as well." On this reasoning, reinforced by observations of conflicting interests within the dominant class, Miliband and others see the capitalist state as reconciling these conflicts, which, in turn, requires some independence from the dominant class. "If the state is to perform this mediating and reconciling function for what are, in effect, different elements or fractions of the bourgeoisie, which have different and conflicting interests, it clearly must have a certain degree of autonomy in relation to the 'ruling class.'"[31]

Relative autonomy can then be said to vary in frequency

with the number and scope of intraclass divisions. Given the great complexity and differentiation of advanced capitalist economies, there is certainly no shortage of such divisions: commercial, industrial, and financial enterprises, large, medium, and small businesses, monopolies, oligopolies, and competitively positioned corporations, exporters, importers, and multinational corporations, enterprises producing for local, regional, and national markets, capital and labor intensive industries, enterprises selling to the private and public sector, enterprises funded by public and private capital, technologically advanced and outmoded industries, raw materials consumers and producers. Along with the number of separate elements of capital and the several axes that divide them, there is their extraordinary interdependence and the inclusive ramifications of public policies, even those directed primarily at one or another element. The great complexity of advanced capitalism requires much involvement on the part of the state in mediating the intraclass disputes for which relative autonomy is required. Were the state to respond to all of the many particular capitalist demands, or respond to the incompatible ones solely on the basis of the politically weightiest resources behind them, its class-neutral legitimizing image would be much tarnished, its financial problems exacerbated, and capitalism's economic contradictions exacerbated.

In addition to the economic divisions within the dominant class, there are its political divisions. Recent writings have expanded upon Marx's recognition that the dominant class is often divided in its political reactions to the dominated class or classes. Within the bourgeoisie there are differing perceptions of the seriousness of the threat from below, as well as varying estimates of its impact upon the interests of particular capital units and sectors. Largely because of these divisions, the bourgeoisie can neither formulate policy preferences that would further its common interest in maintaining a politically predominant position, nor bring together its political fractions within a unified, highly mobilized political party to compete effectively with the political organizations of the dominated class for control over the state. Here too there is a need for autonomy. The most effective policy options for dealing with the dominated class usually develop out of the "State organization's own routines and formal structures," public officials distilling and integrating collective bourgeois interests which are then translated into public policy despite the opposition of narrowly based, shortsighted, situation-bound capitalists and their political organizations.[32] It is as an autonomous tutelary entity that the capitalist state works to preserve the bourgeoisie's political dominance, its precariousness thus being closely associated with the occurrence of Type I autonomy.

The connections between the bourgeoisie's political divisions and the precariousness of its political predominance, on the one hand, and state autonomy on the other, can be amplified and the frequency of autonomous actions emphasized by turning to the problematics of state legitimacy. It is a central tenet of Marxist political theory that the continuing accumulation of capital hinges upon the legitimization of the state in the eyes of the dominated class or classes, the mystifying belief that the state is class neutral, the maintenance of social peace. When legitimacy becomes problematic, it is commonly the relatively autonomous state whose actions deflect or dissipate the challenge. It is public officials who quickly recognize the precariousness of social peace, and not being overly concerned with short-term profits and losses, they are prepared to accept at least some forcefully presented working-class demands as a way of guaranteeing the reproduction of capitalism. The members of the dominant class are certainly "conscious of their interests as capitalists," but they are not "conscious of what is necessary to reproduce the social order in changing circumstances."[33]

The capitalist state's autonomous actions on behalf of social peace most often take the form of reformist policies. "Reform has been a major characteristic of capitalist regimes — not surprisingly since reform has been a *sine qua non* of their perpetuation. What is perhaps less obvious is that it is the state upon which has fallen the prime responsibility for the *organization* of reform. [Public officials] have been well aware of the responsibility, and have acted upon that awareness, not because they were opposed to capitalism, but because they wanted to maintain it." Miliband goes on to point out that the organizers of reform, needing "some elbow room, an area of political maneuver in which *statecraft* in its literal sense could be exercised," have acted independently of the dominant class. "What to concede and when to concede are matters of some delicacy, which a 'ruling class,' with its eyes fixed on immediate interests and demands, cannot be expected to handle properly." Autonomy also obtains given the bourgeoisie's unwillingness to bear the public costs of social and economic reforms. "Much, if not most of the reform which power-holders have organized in capitalist societies has generally been strongly and even bitterly opposed by one or another fraction of the 'ruling class,' or by most of it."[34]

These comments on reform give some sense of the frequency with which legitimacy problems have prompted autonomous state actions. A similar conclusion derives from Marxism's central assertion about the capitalist state's legitimacy: it is often, some say continuously, problematic because of the inherent contradictions between legitimacy and private accumulation, social peace and profitability, democracy and capitalism. Alan Wolfe describes three attempts to overcome these contradictions since 1945: "the franchise state," "the dual state," and "the transnational state." None has succeeded.[35] Jurgen Habermas contends that the great expansion of state activities entails "a growing need for legitimation," and thus a "new level of susceptibility of crisis."[36] With contemporary capitalist states regularly experiencing more or less severe "legitimacy crises," the relative autonomy proposition takes on considerable applicability.

Lastly, relative autonomy relates to the containment of capitalism's contradictory economic imperatives. The incompatible rationalities of individual capitalists and capitalism as a system that Marx identified have been modified to take into account the modern capitalist state's multifaceted involvement in the accumulation process, as in James O'Connor's *The Fiscal Crisis of the State.*[37] Its increasing provision of "social capital" and "social expenses" that indirectly make for greater profitability, in conjunction with the continued "private appropriation of profits creates a fiscal crisis, or 'structural gap,' between state expenditures and state revenues. The result is a tendency for state expenditures to increase more rapidly than the means for financing them . . . The accumulation of social capital and social expenses is a highly irrational process from the standpoint of administrative coherence, fiscal stability, and potentially profitable private capital accumulation."[38]

Whatever specific economic contradictions and irrationalities are emphasized, according to the relative autonomy proposition their containment requires the state to act as the "ideal collective capitalist." The liberal capitalist state has done so via its pervasive intervention in the accumulation process. While it has often intervened at the behest of particular bourgeois interests, its responses to the crisis tendencies of an otherwise anarchic, uncontrolled economic system — price controls, monetary and fiscal policies, regulatory activities, economic planning, nationalization — have also been undertaken in the face of determined capitalist opposition. Claus Offe and others have stressed that once the state has become interventionist, it is even more important for it to adopt public policies that serve the "collective interests" of capital. In fact, interventionism itself may have further heightened state autonomy. "As the state becomes more and more implicated in the productive sphere itself, as larger realms of social activity become *de*commodified (in the sense that production becomes organized around politically determined use-values rather than exchange-values), the state can develop a much greater degree of autonomy than is understood by the conventional Marxist notion of 'relative autonomy.' This further suggests that it may make sense to talk of the state as such having an emergent 'interest,' rather than simply seeing the state as in some sense reflecting the interests of the bourgeoisie."[39]

Here again a reliance on Marxist analyses indicates that it is not uncommon for the state to act on its preferences when these diverge from those of the effective demand group. When taken together with its responses to the economic divisions within the dominant class, the political conflicts among its fractions, the precariousness of state legitimacy, and the bourgeoisie's opposition to reformist measures, none of which is uncommon, the liberal capitalist state turns out to be taking Type I autonomy actions far more often than acknowledged or implied in Marxist writings.

But how is it able to do so with such frequency? Does it have the necessary Type I autonomy-enhancing capacities and opportunities? Where are the generalized and regularized ones required by our fifth guideline to be found? In the previous chapter it was said that Marxism identifies only two Type I autonomy-enhancing capacities and opportunities — exploiting the near balance of strength between the opposing classes and manipulating the class conflict in playing them off against one another. These were also said to be overly limited in number, availability, and applicability in accounting for more than an occasional Type I autonomy action. In claiming that the liberal capitalist state acts autonomously with some frequency, we must either accept Marxism's implicit assumption that one or both of these capacities and opportunities are available, applicable, and effective whenever needed, or indicate that a larger and more diverse number are available to the liberal capitalist state.

To suggest that the latter is indeed the case is not to contradict any general or specific Marxist generalizations or analyses. A review of table 3 indicates that all of the Type I autonomy-enhancing options identified there are available to the capitalist state, and that half of them can be effectively applied to counter the bourgeoisie's constraining efforts. Without belaboring the point, it should be evident that at least eight options are in no way restricted in their applicability and effectiveness vis-à-vis the bourgeoisie, and that their use is not incompatible with the capitalist state's furtherance of that class's common, long-term interests. These are options 1, 3, 5, 6, 7, 12, 13, and 15, and quite possibly 2, 8, 10, and 14. Suffice it to say that were the same kind of analysis of the Marxist variant undertaken as was just done for the other three variants, it could easily be shown that at least the first group of options is available, applicable, and effective with respect to the bourgeoisie despite and/or because of Marxism's descriptive and explanatory generalizations.

At a minimum, this chapter has shown that empirical democratic theory can be reinterpreted to make room for the Type I autonomy proposition. The plausibility it derives from being placed within this theoretical context very much depends on just how demanding the methodological guidelines are thought to be. If it is thought that the hurdles placed in the way of the proposition's survival are low to moderate and that they were cleared fairly and squarely, some additional doubts will have been raised about the societal constraint assumptions' denial of Type I state autonomy. If it is thought that the proposition was able to clear rather high hurdles while carrying some fairly heavy weights in several inhospitable settings, then we have succeeded in providing a good deal of additional plausibility for the most ambitious of the state-centered propositions.

# 7

## Variations in Type I and Type II State Autonomy: The American State in Comparative Perspective

To claim that the democratic state is frequently autonomous under conditions of divergence does not, of course, mean that each state at every point in time is similarly autonomous. It would surely be surprising—more precisely, it would be intuitively most implausible—if there were no substantial variations in Type I and Type II autonomy. A focus upon differences in state autonomy under conditions of divergence immediately raises certain questions. Are there one or more national states that act autonomously so infrequently as to deviate from our propositions? How much autonomy is attributable to the state that is commonly thought of as among the least, if not the least autonomous one among the advanced industrial democracies? Are variations in state autonomy of a highly specific, ad hoc variety about which it is virtually impossible to generalize, or does state autonomy vary in some determinate manner over historical time, across geographical space, and among issue areas? To the extent that generalization is possible, what are the variables that can account for differences in state autonomy? Are the most important ones to be found within the state, civil society, or both?

### The American National State

There are several reasons for focusing on the American national state when working our way through questions about variations in state autonomy. It has for so long been considered an inordinately weak state that it is barely thought to be deserving the name. If there is a national state among the advanced industrial democracies that constitutes an exception to our generalizations it is then more than likely to be the American one; if it does not deviate from the Type I and Type II autonomy propositions perhaps none does so. Since the American state is said to be among the most, if not the most, societally constrained state among the advanced industrial democracies, by estimating how much or little autonomy the federal government enjoys we can approximate one end point on the state autonomy–societal constraint continuum. Just as there is little, if any, disagreement about the American state's weakness, so too there is widespread concurrence in accounting for it. The federal government is first and foremost characterized by an uncommonly great dispersal of decision sites; its authority is at least as fragmented as that of any other among the advanced industrial democracies and far more so than most — a statement that holds even without reference to the exceptional policymaking powers of the American judiciary. The American state is taken as specially telling evidence for the general proposition that the fragmentation of public authority sharply detracts from state autonomy. This widely accepted explanation for variations in state autonomy can then be assessed advantageously in the American context.

Besides elucidating these several issues pertaining to variations in state autonomy, this discussion takes on a quite different kind of significance. Several fundamental doubts will be raised about the conventional interpretation of the federal government as inordinately constrained by society — doubts that could form the basis of a revisionist interpretation of the American state as one that is far more autonomous than is almost invariably claimed. They take on a good deal of generalized significance because the American national state is most certainly a least likely case for the generation of evidence that is supportive of the Type I and Type II autonomy propositions. Since there is more than ample reason for thinking that this case in particular will not bear them out — it is close to being an unquestionably least likely case—their survival goes a long way in enhancing the propositions' overall plausibility. Historians, political scientists, and political commentators, critics, supporters, and apologists alike have consistently and forcefully been struck by the extent to which the American state is constrained by society, primarily due to the great fragmentation of its authority. Given the numerical predominance of American political scientists and the enormous scholarly attention they have lavished upon American politics, this case has been far more extensively studied than any other. The American national state is the case that far more than any other, of whatever variety, has given both enormous support and widespread prominence to the rival society-centered model. Most political scientists are Americans, and their frame of reference in thinking about democratic politics is very much shaped by the regime with which they are most familiar. The United States enjoys a decided prominence in the eyes of citizens, journalists, and scholars alike. It is viewed as the "first new nation," the democratic mainstay in the East-West struggle, as well as the economic, social, and political harbinger of things to come. In reverse fashion, with the American national state constituting an exceptionally significant most likely case for the validation of the rival society-centered model, to question the conventional interpretation is to raise some telling doubts about the model's explanatory power.

The Founding Fathers purposefully wrote a constitution with separated powers that turned the public officials who shared them into arch competitors. As defended in *The Federalist Papers* (especially Madison's number 51), the multifaceted arrangment of checks and balances is intended to weaken any one set of public officials relative to others and the state as a whole vis-à-vis society. The past has been reproduced, even amplified, in the present. "America perpetuated a fusion of functions and a division of power," writes Samuel P. Huntington, "while Europe developed a differentiation of functions and a centralization of power. The passion of the Founding Fathers for the division of power, for setting ambition against ambition, for creating a constitution with a complicated system of balances exceeding that of any other is, of course, well known." The state was purposefully divided, and continues to be, according to Nelson W. Polsby, so that the parts "would be captured by different interests." Walter Dean Burnham writes that throughout its history, "the political system from parties to policy institutions has remained astonishingly little transformed in its characteristics and methods of operation." Perhaps chief among them is its "dedicat[ion] to the defeat, except temporarily and under the direct pressure of overwhelming crisis, of any attempt to generate domestic sovereignty." Richard E. Neustadt maintains that the American state continues to be unmistakenly and uncommonly one of "separated institutions *sharing* powers." David B. Truman points to a direct connection between this "diffusion of leadership and [the] disintegration of policy." Despite the confidence with which these and many similar assertions are put forward, James MacGregor Burns is able to write that "we still underestimate the extent to which our system was designed for deadlock and inaction . . . [The] system of checks and balances and interlocked gears of government requires the consensus of many groups and leaders before the nation can act; and it is [this] system that exacts the heavy price of delay and devitalization." Even Stephen D. Krasner, who has highlighted instances of Type I and Type II autonomy, takes "the central feature of American politics [to be] the fragmentation and dispersal of power and authority," which has the consequence of making "obstruction easy, positive action difficult." There is surely no doubting, although much bemoaning, the absence of cohesive national parties that can pull together what has been constitutionally and institutionally rendered asunder. According to Burns's interpretation of American political history, the "four-party system that compels govenment by consensus and coalition" is deeply rooted in the Madisonian constitutional and governmental model.[1]

In short, the great dispersal of decision sites — the occupants of more than a dozen are frequently involved in a single authoritative action[2] — is the distinctive and central feature of the

American state. The state is thus highly permeable, offering easy access to just about all sizable groups, as well as distinctly vulnerable and malleable, continuously subject to the demands of all manner of large and small "veto" groups. It is regularly unable to adopt decisive, coherent, positive, forward-looking public policies.[3] The conventional interpretation may be valid; the federal government may well be exceptionally weak, inordinately constrained by society, and largely devoid of autonomy primarily because of its constitutional and institutional arrangements. But then again, since the conventional wisdom has not been subjected to any serious questioning, it may turn out to be decidedly invalid. The queries and observations generated by the state-centered perspective need to be considered.

Much of the putative evidence for the weakness or heteronomy of the American state is found in the "devitalization" and "disintegration of policy," in "deadlock and inaction"—its authoritative inactions, slowness in acting, indecisiveness, and the incoherent compromises emanating from the pulling and hauling that characterizes the policy formation process. But as has been said before, the relevant issue for assessing state autonomy is not the attributes of public policy per se; it is rather the explanations underlying such characteristics as policy incoherence, indecisiveness, or their opposites. Explanations based on societal groups dissuading American officials from making decisions they themselves prefer are undoubtedly valid in some instances, but not necessarily in most. More than likely, there are other important explanations having to do with the officials themselves being unable to agree upon what, if any, actions to take, what the most desirable and effectual policies are thought to be. In fact, the conventional interpretation itself lends this point some credence: the sharing of dispersed powers turns public officials into competitors for power, while their distinctive responsibilities help generate incompatible policy preferences. There is also reason to suppose that American officials subscribe to values and beliefs which do *not* place much store upon promptly adopted, coherent, positive, decisive authoritative actions to begin with. On either interpretation the state's preferences are fulfilled; it is acting autonomously.

The apparently minimal leadership provided by the American national state—the many trial balloons relative to sustained policy initiatives, the paucity of efforts to enlist widespread support for less than popular views—is commonly taken as a patently telling manifestation of its weakness. However, it is one thing to stress the near absence of coherent leadership on something approaching a national scale. It is quite another to ignore or assume away the possible existence of far less visible leadership relations between many national officials and small groups of private actors. Once the distinction is made between coherent, national leadership and dispersed leadership, what reasons are there for thinking that the latter is especially scarce? None are provided or implied by the conventional interpretation. If it were somehow possible to estimate the number of successful leadership efforts made by all national officials, the total would probably be much larger than is widely supposed. Take the Congress, whose uncommonly great dispersal of decision sites is said to account for the little, if any, leadership it exercises. If the statement is limited to well-articulated national leadership, there is no doubting it; but if it also refers to the relations of Congress's 535 discrete members with their particular constituents, supporters, and clients, then it is questionable. Recall the quotation from the Bauer, Pool, and Dexter study in the chapter on Type II autonomy. The congressman is portrayed as leading *his* coalition. When he alters his policy stands its members are inclined to change theirs, or to provide continuing support while holding divergent preferences.[4] And it should be apparent that coherent national leadership does not have any special import for gauging the overall autonomy of the state. A state featuring an equal measure of leadership on the part of dispersed officials in their relations with relatively small numbers of constituents, supporters, and clients is, on this score, equally autonomous.

What then of the oft-heard, rarely disputed assertion that the federal government is very much subject to the constraints of a panoply of large and small veto groups? Given the great dispersal of authority, it supposedly becomes all too easy for societal groups opposed to an alteration of the status quo to prevent the state from adopting positive public policies. They need only win at any one of several relevant decision sites, whereas those who want the state to undertake additional responsibilities must win at all of them. But is it actually the case that the American state is continuously constrained by the many private actors who want to block the adoption of new public policies, specifically, because they can do so at any one of several decision sites? These societal groups are certainly much advantaged relative to their societal rivals who prefer policy changes. But this point should not be conflated, as it usually is, with a societal constraint of the state assertion according to which these groups are especially successful in vetoing the preferences of public officials. Many or most of these groups' preferences are apparently realized, but the explanation could have at least as much to do with public as private actors. It is entirely possible that most national officials favor the policy status quo as much as do the veto groups, thereby obviating a one-sided societal constraint account. Moreover, the dispersal of decision sites that affords the latter an enormous advantage relative to their societal rivals affords the exact same advantage to those officials who prefer to block policy changes vis-à-vis others who hold quite different policy views. Public officials who favor the policy status quo need only prevail at one decision site, whereas their opponents must win at several, at all those whose assent is needed for the adoption of public policies. Since state preferences refer to the policy views of public officials as weighted by their resources, the occupancy of strategic decision sites being among the weightiest ones, state preferences would then coincide with authoritative inactions. Thus in and of itself the conjuncture of numerous veto groups and dispersed decision sites does not indicate that the state is inordinately constrained. It is quite possible that the federal government is autonomous despite and because of its fragmented authority.

These queries and observations raise some serious doubts about the conventional interpretation. In addition, its explanatory linchpin needs to be examined. The validity of the conventional interpretation hinges upon an affirmative answer to the question: Does the fragmentation of public authority actually maximize societal constraint of the state? Whereas the previous points speak to the question of whether the state is in fact constrained, this question asks whether the dispersal of decision sites sharply detracts from its autonomy.

The existence of numerous decision sites undoubtedly goes a long way in lowering the barriers for gaining access to the state, and getting one's foot in the door or body into the office is literally and figuratively a significant step toward societal constraint. But the relative importance of access in the conventional interpretation is much exaggerated. Relatively easy access to the state, its high level of permeability, does facilitate societal constraint, yet it is far from being either a necessasry or sufficient condition. There is a sizeable gap between the state's permeability and its constraint by private actors. Other variables of an analytically similar cast impinge far more heavily upon state autonomy—the state's malleability, vulnerability, resistance capacities, and dependence upon private actors. The other doubts to be raised about the presumed relationship between a dispersed state structure and societal constraint speak to these variables.

What reason is there to suppose that a state featuring numerous, dispersed decision sites is more malleable, more vulnerable, or less capable of resisting the pressures of societal groups than one with a much smaller number of concentrated decision sites? The former looks weaker, but is it actually so? A structurally fragmented state offers relatively easy access to a great number of large and small groups. But this does not mean that the state as a whole is less capable of resisting the blandishments and pressures of the effective demand groups taken all together; nor does it allow for the assertion that any one state unit is necessarily less capable of doing so with respect to any given demand group.

The critical or proximate factor in assessing the consequences of state structure for societal constraint is not state structure, but the fit between it and the structure of the demand group universe. In principle there are four possible patterns: state authority and societal resources are dispersed; state authority and societal resources are concentrated; state authority is concentrated and societal resources are dispersed; state authority is dispersed and societal resources are concentrated. Of these, only the last would place the state at a disadvantage. A structurally dispersed state is at a decided disadvantage in confronting a small number of societal groups with concentrated resources, such as nationally organized labor and employers' associations whose members include practically all sectorally situated individuals, firms, and more specialized associations. Yet a fragmented state facing concentrated societal groups is not a commonly realized conjuncture, and it has in fact never appeared in the United States. Public and private actors tend to adapt themselves organizationally to one another. It is the concentration of authority within the state, sometimes along with the encouragement and help of public officials, that moves societal actors to concentrate their resources; a dispersed state provides neither public nor private actors with special incentives to move in this direction. There are thus only two common patterns: a fragmented state facing a dispersed demand group universe, which applies to the United States, and a structurally concentrated state confronting societal actors with similarly concentrated resources. Between these two state-society patterns it is difficult, if not impossible, to say which results in greater or lesser societal constraint. The total political resources brought to bear upon any one state unit and upon the state as a whole is presumably little different whichever pattern obtains.

With the degree of societal constraint being closely related to the state's autonomy-enhancing capacities and opportunities, we need to determine whether there is a significant difference between structurally dispersed and concentrated states with respect to these capacities and opportunities. Only if it is shown that the fragmented state structure substantially diminishes their availability, applicability, effectiveness, or employment can a fully convincing case be made that the federal government is inordinately constrained. There are two variants of empirical democratic theory that have state-society relations in America as their primary focus, pluralism and neopluralism, and both accord much descriptive and explanatory importance to the fragmentation of state authority. Our demonstration that both the liberal and the distorted liberal state do in fact enjoy a good number of regularly available and commonly applicable Type I autonomy-enhancing capacities and opportunities now takes on added significance. These are present despite *and* because of the dispersed decision sites. Moreover, a review of the thirty Type I and Type II autonomy-enhancing options indicates that nearly all of them are no less available, applicable, effective, or employable on the part of those public officials who occupy numerous dispersed decision sites than for those in a concentrated ensemble of state units.[5]

Over and above its import for gauging and explaining variations in state autonomy, this assessment of the American state's autonomy has several other implications. It might well serve as the basis for a revisionist interpretation of state-society relations in America, one in which national officials are portrayed as far more autonomous than has been allowed, in both absolute and relative terms. At a minimum, such a revisionist interpretation should not be ruled out; if the conventional interpretation continues to be accepted in full, the serious misgivings that were just raised need to be allayed.[6] With the American national state constituting an exceptionally telling least likely case for the Type I and Type II state autonomy propositions, or in reverse fashion, a most likely case for the rival societal constraint assertions, even this preliminary inquiry lends considerable plausibility to the state-centered model's most ambitious propositions. To the extent that this discussion has identified some fundamental difficulties with a widely subscribed, nearly unquestioned interpretation, the reason is patently explicable: an issue that has almost exclusively been examined from a society-oriented perspective was addressed from the vantage point of the state.

### Explaining Variations in State Autonomy

The first place to look for the variables that can account for Type I and Type II autonomy, at least in a state-centered study, is within the state itself. There are four seemingly plausible state-centered explanations having to do with state structure, state capacities, the attitudes of public officials, and their autonomy enhancing capacities and opportunities. Yet they begin to look less, rather than more, tenable after a preliminary consideration, which leads us to look wihin civil society for the answers.

One explanation has, of course, just been discussed and found wanting. At first glance it is indeed plausible to suppose that state structure has a decided bearing upon state autonomy, with the concentration of public authority in a small number of decision sites facilitating state autonomy and their dispersion detracting from autonomy. Certainly the French state since 1958, for example, appears to be stronger, considerably more autonomous, than the national state in America. Yet, as just discussed, state structure is an inadequate explanation in several important respects. Most of them apply not just to the state in America, but to the proposition as formulated in a generalized manner, one that speaks to variations in autonomy among all democratic states.

The proposition runs up against an additional difficulty. If differences in state structure are to account for significant variations in autonomy, then they must differ to a considerable extent. Unless there are significant variations in the independent variable, they cannot be related to extensive variations in state autonomy as the dependent variable. There is no doubting that the American state is located very close to one end of the concentration-dispersion continuum, but it is far from clear that marked differences exist among most of the other advanced industrial democracies. On an impressionistic basis, it would appear that almost all of them—the British, Irish, Dutch, Belgian, Norwegian, Finnish, Swedish, German, Danish, Austrian, and Canadian states—feature basically similar degrees of concentration at the national level. With the exception of the American, Italian, and possibly Swiss states, others are likely to be found toward the concentrated authority end of the continuum were this variable to be measured in a systematic manner. If so, some, but not very much, variation in state autonomy could be accounted for in terms of state structure.

Another explanation for variations in state autonomy also features a seemingly plausible rationale. The more extensive a state's capacities and the more deeply its activities penetrate into the economy and society, the greater its autonomy. Public officials who are assigned enormous authoritative powers are doubly advantaged vis-à-vis private actors: they have abundant resources at their disposal and many policy levers to pull, while private actors are heavily dependent upon them for public assistance in realizing their policy preferences. But as noted in Chapter 1, this hypothesis is not nearly as convincing as its widespread acceptance would suggest. It is overly simplistic in ignoring two hardly improbable considerations— considerations that are even suggestive of an inverse relationship between state autonomy and state capacities. The number of demands made upon the state and the intensity with which they are pressed upon it are to some significant extent triggered by its impact upon, and importance for, private actors. A state engaged in wide-ranging and penetrative activites tends to be confronted with greater societal pressures and is thus potentially more susceptible to societal constraints than is one whose activities are more restricted in their scope and less ambitious in their goals. Moreover, the dependence of one set of actors upon another may be a two-way street. The decided dependence of societal actors upon the public officials of a highly developed mixed-economy welfare state is mitigated by their dependence upon the cooperation of private actors for the fulfillment of some ambitious social and economic guidance goals. These comments are not intended to deny the existence of a positive relationship between state autonomy and capacities. But if such a relationship does in fact obtain, it is hardly a simple, straightforward one. Extensive state capacities do place public officials in an advantaged position, but their other consequences need also to be taken into account.

A third explanation is an attitudinal one. Some combination of the beliefs, values, and norms held by public officials more or less strongly predisposes them to act on their preferences in the face of societal opposition. This too would seem to be a promising explanatory avenue. Attitudes have a discernible impact upon behavior and they presumably vary over time and space, in this instance, among public officials who have (if nothing else) lived through and been indirectly influenced by some very different constellations of historical events. Still, too much importance should not be attached to attitudinal or cultural explanations, at least in this book and at this point in the study of state autonomy. And this for the paradoxical reason that cultural explanations may be all too important. They should not, as they often are, be conflated with behavioral statements, nor treated as a grab bag of residual explanations for behavioral patterns that cannot readily be accounted for with the variables at hand. So while an attitudinal explanation of autonomous behavior is eminently persuasive in principle, the conceptual and empirical work is not yet sufficiently developed to turn it into a coherent, graspable explanation. For example, none of the survey studies that have tested for the presence of Burkean type officials distinguish between attitudinal and cost-benefit accounts of autonomous behavior. Public officials who say that they would act on their own preferences when these diverge from those of their constituents were not asked whether they would do so because of their beliefs and norms, or whether they would act autonomously in the expectation that societal sanctions would not follow. To the extent that the latter obtains, we have instances of public officials recognizing their relatively low-cost capacities and opportunities for autonomous behavior, rather than Burkean type officials who give normative priority to their personal judgment, conscience, conceptions of representation, or leadership roles.

A fourth explanation derives from the particular structural perspective that was applied throughout much of this book; it points to the kinds of variables that would seem to be leading candidates. These are, of course, the number, applicability, and effectiveness of the autonomy-enhancing capacities and opportunities. Having used them to argue for the autonomy of the democratic state, it follows that they may be equally well employed in accounting for variations in its autonomy. But here too we encounter a serious problem. While the argument of the book strongly suggests that these variables should be able to explain variations in autonomy, much of its substance just as clearly indicates that they probably cannot do so. For nowhere was there seen to be a shortage in the number of readily available Type I or Type II autonomy-enhancing capacities and opportunities; nor was their availability seen to be significantly diminished by any common set of state or societal patterns. The Type I autonomy-enhancing capacities and opportunities were shown to be well represented in the midst of each of the very different state and societal constellations delineated by the pluralist, neopluralist, and social corporatist variants. Although significant differences appeared in the applicability and effectiveness of many autonomy-enhancing options with respect to more or less complex issues and societal actors who stand at a greater or lesser distance from the state, taken singly or as a whole, these do not form some generalized pattern capable of accounting for substantial variations in state autonomy. The problem, as it were, is that public officials are all too often endowed with autonomy-enhancing capacities and opportunities. These go a long way in explaining the frequent and marked autonomy of most, if not all, national states among the advanced industrial democracies, without however accounting for variations across geographical space, over time, or among issue areas.

In contrast to these four state-centered hypotheses whose applicability and/or rationale are at least moderately problematic,[7] the societal perspective immediately produces a single, encompassing, virtually axiomatic explanation. The incidence of Type I and Type II autonomy is most assuredly related to the degree of societal opposition to state preferences, and there is no doubting the extensive variations in societal opposition. The degree of societal opposition has a sharp impact upon state autonomy in two respects. It affects the probabilities of public officials engaging in the kinds of autonomy-enhancing efforts set out in tables 2 and 3 and the chances of success on the part of those who make such efforts.

The frequency with which public officials strive to act autonomously is affected by not only the probabilities of societal sanctions following in their wake, but also by the severity or telling consequences of sanctions if and when imposed. It is one thing to act in ways that might involve the loss of some societal support, it is quite another to do so when the risk involves the imposition of enormously consequential sanctions. And it is variations in the extent of societal opposition to state preferences that relate closely to the severity of societal sanctions. When the interested private actors control almost all the effective resources, societal sanctions are almost sure to be more severe than when they control only marginally greater resources than those who support the state on the issue at hand. Public officials are far less discouraged from engaging in autonomy-enhancing attempts in the latter case. Similarly, the success of public officials in capitalizing upon the autonomy-enhancing capacities and opportunities is not only related to their applicability and effectiveness. The degree of societal opposition is also relevant. Whether public officials are able to transform divergent into nondivergent societal preferences (Type II autonomy), or ignore, neutralize, or overcome the imposition of societal constraints under conditions of divergence (Type I autonomy), is clearly affected by the overall proportion of currently engaged resources controlled by those who hold divergent preferences. The latter helps determine whether the task is more or less demanding, and thus more or less likely to be successful.

Still, this explanation is not entirely satisfactory. The extent of societal opposition to state preferences is overly general; it tells us where to look for explanations of variations in state autonomy without however identifying the more readily graspable variables themselves. In part, it is just because this societal explanation is an encompassing one that it is so persuasive and powerful. For it to become a fully satisfactory explanation a great deal needs to be done to explicate patterns of societal opposition. But to delve into the when, where, and why of variations in societal opposition would extend much beyond the bounds of a state-centered study.

## State Autonomy and Societal Opposition

The critical explanations for the incidence of Type I and Type II autonomy are to be found in the state's autonomy-enhancing capacities and opportunities and the degree of societal opposition to state preferences. The former do not vary substantially. They are usually sufficient in number, applicability, and effectiveness to encourage public officials to strive for autonomy and to make success at least moderately probable. There are wide variations in societal opposition and they have a decided impact upon both the probability of the attempts being made and their success. These are the most important conclusions to be drawn from the previous section.

The question then becomes: Just how much effect do variations in societal opposition have upon public officials successfully undertaking Type I and Type II autonomy actions? More precisely, to what extent are the state's autonomy-enhancing capacities and opportunities offset by varying degrees of societal opposition? This question allows for three issues to be addressed simultaneously. First, to answer the question is to delineate what is perhaps the most important patterned or generalizable variation in the incidence of Type I and Type II autonomy. Second, in identifying a state and a societal variable as the most important explanations for state autonomy under conditions of divergence brings us back to our broadest thesis: the state- and society-centered models complement one another; both are needed to understand the authoritative actions of the democratic state. Gauging the extent to which societal opposition diminishes the use and effectiveness of the autonomy-enhancing capacities and opportunities gives this thesis a more precise cast. Third, our own answer to the question will be contrasted with two others, one of which is far less state-centered and the other far more so. The discussion may then be read as a partial summary of the way in which our state-centered claims differ from their rivals.

The three sets of curves in figure 2 depict the rival assertions about the impact of societal opposition upon state autonomy — our own, those of the society-centered model, and Marxism's

2. THREE SETS OF RELATIONSHIPS BETWEEN STATE AUTONOMY AND SOCIETAL OPPOSITION TO STATE PREFERENCES.

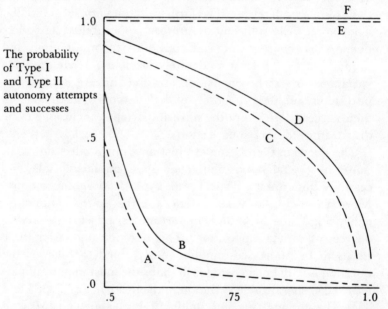

The resources controlled by those opposed to the state's preferences as a proportion of all engaged resources.

(The solid curves represent Type I and Type II autonomy attempts. The dashed curves represent Type I and Type II autonomy successes.)

"relative autonomy" of the state proposition. The degree of societal opposition is found on the horizontal axis; the numerical values represent the proportion of total resources controlled by those private actors who oppose the state's preferences. For example, the .5 position (or coordinate) on the extreme left-hand side represents those instances in which the societal actors who hold divergent preferences control half of the engaged resources, or put differently, the state's opponents and supporters on the issue at hand control equally weighty resources.[8]

Although not commonly done, the vertical axis in figure 2 can be taken to represent two variables. It can be done here because both the probability of Type I and Type II autonomy efforts being made and their probability of success when undertaken relate to the degree of societal opposition in the same way, no matter which interpretation of the relationships is accepted. Thus the 1.0 position, for example, represents those instances in which it is for all practical purposes certain that the efforts are both undertaken and successful. The solid curves represent the probability of autonomy-enhancing efforts being made, the dashed curves refer to the probability of their succeeding. Although not explicitly done here because it would make figure 2 overly complex, the success of Type I and Type II autonomy efforts could equally well be gauged in another manner. The vertical axis could be taken to represent the extent to which state preferences are translated into public policy, that is, as a measure of the substantive fit between preferences and policies. For instance, the .5 position would then represent instances in which the state gets half a loaf of what it prefers in the way of authoritative actions. If assigning numbers to the different positions on the two axes gives the impression of greater precision than is warranted, such corresponding terms as "high," "moderate," and "low" could be substituted.

The three sets of curves and the differences among them summarize much of what we have been saying about state autonomy under conditions of divergence and contrasts our claims with two others. Curves $A$ and $B$ depict the relationship between state autonomy attempts and successes and the degree of societal opposition drawn from the society-centered perspective. Type I and Type II autonomous actions are almost entirely limited to situations in which there is a nearly equal balance in the resources of the private actors who oppose and support the state. As soon as the former begin to predominate, the autonomy-enhancing efforts and successes of public officials drop off sharply, and then remain at a very low level along practically the entire length of the horizontal axis. The three empirical variants of liberal democratic theory—pluralism, neopluralism, and social corporatism—are largely built on the double barreled premise that public officials are regularly unable and/or unwilling to free themselves from the constraints imposed by the private actors who make up the effective demand group universe. They are supposedly very much lacking in autonomy-enhancing capacities and opportunities, while manifesting a decided concern, sometimes even an anxiety, about the probable, sometimes even possible, imposition of societal sanctions. They are consequently dissuaded from undertaking autonomy-enhancing efforts except under relatively propitious conditions—those found toward the extreme left-hand side of figure 2, where societal opposition to the state is very nearly balanced by societal support. It is only under such circumstances that public officials manage to act on their preferences without suffering much in the way of societal retributions.

The Marxist variant provides two assertions about state autonomy under conditions of divergence. Although they could hardly be more different, they are not inconsistent. There is Marxism's primary society-centered thrust from which is derived the assertion that the state in capitalist society is an instrument in the hands of capital. With the state being viewed as the agent of the economically dominant class that makes up the effective demand group universe, the Marxist interpretation of state-society relations falls directly on the $A$-$B$ society centered curves. As such it does not differ from the liberal variants of democratic theory in depicting the broad contours of state-society relations. They are at one in denying, ignoring, or downplaying the possibilities and actualities of Type I and Type II autonomy due to the powerful constraints and telling sanctions that the effective demand groups can impose upon the state. It is therefore the other, very different assertion offered by Marxist theory that needs to be depicted in figure 2.

The $E$ and $F$ curves represent the relative autonomy of the state proposition found in both the instrumental and structural versions of Marxist theory. From their shape and position it is readily apparent that they constitute Marxism's distinctive state-centered assertion. The two curves are located at the up-permost point on the vertical axis and remain there even in the presence of overwhelming societal opposition to state preferences. The state is almost invariably successful in acting on its preferences for the promotion of capital's collective in-terests, even when opposed by virtually the entire bourgeoisie, that is, by nearly all of the actors making up the effective de-mand group universe. Since the state's primary and invariable activities in ensuring the reproduction of capitalism occasion-ally require the adoption of public policies which are opposed by the shortsighted, narrow-minded bourgeoisie, and since capitalist relations of production have survived in all the ad-vanced industrial democracies, the state must have been con-sistently successful in translating its preferences into public policy. With the capitalist state's autonomy barely (if at all) affected by the extent of societal opposition, the relative autonomy proposition is clearly an inordinately ambitious state-centered assertion.

Comparing the different positions and shapes of the $C$-$D$ curves representing our state-centered propositions and Marx-ism's $E$-$F$ curves indicates that the latter are overinflated. The claim that state autonomy is unaffected by the degree of societal opposition runs counter to a common sense axiom and is without the benefits of a reasoned argument. Nor have Marx, Engels, and Marxist scholars identified a sufficiently numerous, diverse, or widely applicable set of autonomy-enhancing capacities and opportunities to undergird a claim for the state's virtually unswerving autonomy in the face of bourgeois opposition. Only two such conditions have been identified, and they are closely enough interrelated to be found together more often than not. On the other hand, the proposition tends toward a minimal state-centered assertion insofar as it is only in rare instances that the state prefers, or needs to act contrary to, bourgeois preferences. In this important respect the proposition is underinflated; on a reading of Marxist theory we saw that the liberal capitalist state has preferences or needs to act in a relatively autonomous manner far more often than Marxists have allowed.

Curves $C$ and $D$ offer a graphic summary of propositions 4, 5, and 6 of the state-centered model as they are affected by variations in the degree of societal opposition. The latter does have a strong impact upon the probability of autonomy-enhancing attempts and successes: the two curves slope downwards along the entire length of the horizontal axis. But except for instances of overwhelming societal opposition, they remain at moderate to high levels. They slope downwards only gradually, for the wide-ranging applicability and marked effectiveness of the state's autonomy-enhancing capacities and opportunities offset the constraining impact of societal opposition. Put differently, the former are significantly independent of the latter. Much of this book's central argument is then summarily depicted in the shape and position of the $C$-$D$ curves and the ways in which they differ from the society-centered $A$-$B$ curves. The large spaces between them represent the very different assertions about public policy formation derived from the state- and society-centered models.

# 8

## The Plausibility and Implications
## of the State-Centered Model

L OOK AT LEAST AS MUCH to the state as to civil society to understand what the democratic state does in the making of
public policy and why it does so; the democratic state is frequently autonomous in translating its own preferences into authoritative actions, and markedly autonomous in doing so even
when they diverge from those held by the politically weightiest
groups in civil society. These two far-reaching assertions are
what this book is all about. They are amplified in the six propositions that constitute the state-centered model. Having
brought them together in the first chapter as an introduction to
the book, there is no point in summarizing them here as a set of
conclusions. But there is good reason to summarize this study
in another way—by highlighting the state-centered model's
plausibility. Then, assuming that the model is indeed highly
plausible, this chapter offers some thoughts about its implications for democratic theory.

### Highlighting the Plausibility of the State-Centered Model

When evaluating the plausibility of a set of empirical propositions, the most important consideration is, of course, the
overall weight of the evidence that bears directly upon them.
When there is a distinct shortage of such empirical findings, as
is the case here, two other critieria take on special sig-

nificance—the persuasiveness of the underlying arguments upon which the propositions rest and the appropriateness of the methodology (broadly conceived) that was used in developing them.

There is no denying that only a limited amount of direct, supportive evidence is available to confirm the state-centered model, while an abundance of putative evidence denies some of its propositions. Yet I would venture to say that overall, the available evidence does not call the propositions into question. Those few studies in the literature on public policy formation and empirical democratic theory that are directly supportive of the model are highly regarded ones. The small number of such studies is hardly surprising; quantity cannot readily be taken as a negative consideration given the widespread adherence to the society-centered perspective. With the overwhelming number of empirical investigations being methodologically guided and substantively informed by the latter it would be unreasonable to expect more than a few studies to provide the kind of evidence that speaks directly to the propositions in an unbiased fashion. While a good portion of the seemingly disconfirming evidence is undoubtedly valid—societal constraint accounts are hardly unpersuasive in and of themselves—most of it was practically foreordained from the outset, at least in its broad contours. The analyses tend toward the tautological insofar as an exclusive reliance upon the societal constraint assumptions is bound to produce societal constraint accounts, or they are undertaken within a closed system which, from the outset, makes the possible emergence of state-centered accounts most unlikely. Nor has the validity of the societal constraint assumptions been demonstrated in a direct, systematic manner; they have certainly not been subjected to a serious attempt at disconfirmation as a way of validating their wide-ranging applicability and explanatory power. In short, the direct evidence does not go very far in helping either to confirm or disconfirm the state-centered model.

The model's persuasiveness consequently comes to rest very much upon the arguments made on its behalf. Consider the following reasons for thinking it to be an eminently plausible one. (1) There is an intuitive *im*plausibility to the rival society-centered model, for it seems most improbable that the modern democratic state — the individuals who populate this large, weighty, resource-laden, institutionalized, highly prized ensemble of authoritative offices — is consistently unwilling and unable to act on its preferences when these diverge from society's. (2) The societal constraint assumptions, which deny some state-centered propositions and turn a deaf ear to others, have distinct limits and limitations with respect to their applicability and explanatory power. (3) The interpretation of contemporary democratic politics that most forcefully denies the autonomy of the state, the "crisis of democracy" or "crisis of authority" thesis, is a problematic one in this regard. (4) The fundamental problems afflicting the virtually unquestioned societal constraint interpretation of the American national state indicate that it is probably far more autonomous than is commonly claimed, while the state-centered model's most ambitious propositions survived even when stacked against this especially telling least likely case. (5) There are numerous Type I, Type II, and Type III autonomy-enhancing capacities and opportunities — almost fifty when adding up the options set out in tables 1, 2, and 3 — that are regularly available to the democratic state. (6) With only a few of these autonomy-enhancing options depending upon unusual circumstances for their activation, and with hardly any requiring public officials endowed with unusual attributes for their effective employment, a significant number are almost always present as live options. (7) Although some of the options are limited in their applicability and effectiveness to certain kinds of societal actors and policy issues, most are widely and diversely applicable, and many can be employed in an especially effective manner under certain quite common conditions. (8) The liberal, distorted liberal, liberal corporatist, and liberal capitalist states each have at least half-a-dozen regularly available and commonly applicable Type I autonomy-enhancing capacities and opportunities. (9) Over and above the autonomy-enhancing options, the democratic state can rely upon its inherent powers to translate its preferences directly into public policy, and these are applicable over an especially wide and diverse political terrain. (10) There are indeed circumstances in which public officials are dissuaded from acting contrary to societal preferences by the likely imposition of societal sanctions, but there are many others in which societal actors are not disposed to sanction the state for doing so, others in which they tend not to act upon their dispositions, and yet others in which public officials can mitigate the likelihood of dispositions being translated into behavior. (11) Even when societal sanctions are likely or expected, public officials sometimes act on their preferences because sanctions are not thought to have an especially telling impact upon them, the officials' preferences are more salient than are the consequences of societal sanctions, or the Burkean model of the modern public official is alive and well among some significant proportion of public actors.

The other important criterion for assessing the plausibility of the state-centered model, or any set of empirical propositions, is the appropriateness of the study's methodology broadly conceived. The manner in which this model was developed was based on the following considerations. (1) The state was defined in as theoretically neutral a manner as possible, and more specifically, it was not assigned any functional imperatives that would have biased the analysis toward state autonomy. (2) State autonomy as a concept and a variable was developed in a way that minimizes analytical or empirical bias, most important, by focusing upon the state's autonomy in relation to the politically stronger rather than weaker societal actors, such as the indigent, the apathetic, and the unorganized. (3) The study was very much guided by the assumption that public officials have as their generalized goals the realization of both autonomy *and* societal support. (4) In developing the state-centered model it was never forgotten that it refers to the *democratic* state, avoiding any and all arguments and scenarios which would, in effect, turn it into something other than a democratic state. (5) The societal constraint assumptions that directly deny and indirectly question the state-centered propositions were addressed head on, examined extensively, and treated with the respect they deserve as eminently plausible, often valid assumptions. (6) While laying great stress upon the state's autonomy-enhancing capacities and opportunities, the special situational contexts and policy areas (national security issues, for example) that clearly place the state in an advantageous position were downplayed. (7) Those cases that provide empirical support for the propositions were not simply set out as such, but wherever possible, the evidence was assessed as more or less persuasive and generalizable. (8) The argument on behalf of the model's most ambitious Type I autonomy proposition was pursued according to some unusually demanding guidelines that stacked the cards against its survival.

Taking together the quality of the existing empirical evidence (both pro and con), the strength of the underlying arguments, and the appropriateness of the methodology, the state-centered model can be characterized as highly plausible — both in and of itself, and as a much needed complement to its society-centered rival.

### Some Implications for Democratic Theory

This book has directly challenged the fundamental empirical premise of liberal democratic theory — the state's consistent constraint by civil society, its barely wavering responsiveness to the demands of the politically best endowed private actors. It consequently is very much in the mainstream of the "realist" tradition that has questioned, criticized, and revised liberal democratic theory since it reached its apogee around 1900. At that time, democratic theory featured an exceptionally optimistic view of the individual as benign in his motives, rational in his actions, and educable where lacking in these respects. It was also characterized by a heady confidence in the capacities of political engineering for designing and constructing a smoothly functioning, decisionally effective, integrative, and representative set of institutional arrangements. Among those who thought about the democratic present and future, the prevailing ideas were those of Locke, Condorcet, Kant, Bentham, and John Stuart Mill. Their widely diffused ideas informed many of the profoundly novel formal-legal and institutional developments of the late nineteenth century — the secret ballot, mass suffrage, freedom of organization, broadly based political parties, electoral accountability, legislative control of the executive, and civil service reform.

Already at its apogee, liberal democracy was confronted with some inordinately powerful challenges; the viability of its theoretical premises, its institutional arrangements, and the very facts of democratic politics were severely questioned. The work of Sigmund Freud and Vilfredo Pareto, which brought to light the self-destructive and nonrational aspects of the individual psyche, challenged some of the central premises upon which democracy's intellectual edifice was built. Gaetano Mosca and Roberto Michels criticized the liberal portrayal of man as freedom loving in pointing out that some (a minority) have a will-to-power and others (the majority) a desire to obey. Pareto, Mosca, and Michels argued that no set of institutional arrangements would allow for control over the democratic state by the many, variously circumscribed as the nonelite, the masses, the electorate, or the great majority of citizens. Along with Marx, they stripped away the formalities, charades, illusions, and delusions of democratic politics to get at the actual practices or facts, concluding that the term democracy hardly begins to serve as an accurate description of political reality. Power in civil society is so highly concentrated in the hands of the few that democratic politics is practically devoid of majority rule in any meaningful sense of the term. By the middle of the twentieth century these powerful challenges to the empirical construct of liberal democracy helped produce a widespread revisionist attitude in the academy, summarily captured in the rapid adoption of Joseph Schumpeter's elitist and exclusively procedural definition of democracy — democracy as the regularized competition among elites for the support of the nonelite, with the latter choosing the governors from among the former. Nearly all the empirical research of the last thirty years has helped to confirm this less than ambitious (that is, realistic) conception of democracy: most voters manifest little or no political interest and awareness; just about all private organizations are oligarchical in being dominated by the leadership; "pressure group politics" frequently if not regularly predominates relative to a more widely based "party politics"; formal powers and informal influence has shifted from the legislature to the executive, and from both to the bureaucracy.

With the present study in the mainstream of this already well-developed body of realist writings, it may reasonably be asked: What if any distinctive contributions does the book make? I do not think it an overstatement to suggest that it both elaborates and extends the realist study of democratic politics. The elaborations are to be found in a good number of more or less specific arguments that have been no more than touched upon in other realist analyses. The present study extends the claims of realist writings in at least two important respects. Nearly all realist writings can be characterized in one or both of two ways that limit the applicability and ambitiousness of their claims relative to those developed here.

Much, quite possibly the central thrust, of the realist case for oligarchy, class rule, minority control, or elite dominance derives from the political debilities of the many—their low levels of political consciousness, awareness, activity, and organization. The focus is upon the political passivity and ineffectualness of the nonelite in permitting, facilitating, and even encouraging elite dominance. The present study both parallels and goes beyond this kind of argument. The parallels are largely to be found in the discussion of Type III autonomy. The democratic state acts autonomously when the nonelite holds preferences that converge with the state's, defers to public officials, and is indifferent to their policy preferences. With the state being autonomous without having to take any purposeful actions to enhance its autonomy, there is considerable overlap with realist writings. According to Michels' "psychological causes of leadership," for instance, oligarchy largely obtains because the nonelite is apathetic, is grateful for leadership, idolizes particular leaders, and believes in the indispensability of the leadership. Public officials also capitalize upon the Type III autonomy-enhancing options to reinforce societal convergence, deference, and indifference for their own purposes, with the great majority of private actors being unaware of when and how the emergence of divergent preferences is forestalled. What I have analyzed in this fashion, emphasizing that the Type III autonomy-enhancing options are most effective with respect to those actors who stand at some distance from the state, would be characterized by the great elite theorists as manifestations of the ready manipulability of the nonelite on the part of dissembling elites. It is in the analysis of Type I and Type II autonomy that the present study extends beyond the existing realist tradition, for here it is argued that the state is autonomous even when the many are politically aware, active, and organized. For instance, several Type I and Type II autonomy-enhancing options were shown to be applicable and effective when the preferences of the activated many diverge from the state's preferences; the Type I autonomy proposition was pursued in the context of pluralism's inclusive demand group universe — one that is practically coterminous with civil society. Going beyond the elite theorists' argument that public officials are able to act on their preferences largely because of the absence of opposition from the many, here it is claimed that they do so despite their opposition.

Some realist writings do not distinguish between public and private elites, but even in those that do, it is not argued that the public officials who make up the democratic state can prevail when opposed by private social, economic, and political elites.[1] Realist claims for the predominance (or autonomy) of public officials is very much limited to their relations with the nonelite — what is thought of as the most politically disadvantaged stratum. Here every effort has been made to examine the ways in which public officials can free themselves from the control of all kinds of private actors, *especially* those who are best endowed with political and politically fungible resources. In fact, it would not be stretching scholarly parlance to substitute the term "elites" for some of the private actors who make up the different effective demand groups — the well-organized and financed groups with narrow policy concerns in neopluralism, the leadership of the great sectoral associations of employers, workers, and farmers in social corporatism, and the owners and managers of large industrial and financial enterprises in Marxism. As such, I am claiming that public elites can and do act contrary to the preferences of private elites. The present study thus helps fill in what are thought to be two patently significant lacunae in realist writings relating to the nonelite and private elites; the democratic state is seen to be markedly more autonomous than claimed even by the elite theorists.

Realist writers reacted very differently to their findings. The newly uncovered realities behind the democratic facade were greeted with varying degrees of applause, satisfaction, acceptance, regret, dismay, and condemnation. A good sampling comes from the great elite theorists who found a vast disparity between democratic ideals and practices. "Marx contended that the disparity could and should be remedied, Michels that it should but could not, Pareto that it neither could nor should."[2] How then are we to react to the frequent and marked autonomy of the democratic state?

On the question of whether the autonomy of the democratic state can be mitigated, my reactions parallel those of Michels and Pareto. Although their claims were put forward in a more uncompromising manner than is done here, several aspects of the present study point to the problematics of diminishing state autonomy. Given the highly valued and salient features of the state that help generate divergent state preferences (see Chapter 1), it is hard to see how the internal characteristics and arrangements of the state might be altered so as to minimize the frequency with which state and societal preferences diverge. In light of the abundance and diversity of autonomy-enhancing capacities and opportunities, it is hard to see how they could be sufficiently reduced in number and narrowed in scope to make an important difference for autonomy-seeking public officials. Having seen that the state is autonomous in relation to those private actors who are politically most aware and best endowed, it is hard to see how prescriptions for expanding and enhancing political consciousness and citizen involvement could substantially redress the special advantages accruing to public officials. Having failed to come up with any persuasive explanations for major variations in state autonomy other than the degree of societal opposition, which is hardly a readily manipulable variable, it is hard to see how a political engineering approach can get a reasonable good handle on the problem and where the leverage or fulcrum for change is to be found. These considerations are not, of course, necessarily the determining ones. However, they may well be, considering that not a single aspect of this study suggests when, where, or how the autonomy of the democratic state can be significantly diminished.

Whatever the possibilities for limiting the state's autonomy, there is a prior question. How do our norms and values lead us to react to the autonomy of the democratic state? Is it to be much applauded, accepted with some modicum of satisfaction or dismay, or condemned outright? To say that there is no easy answer to a question fraught with so many ambiguities, that it cannot begin to receive a comprehensive answer apart from some fully developed normative and empirical theory of democracy, that the answer depends upon numerous and varying contextual conditions so that no single answer could possibly be viable, that far more empirical work needs to be done before a satisfactory answer can be attempted—to respond in any one of these ways might be seen as patently trite or glib. Still, it must be said that these are indeed the appropriate ones. As such, the observations ventured here do little more than sketch in a few surface aspects of some normative reactions to the democratic state's autonomy.

The delineation of the three types of state autonomy provides a good analytical handle on the problem. Little need be said about the state acting on its preferences in the absence of a state-society divergence, but much should certainly be made of the activist Type III autonomy efforts, those intended to reinforce nondivergent societal preferences. Here the implications are decidedly unpalatable. Public officials are purposefully reinforcing societal deference, indifference, and convergence so as to forestall the emergence of divergent preferences; they are doing so in a manipulative and dissembling manner, what might more charitably be expressed as symbolic politics; they are most unlikely to be held accountable for their autonomy-enhancing efforts since neither the intentions behind them nor their consequences are usually visible; and the result is the placing of distinct limitations on the unbiased evaluation of alternative policy options on the part of private actors, or — more broadly — a partial stifling of political change.

By and large, Type II autonomy actions probably engender just the reverse implications. One strategy for engineering a change in societal preferences involves public officials persuading those with divergent preferences to alter them, another the eliciting of support from those private actors who are currently indifferent to the issue at hand, and the other, increasing the active participation of those who are already politically engaged. The Type II autonomy-enhancing capacities and opportunities are used in a forthright manner; the actions of public officials are visible and their intentions known. They can then be held responsible for both their goals and behavior. Rather than limiting the open-minded consideration of policy alternatives, Type II autonomous actions sometimes expand the political agenda. A positive reaction is likely to be forthcoming from those who value public initiative and leadership as a way of enhancing democratic performance. Of course Type II autonomy is at variance with the broad notion of the state representing, acting on behalf of, and responding directly to private actors and their preferences. But the variance is hardly sufficient to characterize it as unresponsiveness; the state does not translate its preferences into public policy unless and until they no longer diverge from society's.

Type I autonomous actions are, on balance, closer to their Type II than Type III counterparts in being direct and visible.

The private actors who hold divergent preferences are aware of the public officials' efforts to free themselves from societal constraints with the intention of taking authoritative actions that run counter to their preferences. Type I autonomous actions deriving from the inherent powers of the state are also forthright and visible, thereby not detracting from the state's accountability to society. On the other hand, several of the Type I autonomy-enhancing options (2, 4, 5, 7, and 11 in table 3) feature the kind of manipulative and dissembling behaviors, and thus conjure up the unpalatable implications, associated with their Type III autonomy-enhancing counterparts. The public officials who rely upon certain Type I autonomy-enhancing options (12 through 16 in table 3) may be seen as taking undue advantage of their control over public resources and authoritative offices — for exploiting the private actors' dependence upon the state and using "sticks" to dissuade those who hold divergent preferences from fully deploying their resources.

Whatever the reactions to the ways in which Type I autonomy is realized, our evaluation will be based primarily upon its stark denial of the central thrust of liberal democratic theory. With democratic states being instituted and maintained to maximize responsiveness to societal preferences, the adoption of public policies that depart from this standard are very likely to engender an adverse reaction. Whether it be one of regret, dismay, or outright condemnation depends upon our belief in and commitment to the several fundamental justifications for public responsiveness to private preferences. One of these is Aristotle's assertion that the collective wisdom of the many is at least as reliable as that of the few. "There is this to be said for the Many: Each of them by himself may not be of a good quality; but when they all come together it is possible that they may surpass — collectively and as a body, though not individually — the quality of the best."[3] This limited appreciation of the collective wisdom of the many is, of course, amplified several times over in Rousseau and the populist-minded writers who came after him. Their unmitigated condemnation of Type I autonomy also derives from its effects upon the individual. In detracting from the individual's active involvement in the discussion and resolution of public policy issues, Type I autonomy denudes the citizen of a sense of self-worth and stultifies his intellectual and benevolent capacities. John Stuart Mill asserted that it is the individuals affected by the state who can best identify and protect their interests. Public officials (as well as social, economic, and political elites) are not generally capable of promoting interests other than their own, even though they may, in good conscience, believe that their own can be equated with the interests of others. "In the absence of its natural defenders, the interest of the excluded is always in danger of being overlooked; and when looked at, is seen with very different eyes from those of the persons whom it directly concerns."[4]

Despite the great appeal of these justifications for the responsiveness of the state to society, an assessment of Type I autonomy need not be entirely this one-sided. There is the long-standing assertion that instead of being responsive to expressed societal interests, the state should pursue the public interest as conceived and perceived by the state itself. Underlying this assertion are two very different kinds of arguments. In the idealist tradition it becomes the unique responsibility of the state to advance the objective interests of society, these being conceived mainly in terms of integration, cohesion, order and stability. But since there are few of us who subscribe to a tradition embodied in the writings of Hegel, Bosanquet, and T. H. Green, and since it is for the most part neither democratic nor liberal, a defense of Type I autonomy in idealist terms becomes singularly problematic. The other argument for the state's fulfillment of the public interest has several components. Private actors are sometimes unaware of their real needs; these differ substantially from their expressed wants; they are often unable to appreciate society's common, long-run interests, and how these are positively related to their own; and when private actors do have a clear conception of the public interest, they are frequently unwilling to accept the sacrifices it entails. The other components of the argument have to do with the state. The distinctive attributes of some sizable number of public officials—their strategic positioning, self-image, role definition, professional expertise, and disinterestedness—help form policy views focused upon long-run, encompassing considerations of society's interests taken in its parts and as a whole.

A less familiar defense of Type I autonomy may be derived from an assumption that is part and parcel of all the justifications for the state's responsiveness to societal preferences: the state is responding to the preferences of the many, of the great majority of citizens. But what if their preferences do not, in fact, have that much weight? If the political resources that determine the societal parallelogram of resource-weighted preferences are narrowly or unequally distributed, in responding to societal preferences the state is not necessarily acting in accordance with those of the many, indeed, it is often acting contrary to their preferences. This assertion is far more than a possibility. It stems directly from two incontrovertible propositions. Resources are distributed unequally, and individuals with fewer resources at their disposal tend to hold different policy preferences than those who are better endowed. The great debate in empirical democratic theory about the contours of civil society revolves primarily around the issue of just *how* narrowly and unequally resources are distributed. Even pluralism acknowledges "dispersed inequalities." Again and again, attitudinal surveys, electoral analyses, and case studies of policy formation have demonstrated a significant association between an individual's socioeconomic status, political resources, and policy preferences; those who stand on the upper rungs of the socioeconomic ladder tend to be better endowed politically and hold different preferences than those on the lower rungs. There is consequently a substantial difference between the resource-weighted parallelogram of societal preferences and a parallelogram of societal preferences in which everyone's preferences have equal weight.

To whom and what in civil society should the state then respond? If it is to respond to the buyers and sellers in the political marketplace in accordance with their disparate resources or the results of the unfettered competitive political process, then a strong negative reaction to Type I autonomy is obviously forthcoming. On the other hand, a set of highly egalitarian representative norms may bring forth a very different reaction. If the pithy "one man, one vote" notion of democracy is expanded beyond election day itself to all the days between elections, and beyond elected officials to appointed ones as well, then we arrive at a highly egalitarian answer to the question: To whom and what in civil society should the state respond? It should act in accordance with the resultant of societal preferences in which those of all individuals are assigned equal weight, despite enormous disparities in the resources they control. A defense of Type I autonomy thus begins to emerge if we subscribe to highly egalitarian representative norms and believe civil society to feature a markedly unequal distribution of resources. This does not, of course, mean that Type I autonomy necessarily entails this largely unconstrained kind of egalitarian responsiveness. However, it does suggest that the preferences of the many receive short shrift when the state adopts public policies in accordance with the constraints imposed upon it. Type I autonomy is a necessary but far from a sufficient condition for the adoption of public policies that correspond to the equally weighted preferences of all citizens. The frequency with which such a match appears remains a wide open empirical question.

In short, to the extent that this book has made a plausible case for the autonomy of the democratic state, another realist wound will have been opened in the body of liberal democratic theory. But as this sketch of some likely reactions to the state's autonomy has suggested, one need not echo Dr. Pangloss to find some comfort. The distasteful implications and unhappy consequences of the Type III autonomy-enhancing actions that help forestall the emergence of divergent societal preferences are at least partly balanced by the attractions of Type II autonomy. While the reactions to Type I autonomy are likely to be negative ones, some positive possibilities are not entirely absent. Moreover, in evaluating the autonomy of the democratic state, it is not enough to look only at the manner in which the three types of autonomy are achieved and the way in which they bear upon the state's responsiveness to society. The issue should also be addressed by asking how autonomy relates to the overall performance of democratic states (or regimes), their success in doing those things and realizing those goals that nearly all of us want and expect of the democratic state. Besides the state's responsiveness to society or representativeness, these criteria include the state's legitimacy, successful management of societal conflicts, decisional effectiveness, and openness to the attractions and possibilities of change. The exceptionally complex question of whether state autonomy has an overall positive or negative effect upon its record in meeting these performance criteria remains very much an open question.

Another implication to be drawn from this book—the desirability of according the state far more prominence in the further development of democratic theory—lies only a small step beyond its central concern. The great debate in empirical democratic theory might well be near a point of exhaustion; it is already beyond the point of diminishing returns because it continues to revolve primarily around some apparently irreconcilable depictions of civil society. Rather than continuing to debate the question of which political resources are the especially effective ones, delineating their distribution again and again, and arguing (or assuming) that one or another set of private actors constitutes the effective demand groups, democratic theory would now be better served by shifting the primary focus to the state. Doing so might allow the apparently irreconcilable generalizations to be partly circumvented or synthesized, while some revisions of the answers could emerge when the question of who constitutes the effective demand groups is posed from the perspective of the state.

Whether these suggestions are or are not acted upon, this book points to the need to make some state-centered modifications and additions to the major variants of empirical democratic theory. Extensive references were made to each variant in highlighting, questioning, and supplementing their heavy reliance upon the societal constraint assumptions. The major arguments for state autonomy were developed in and of themselves, and also by confronting the underlying assumptions and filling in the gaps of the society-centered variants. If the state-centered model now enjoys the plausibility which it is thought to deserve, it becomes especially important to think about the placing of one or another state-centered "cap" upon each of the society-centered variants of democratic theory. This is not to suggest that the present model should necessarily serve as that cap, nor that the same model should complement each variant. But however it is to be accomplished, some major revisions and additions are called for to take account of the frequent and marked autonomy of the democratic state.

Finally, this study has highlighted and amplified what is already well known about democratic politics. Democracy—as an ensemble of behaviors and practices, institutions and rules, ideas and ideals—is replete with tensions, trade-offs, dilemmas, incompatibilities, and conflicts. This study has shown how the contradictions between state autonomy and societal constraint can be used to capture and elaborate upon the distinctive and characteristic features of democratic politics.

# Notes

## 1. State, Society, and Public Policy

1. In addition to the likely inaccuracy of their perceptions, journalists and public officials, congressmen in particular, have self-serving reasons for overemphasizing the societal pressures placed upon the state. See Raymond A. Bauer, Ithiel De Sola Pool, and Lewis Anthony Dexter, *American Business and Public Policy: The Politics of Foreign Trade* (Cambridge, Mass.: MIT Press, 1963), p. 486.

2. Herbert A. Simon, Donald W. Smithburg, and Victor A. Thompson, *Public Administration*, the section on "The Struggle for Organizational Survival," reprinted in Francis E. Rourke, ed., *Bureaucratic Power in National Politics* (Boston: Little, Brown, 1965), p. 49. Similarly, there is the assertion the "The administrator, like the politician, must nurse his constituency to ensure his own survival, and the task of creating a continuing fund of public support is an indispensable part of bureaucratic statecraft," in Francis E. Rourke, *Secrecy and Publicity: Dilemmas of Democracy,* the section on "Bureaucracy and Public Opinion," reprinted ibid., p. 187.

3. Samuel P. Huntington, "Uneasy Coexistence: The Anti-Power Ethic vs. the 'State' in America," a paper presented to the MIT-Harvard Joint Seminar on Political Development, May 2, 1979.

4. As quoted in Colin Campbell and George J. Szablowski, *The Super-Bureaucrats: Structure and Behavior in Central Agencies* (Toronto: Macmillan, 1979), p. 9, italics added.

5. Gianfranco Poggi, *The Development of the Modern State: A Sociological Introduction* (Stanford: Stanford University Press, 1978), p. 1.

6. Scott C. Flanagan, "Models and Methods of Analysis," in Gabriel A. Almond, Scott C. Flanagan, and Robert J. Mundt, eds., *Crisis, Choice and Change: Historical Studies of Political Development* (Boston: Little, Brown, 1973), p. 75.

7. See Chapter 7, where some basic doubts are raised about the ap-

parently unquestioned assertion that the American national state is a decidedly weak one because its authority is dispersed and its institutions are fragmented.

8. Stephen D. Krasner, *Defending the National Interest: Raw Materials Investments and U.S. Foreign Policy* (Princeton: Princeton University Press, 1978);
Theda Skocpol, *States and Social Revolutions: A Comparative Analysis of France,
Russia, and China* (Cambridge, Eng.: Cambridge University Press, 1979). Although one is not explicitly laid out, there are also hints of a relational conception of autonomy to be found in Alfred Stepan, *The State and Society: Peru in
Comparative Perspective* (Princeton: Princeton University Press, 1978).

9. Krasner, *Defending the National Interest*, pp. 55-57.

10. Skocpol, *States and Social Revolutions*, pp. 24-31.

11. Richard Fenno, Jr., *Home Style: House Members in Their Districts* (Boston: Little, Brown, 1978), p. 240; Hanna Fenichel Pitkin, ed., *Representation*
(New York: Atherton Press, 1969); J. Roland Pennock and John W. Chap-
man, eds., *Representation*, vol. X, Nomos Yearbook of the American Society
for Political and Legal Philosophy (New York: Atherton Press, 1968).

12. Also included here are societally constrained authoritative actions
taken subsequent to unsuccessful Type I and Type II state autonomy attempts.

13. It might be thought that an important kind of societal explanation
has been omitted from figure 1. State and societal preferences are divergent at
first, private actors then bring about a shift in state preferences to make them
consonant with their own, and public officials translate their now modified
preferences into public policy. However, a brief look at the three ways in
which private actors can alter state preferences indicates why this kind of explanation does not form a distinctive part of the basic typology. First, private
actors can pressure public officials and offer them inducements to alter their
policy views. But it would then become difficult, if not impossible, to refer to
the genuine preferences of public officials, or alternatively, the account would
constitute part of a societal constraint explanation — one that focuses upon the
beliefs rather than the consequent behavior of public officials. Second, societal
actors can alter state preferences at election time by voting for challengers
whose policy views are closer to their own than are those of the incumbents.
This is to say that votes constitute a highly effective set of resources and sanctions, but these are, of course, already included as part of the societal constraint explanation. Third, private actors can use all sorts of information, intellectual arguments, and emotional appeals to convince public officials to
modify their policy preferences. Such efforts speak to the issue of how state
preferences are formed, rather than the present one of determining if and how
public officials can translate them into public policy. And in setting out the
concept of state preferences it was stressed that they may be derived from any
source and in any manner, including societal persuasion, just as long as they
are formed in a societally unconstrained manner. Also relevant here is a

previously made observation. In this study state preferences serve as the reference point; these are taken as given, with societal preferences varying in their fit with the state's.

14. Richard E. Neustadt, *Presidential Power: The Politics of Leadership* (New York: John Wiley, 1960).

15. Charles W. Anderson, "The Logic of Public Problems: Evaluation in Comparative Policy Research," in Douglas E. Ashford, ed., *Comparing Public Policies: New Concepts and Methods*, vol. IV, Sage Yearbooks in Politics and Public Policy (Beverly Hills: Sage Publications, 1978), pp. 20, 35-36, italics in original.

16. Ibid., p. 36, italics added.

17. For a conceptualization of the public interest as a consistent rank ordering of generalized goals over time, one which turns out not to be empirically inconsonant with ours, see Krasner, *Defending the National Interest,* pp. 42-45. His formulation is discussed briefly in Chapter 5.

## 2. Societal Constraint of the State

1. Earl Latham, *The Group Basis of Politics* (Ithaca: Cornell University Press, 1952), pp. 35-36.

2. David B. Truman, *The Governmental Process* (New York: Alfred Knopf, 1952); Robert A. Dahl, *Who Governs?* (New Haven: Yale University Press, 1961). See also Arthur F. Bentley, *The Process of Government* (Cambridge, Mass.: Harvard University Press, 1967, first published 1908); Nelson W. Polsby, *Community Power and Political Theory*, 2d ed. (New Haven: Yale University Press, 1980); Emmette S. Redford, *Democracy in the Administrative State* (New York: Oxford University Press, 1969); V. O. Key, Jr., *Public Opinion and American Democracy* (New York: Alfred Knopf, 1965); Leon D. Epstein, *Political Parties in Western Democracies* (New York: Praeger, 1967); Robert A. Dahl and Charles E. Lindblom, *Politics, Economics, and Welfare* (New York: Harper and Row, 1953); Robert A. Dahl, *A Preface to Democratic Theory* (Chicago: University of Chicago Press, 1954); Lester W. Milbrath, *Political Participation* (Chicago: Rand McNally, 1965); Seymour Martin Lipset, *Political Man* (New York: Doubleday, 1960); Christopher J. Hewitt, "Elites and the Distribution of Power in British Society," in Philip Stanworth and Anthony Giddens, eds., *Elites and Power in British Society* (Cambridge, Eng: Cambridge University Press, 1974), pp. 45-64.

3. Grant McConnell, *Private Power and American Democracy* (New York: Alfred Knopf, 1967); Theodore J. Lowi, *The End of Liberalism: Ideology, Policy, and the Crisis of Public Authority* (New York: Norton, 1969). See also William E. Connolly, ed., *The Bias of Pluralism* (New York: Atherton, 1969); Henry S. Kariel, ed., *Frontiers of Democratic Theory* (New York: Random House, 1970).

4. Stein Rokkan, "Norway: Numerical Democracy and Corporate Pluralism," in Robert A. Dahl, ed., *Political Opposition in Western Democracies*

(New Haven: Yale University Press, 1966), pp. 70-115; Phillippe Schmitter, "Still the Century of Corporatism?" *Review of Politics,* 36 (1974), 85-131; Phillippe Schmitter, "Modes of Interest Intermediation and Models of Societal Change in Western Europe," *Comparative Political Studies,* 10 (1977), 7-38. See also Gerhard Lembruch, "Liberal Corporatism and Party Government," *Comparative Political Studies,* 10 (1977), 89-126; Alan Cawson, "Pluralism, Corporatism and the Role of the State," *Government and Opposition,* 13 (1978), 178-198; Samuel H. Beer, *British Politics in the Collectivist Age* (New York: Alfred Knopf, 1969); G. Ionescu, *Centripetal Politics: Government and the New Centres of Power* (London: Hart-Davis, MacGibbon, 1975); Martin O. Heisler, ed., *Politics in Europe: Structures and Processes in Some Postindustrial Democracies* (New York: David McKay, 1974); Martin O. Heisler, "Corporate Pluralism Revisited: Where Is the Theory?" *Scandinavian Political Studies,* new ser., 2 (1979), 277-298, and the other articles in this issue dealing with Norwegian, Finnish, and Danish politics; Hans Meijer, "Bureaucracy and Policy Formation in Sweden," *Scandinavian Political Studies,* 4 (1969), 103-116.

5. Robert C. Tucker, ed., *The Marx-Engels Reader* (New York: Norton, 1972); Ralph Miliband, *Marxism and Politics* (New York: Oxford University Press, 1977); Nicos Poulantzas, *Political Power and Social Classes* (London: New Left Books, 1973). See also Claus Offe, "Structural Problems of the Capitalist State," in Klaus von Beyme, ed., *German Political Studies* (Beverly Hills: Sage Publications, 1974), pp. 31-57; James O'Connor, *The Fiscal Crisis of the State* (New York: St. Martin's Press, 1973); Ralph Miliband, *The State in Capitalist Society: An Analysis of the Western System of Power* (New York: Basic Books, 1969); Alan Wolfe, *The Limits of Legitimacy: Political Contradictions of Contemporary Capitalism* (New York: The Free Press, 1977); Jurgen Habermas, *Legitimation Crisis* (Boston: Beacon Press, 1975); David A. Gold, Clarence Y. H. Lo, and Erik Olin Wright, "Recent Developments in Marxist Theories of the State," *Monthly Review* (1975), part I, pp. 28-43, part II, pp. 36-51; Fred Block, "The Ruling Class Does Not Rule: Notes on the Marxist Theory of the State," *Monthly Review* (1977), pp. 6-28.

6. The other major features of the four variants are set out in Chapter 6. The extensive body of writings on consociational democracy is not considered here even though the focus is upon political elites, more specifically, the leaders of hostile societal segments. Arend Lijphart has made the most important contributions to the development of the consociational model. His most recent statement is in *Democracy in Plural Societies: A Comparative Exploration* (New Haven: Yale University Press, 1977). Also relevant insofar as it assigns far more importance to political elites than does Lijphart, is Eric A. Nordlinger, *Conflict Regulation in Divided Societies* (Cambridge, Mass.: Center for International Affairs, Harvard University, 1972). There are several reasons why this body of writings is not considered as a fifth variant of democratic theory. First, in terms of the close interactions among political elites and their working out of mutually acceptable public policies, there is

considerable overlap with the social corporatism variant. Second, consociationalism's distinctiveness has to do with its explanations for the absence of violence in segmented or deeply divided societies. Since such divisions have characterized only a few advanced industrial democracies, such as Austria between 1945 and 1965 and Belgium since 1945, the universe to which consociational hypotheses are applicable is overly restricted relative to this study's concerns. Indeed, so is the exclusive analysis of public policies that bear upon the avoidance of violence. Third, it is exceptionally difficult to characterize this literature as state-or society-centered. Consociationalism does not distinguish between, even merges, those political elites found within and those outside the state. Even if the distinction could be made, a lengthy and arguable exegesis would be required with respect to the explanatory importance of public elites in preserving political stability. In my own study of conflict regulation I point out that Lijphart's explanatory hypotheses actually assign far greater importance to societal than elite variables, even if he himself seems to be unaware of it, and his doing so is highly questionable. It is the independent actions of political elites, often taken in opposition to their followers' demands, rather than societal variables, that best account for conflict regulating successes and failures in democratic regimes.

7. Dahl, *Who Governs?* p. 228.

8. Karl Marx, "The German Ideology," reprinted in Tucker, ed., *Marx-Engels Reader*, p. 151.

9. Somewhat different and more extensive discussions of the society-centered premises of liberal and Marxist political theory are found in several recent books. See Alfred Stepan, *The State and Society: Peru in Comparative Perspective* (Princeton: Princeton University Press, 1978); Stephen D. Krasner, *Defending the National Interest: Raw Materials Investments and U.S. Foreign Policy* (Princeton: Princeton University Press, 1978); Theda Skocpol, *States and Social Revolutions* (New York: Cambridge University Press, 1979).

10. Graham Allison, *Essence of Decision: Explaining the Cuban Missile Crisis* (Boston: Little, Brown, 1971).

11. E. E. Schattschneider, *The Semi-Sovereign People* (New York: Holt, Rinehart and Winston, 1960); James Q. Wilson, *Political Organizations* (New York: Basic Books, 1973); Theodore J. Lowi, "American Business, Public Policy, Case Studies, and Political Theory," *World Politics*, 16 (1964), 685-714; Theodore J. Lowi, "Four Systems of Policy, Politics, and Choice," *Public Administration Review*, 32 (1970), 298-310.

12. Schattschneider, *The Semi-Sovereign People*, p. 2, italics in original.

13. Ibid., p. 35.

14. Wilson, *Political Organizations*, pp. 333-334, italics in original.

15. James Q. Wilson, "The Politics of Regulation," in James Q. Wilson, ed., *The Politics of Regulation* (New York: Basic Books, 1980), pp. 366-372.

16. Theodore J. Lowi, "Public Policy and the Bureaucracy in the United States and France," in Douglas E. Ashford, ed., *Comparing Public Policies: New*

Concepts and Methods, vol. IV, Sage Yearbooks in Politics and Public Policy (Beverly Hills: Sage Publications, 1978), pp. 177-196.

17. Daniel Tarschys, "The Growth of Public Expenditures: Nine Modes of Explanation," *Scandinavian Political Studies,* 10 (1975), 9-31.

18. The reference is to Alan R. Peacock and Jack Wiseman, *The Growth of Public Expenditure in the United Kingdom,* 2d ed. (London: Allen and Unwin, 1967).

19. Hugh Heclo, *Modern Social Politics in Britain and Sweden* (New Haven: Yale University Press, 1974), pp. 2, 6-9.

20. David R. Cameron, "The Expansion of the Public Economy: A Comparative Analysis," *American Political Science Review,* 72 (1978), 1243-1261.

21. Ibid., p. 1245. The reference is to Aaron Wildavsky, *Budgeting: A Comparative Theory of the Budgetary Process* (Boston: Little, Brown, 1975), pp. 232-235.

22. Cameron, "Expansion of the Public Economy," pp. 1246-1248.

23. Ibid., p. 1246. The references are to Gerald H. Kramer, "Short-Term Fluctuations in U.S. Voting Behavior, 1896-1964," *American Political Science Review,* 65 (1971), 131-143; Edward R. Tufte, *Political Control of the Economy* (Princeton: Princeton University Press, 1978).

24. Cameron, "Expansion of the Public Economy," pp. 1245-1246.

25. Ibid., pp. 1249-1259.

26. Ibid., pp. 1248-1249. The references are to Anthony Downs, *Inside Bureaucracy* (Boston: Little, Brown, 1964); William A. Niskanen, *Bureaucracy and Representative Government* (Chicago: Aldine Publishing, 1971); Aaron Wildavsky, *The Politics of the Budgetary Process,* 2d ed. (Boston: Little, Brown, 1974); Tarschys, "Public Expenditures."

27. Nehemiah Jordan, "The Asymmetry of Liking and Disliking: A Phenomenon Meriting Further Reflection and Research," *Public Opinion Quarterly,* 29 (1965), 315-322; David E. Kanouse and L. Reid Hanson, "Negativity in Evaluations," in Edward E. Jones and others, eds., *Attribution: Perceiving the Causes of Behavior* (Morristown, N.J.: General Learning Press, 1971), pp. 47-62; Margaret W. Matlin and David J. Stang, *The Pollyanna Principle: Selectivity in Language, Memory and Thought* (New York: Schenkman, 1978).

28. Compare two outstanding studies of the U.S. Congress as they relate to this point. In his *Congress: The Electoral Connection* (New Haven: Yale University Press, 1974), David Mayhew makes a powerful case for the proposition that the best way in which to understand congressional behavior is to recognize that congressmen are "single-mindedly interested in reelection." This proposition is used to explain why congressmen are so active in securing particularized benefits for their districts, in claiming credit for these benefits, and in taking positions which will be popular in their districts. Partly because so many decisions are, in effect, made in committee, Richard F. Fenno, Jr., focuses upon them in his *Congressmen in Committees* (Boston: Little, Brown, 1974). He argues that the single most important determinant of committee de-

cisions is probably the goals of its members, and on the basis of their goals he distinguishes between three kinds of committees. There are those, like Ways and Means and Appropriations, whose members are legislative "insiders," and as such, primarily oriented toward influence in the House and legislative success; those, like Foreign Affairs, Labor, and Education, whose members are primarily interested in the substance of public policy; and those, like Interior and Post Office, whose members are more constituent oriented.

29. Heinz Eulau, John C. Wahlke, William Buchanan, and LeRoy C. Ferguson, "The Role of the Representative: Some Empirical Observations on the Theory of Edmund Burke," in Heinz Eulau and John C. Wahlke, eds., *The Politics of Representation: Continuities in Theory and Research* (Beverly Hills: Sage Publications, 1978), pp. 73-90.

30. Philip E. Converse and Roy Pierce, "Representative Roles and Legislative Behavior in France," *Legislative Studies Quarterly,* 4 (1979), especially pp. 536-538; Warren E. Miller and Donald E. Stokes, "Constituency Influence in Congress," *American Political Science Review,* 57 (1963), especially pp. 45-46; Hans Daalder and Jerrold G. Rusk, "Perceptions of Party in the Dutch Parliament," in Samuel C. Patterson and John C. Wahlke, eds., *Comparative Legislative Behavior: Frontiers of Research* (New York: John Wiley, 1976), especially pp. 158-162. See also Roland Cayrol and others, "French Deputies and the Political System," *Legislative Studies Quarterly,* 1 (1976), especially p. 77. In this survey of another Fifth Republic legislature, the ratio between those deputies who say that they would act in accordance with their own conscience and those who say that they would act in accordance with the voters' preferences is even higher (10 to 1). A difficulty in giving a specifically Burkean interpretation to all these survey studies and the one cited in the previous note is discussed in Chapter 7.

31. Raymond A. Bauer, Ithiel De Sola Pool, and Lewis Anthony Dexter, *American Business and Public Policy: The Politics of Foreign Trade,* 2d ed. (Chicago: Aldine Publishing, 1972), p. ix.

32. Ibid., p. 414, italics in original.

33. Michel Crozier, Samuel P. Huntington, and Joji Watanuki, *The Crisis of Democracy: Report on the Governability of Democracies to the Trilateral Commission* (New York: New York University Press, 1975); Leon N. Lindberg, ed., *Politics and the Future of Industrial Society* (New York: David McKay, 1976), especially the literature summarized on pp. 222-252; Samuel Brittan, "The Economic Contradictions of Democracy," *British Journal of Political Science,* 5 (1975), 239-259; James Douglas, "Review Article: The Overloaded Crown," *British Journal of Political Science,* 6 (1976), 488-500; several essays in *The Public Interest,* 10 (1975), a special issue devoted to "The American Commonwealth, 1976."

## 3. Type III State Autonomy

1. See the references in Chapter 2, notes 2–5. A full summary of each variant is found in Chapter 6.

2. John Odell, "The United States in the International Monetary System: Sources of Foreign Policy Change" (Ph.D. diss. University of Wisconsin, 1976).

3. Eric A. Nordlinger, *The Working Class Tories: Authority, Deference, and Stable Democracy* (Berkeley: University of California Press, 1967), pp. 82-90. Also worth noting are the responses to two questions designed to elicit the workers' acquiescent representational norms. "Do you think that people like yourself have any say in how the country is run? Do people like you have a good deal of say, a little, or none at all?" Almost 90 percent replied with "a little" or "none at all." This may not be especially surprising. But when asked "Do you think that this is the way things *ought* to be?,", more than two-thirds of those who believed that people like themselves have little influence on how the country is run registered their satisfaction with this perceived state of affairs, and nearly one-third of those who said that people like themselves have no influence at all provided the same response. See pp. 97-103.

4. An additional one should be mentioned for analytical completeness. Public officials prefer $X$, they know that most of the societal actors within their constituencies (electoral or other) prefer $Y$, and they translate the latter into public policy. But they do so not because of actual or anticipated societal sanctions, which would turn this into a societal constraint explanation. Rather, these public officials subscribe to representational norms that enjoin them to act according to their constituents' preferences, even when these diverge from their own. Such officials believe that they ought to prefer $Y$, and come genuinely to do so, without being influenced by actual or anticipated societal pressures to alter their own preferences from $X$ to $Y$.

5. Ezra N. Suleiman, *Politics, Power, and Bureaucracy in France: The Administrative Elite* (Princeton: Princeton University Press, 1974), pp. 316-351, but especially pp. 337-340.

6. Murray Edelman, *The Symbolic Uses of Politics* (Urbana: University of Illinois Press, 1964), pp. 124-125.

7. Nicos Poulantzas, *Political Power and Social Classes* (London: New Left Books, 1973), pp. 137-140.

8. Edelman, *Symbolic Uses*, pp. 1-2. See also the chapter on "The Credenda and Miranda of Power," in Charles E. Merriam, *Political Power* (New York: Collier Books, 1964, first published 1934), and Gaetano Mosca's conception of the "political formula," in *The Ruling Class* (New York: McGraw-Hill, 1939).

9. Edelman, *Symbolic Uses*, pp. 7, 75.

10. Ibid., p. 172, italics added. Nor do I use his institutional and other generalized situations, settings, and characteristics of public officials as explanations, since these are givens, not variables that are purposefully exploited.

11. Ibid., pp. 172, 114-115.

12. Ibid., pp. 30-31, 80-81, 17.

13. Ibid., pp. 76-78.

14. Peter Bachrach and Morton Baratz, "Two Faces of Power," *American Political Science Review,* 56 (1962), 948. See also Peter Bachrach and Morton Baratz, "Decisions and Nondecisions: An Analytical Framework," *American Political Science Review,* 57 (1963), 632-642; Matthew A. Crenson, *The Unpolitics of Air Pollution* (Baltimore: Johns Hopkins University Press, 1971).

15. Peter Bachrach and Morton Baratz, *Power and Poverty: Theory and Practice* (New York: Oxford University Press, 1970), pp. 44-45.

16. Charles E. Lindblom, *Politics and Markets: The World's Political-Economic Systems* (New York: Basic Books, 1977), p. 205.

17. See Daniel Nimmo, *Popular Images of Politics* (Engelwood Cliffs: Prentice-Hall, 1974), especially chap. 6; W. Lance Bennett, *Public Opinion in American Politics* (New York: Harcourt, Brace and Jovanovich, 1980), especially chap. 9.

18. Murray Edelman, *Political Language* (New York: Academic Press, 1977), especially chaps. 3 and 7.

## 4. Type II State Autonomy

1. Robert A. Dahl, *Who Governs?* (New Haven: Yale University Press, 1961), pp. 115-140, italics in original.

2. Harry Eckstein, "Case Study and Theory in Political Science," in Fred I. Greenstein and Nelson Polsby, eds., *Handbook of Political Science: Strategies of Inquiry,* vol. VII (Reading, Mass.: Addison-Wesley Publishing, 1975), pp. 79-138.

3. Hadley Arkes, *Bureaucracy, the Marshall Plan, and the National Interest* (Princeton: Princeton University Press, 1972); Harry Bayard Price, *The Marshall Plan and Its Meaning* (Ithaca: Cornell University Press, 1955).

4. Andrew Shonfield, *Modern Capitalism: The Changing Balance of Public and Private Power* (London: Oxford University Press, 1965); Stephen Cohen, *Modern Capitalist Planning* (Cambridge, Mass.: Harvard University Press, 1969); John Zysman, *Political Strategies for Industrial Order: State, Market, and Industry in France* (Berkeley: University of California Press, 1977).

5. Shonfield, *Modern Capitalism,* pp. 128-129.

6. Raymond A. Bauer, Ithiel De Sola Pool, and Lewis Anthony Dexter, *American Business and Public Policy: The Politics of Foreign Trade,* 2d ed. (Chicago: Aldine Publishing, 1972), p. 423. See also Lewis Anthony Dexter, *The Sociology and Politics of Congress* (Chicago: Rand McNally, 1969).

7. Hugh Heclo, *Modern Social Politics in Britain and Sweden* (New Haven: Yale University Press, 1974), p. 303.

8. Stephen D. Krasner, *Defending the National Interest: Raw Materials Investments and U.S. Foreign Policy* (Princeton: Princeton University Press, 1978), p.5.

9. Ibid., p. 74.

10. Ibid., pp. 75-82.

## 5. Type I State Autonomy

1. David A. Gold, Clarence Y. H. Yo, Erik Olin Wright, "Recent Developments in Marxist Theories of the State," *Monthly Review* (1975), part I, pp. 28-43, part II, pp. 36-51.

2. Ralph Miliband, *Marxism and Politics* (New York: Oxford University Press, 1977), p. 87.

3. Nicos Poulantzas, *Political Power and Social Classes* (London: New Left Books, 1973), pp. 285-286, italics in original.

4. Claus Offe, "Structural Problems of the Capitalist State," in Klaus von Beyme, ed., *German Political Studies* (Beverly Hills: Sage Publications, 1974), p. 35.

5. Miliband, *Marxism*, p. 87.

6. Karl Marx, *The Eighteenth Brumaire of Louis Bonaparte*, in Robert C. Tucker, ed., *The Marx-Engels Reader* (New York: Norton, 1972), p. 515.

7. Karl Marx, *The Civil War in France*, in Tucker, ed., *Marx-Engels Reader*, p. 555.

8. Friedrich Engels, *The Origin of the Family, Private Property, and the State*, in Tucker, ed., *Marx-Engels Reader*, pp. 653-654.

9. Poulantzas, *Political Power*, pp. 285-286.

10. Stephen D. Krasner, *Defending the National Interest: Raw Materials Investments and U.S. Foreign Policy* (Princeton: Princeton University Press, 1978), p. 10.

11. Ibid., p. 13.

12. Ibid., p. 63, italics added.

13. Ibid., p. 73.

14. Ibid., pp. 149-150.

15. Ibid., p. 89.

16. Ibid., pp. 83-86.

17. Ibid., p. 87.

18. This is not to suggest that the mixed-economy welfare state is generally more autonomous than its less developed predecessors. As pointed out in Chapter 1, there are also good reasons for thinking that it is not. Here we only want to emphasize the regular availability of half the Type I autonomy-enhancing options by noting their close connections with some characteristics of the state in all the advanced industrial democracies.

19. David R. Mayhew, "Congressional Elections: The Case of the Vanishing Marginals," *Polity*, 6 (1974), 295-317; Morris P. Fiorina, *Congress: Keystone of the Washington Establishment* (New Haven: Yale University Press, 1977).

20. Fiorina, *Congress*, p. 53.

21. Bruce E. Cain, John A. Ferejohn, and Morris P. Fiorina, "What Makes Legislators in Great Britain and the United States Popular?" California Institute of Technology, forthcoming.

22. Edward R. Tufte, *Political Control of the Economy* (Princeton: Princeton University Press, 1978), p. 19. The same conclusions emerge from an analysis of comparable Australian data. See Friedrich Schneider and Werner W. Pommerehne, "Illusions in Fiscal Policy: A Case Study," University of Zurich, forthcoming.

## 6. Type I State Autonomy and Empirical Democratic Theory

1. Harry Eckstein, "Case Study and Theory in Political Science," in Fred I. Greenstein and Nelson Polsby, eds., *Handbook of Political Science: Strategies of Inquiry*, vol. VII (Reading, Mass.: Addison-Wesley Publishing, 1975), pp. 79-138.

2. For references to the pluralist literature see Chapter 2, note 2.

3. David B. Truman, *The Governmental Process* (New York: Alfred Knopf), 1952.

4. Robert A. Dahl, *Who Governs?* (New Haven: Yale University Press, 1961), p. 228.

5. Emmette S. Redford, *Democracy in the Administrative State* (New York: Oxford University Press, 1969), pp. 27-28.

6. Truman, *Governmental Process*, p. 164.

7. For references to the neopluralist literature see Chapter 2, note 3.

8. Grant McConnell, *Private Power and American Democracy* (New York: Knopf, 1967), p. 147.

9. Ibid., pp. 163, 356-357.

10. Theodore J. Lowi, *The End of Liberalism: Ideology, Policy, and the Crisis of Public Authority* (New York: Norton, 1969), p. 71.

11. McConnell, *Private Power*, pp. 162-164.

12. Ibid., p. 147 et passim.

13. Lowi, *End of Liberalism*, p. 124.

14. Ibid., p. 85.

15. McConnell, *Private Power*, pp. 122, 342; Lowi, *End of Liberalism*, p. 88.

16. For references to the social corporatist literature see Chapter 2, note 4.

17. One of social corporatism's better known exponents combines it with the Marxist variant in arguing that corporatist state-society patterns constitute a structural rescue effort of late capitalism, specifically, in controlling trade union demands. See Leo Panitch, *Social Democracy and Industrial Militancy: The Labour Party, the Trade Unions and Incomes Policy*, 1945-1974 (Cambridge, Eng.: Cambridge University Press, 1976), and Leo Panitch, "The

Development of Corporatism in Liberal Democracies," *Comparative Political Studies*, 10, (1977).

18. Stein Rokkan, "Norway: Numerical Democracy and Corporate Pluralism," in Robert A. Dahl, ed., *Political Oppositions in Western Democracies* (New Haven: Yale University Press, 1966), p. 107.

19. Martin O. Heisler, with Robert B. Kvavik, "Patterns of European Politics: The 'European Polity' Model," in Martin O. Heisler, ed., *Politics in Europe: Structures and Processes in Some Postindustrial Democracies* (New York: David McKay, 1974), p. 56.

20. Phillippe Schmitter, "Modes of Interest Intermediation and Models of Societal Change in Western Europe," *Comparative Political Studies*, 10 (1977), p. 34.

21. Phillippe Schmitter, "Still the Century of Corporatism?" *Review of Politics*, 36 (1974), p. III.

22. Ibid.

23. Schmitter, "Modes of Interest Intermediation," p. 35.

24. Ibid., p. 9.

25. Hans Meijer, "Bureaucracy and Policy Formation in Sweden," *Scandinavian Political Studies*, 4 (1969), pp. 106-109.

26. Tom Christensen and Morton Egeberg, "Organized Group-Government Relations in Norway: On the Structured Selection of Participants, Problems, Solutions, and Choice Opportunities," *Scandinavian Political Studies*, new ser., 2 (1979), p. 251.

27. Voitto Helander, "Interest Representation in the Finnish Committee System in the Post-War Era," *Scandinavian Political Studies*, new ser., 2 (1979), p. 232.

28. For example, there are the critically important and continuous contributions of Norwegian civil servants in preparing the government's budget. See John Higley, Karl Erik Brofoss, and Knut Groholt, "Top Civil Servants and the National Budget in Norway," in Mattei Dogan, ed., *The Mandarins of Western Europe: The Political Role of Top Civil Servants* (New York: John Wiley, 1975), pp. 252-274.

29. Robert B. Kvavik, "Interest Groups in a 'Cooptive' Political System: The Case of Norway," in Heisler, ed., *Politics in Europe*, p. 113. For Austria and Germany see Gerhard Lembruch, "Liberal Corporatism and Party Government," *Comparative Political Studies*, 10 (1977), pp. 91-126.

30. Kvavik, "The Case of Norway," p. III.

31. Ralph Miliband, *Marxism and Politics* (New York: Oxford University Press, 1977), pp. 68-69.

32. Claus Offe, "Structural Problems of the Capitalist State," in Klaus von Beyme, ed., *German Political Studies* (Beverly Hills: Sage Publications, 1974), pp. 35-37; Nicos Poulantzas, *Political Power and Social Classes* (London: New Left Books, 1973) pp. 284-287.

33. Fred Block, "The Ruling Class Does Not Rule: Notes on the Marxist

Theory of the State," *Monthly Review* (1977), p. 10.

34. Miliband, *Marxism*, pp. 87-88, italics in original.

35. Alan Wolfe, *The Limits of Legitimacy: Political Contradictions of Contemporary Capitalism* (New York: The Free Press, 1977).

36. Jurgen Habermas, *Legitimation Crisis* (Boston: Beacon Press, 1975), pp. 53, 59.

37. James O'Connor, *The Fiscal Crisis of the State* (New York: St. Martin's Press, 1973).

38. Ibid., pp. 7-10.

39. David A. Gold, Clarence Y. H. Lo, and Erik Olin Wright, "Recent Developments in Marxist Theories of the State," *Monthly Review* (1975), part II, p. 48.

## 7. Variations in Type I and Type II State Autonomy: The American State in Comparative Perspective

1. Samuel P. Huntington, *Political Order in Changing Societies* (New Haven: Yale University Press, 1968), p. 110; Nelson W. Polsby, *Congress and the Presidency,* 2d ed. (Englewood Cliffs: Prentice-Hall, 1971), pp. 140-141; Walter Dean Burnham, *Critical Elections and the Mainsprings of American Politics* (New York: Norton, 1970), p. 176; Richard E. Neustadt, *Presidential Power: The Politics of Leadership* (New York: John Wiley, 1960), p. 33, italics in original; David B. Truman, *The Governmental Process: Political Interests and Public Opinion* (New York: Alfred Knopf, 1951), p. 529; James MacGregor Burns, *The Deadlock of Democracy: Four-Party Politics in America* (Englewood Cliffs: Prentice-Hall, 1963), pp. 6-7; Stephen D. Krasner, *Defending the National Interest: Raw Materials Investments and U.S. Foreign Policy* (Princeton: Princeton University Press, 1978), pp. 61, 70.

2. The adoption of a sizeable proportion of public policies requires the assent of the president, the Office of Management and Budget, two or more executive departments with overlapping jurisdictions, and two or more bureaus within each, as well as both houses of Congress, and within each, the Rules Committee and its Senate equivalent, the Appropriation Committee, two or more full committees with overlapping responsibilities, their subcommittees, and a conference committee made up of members from both houses.

3. For the distinctly minority position on the evaluative aspects of this point see Kenneth Waltz, *Foreign Policy and Democratic Politics: The American and British Experience* (Boston: Little, Brown, 1968). Waltz argues that the dispersal of decisionmaking sites promotes consideration of a wider range of policy options and indirectly facilitates greater responsiveness to societal interests.

4. Raymond A. Bauer, Ithiel De Sola Pool and Lewis Anthony Dexter, *American Business and Public Policy: The Politics of Foreign Trade,* 2d ed. (Chicago: Aldine Publishing, 1972), p. 423.

5. Parenthetically, a review of the fifteen Type III autonomy-enhanc-

ing options set out in table 1 indicates that these are no less regularly available, widely applicable, markedly effective, or frequently employable on the part of American officials than they are in the case of public officials whose powers and units are structurally concentrated. Although this point does not speak to the validity of the conventional interpretation which is limited to situations in which state and societal preferences diverge, it does suggest that the American state is not disadvantaged in realizing its autonomy indirectly, by forestalling the emergence of divergent preferences.

6. Although the most widespread and virtually unquestioned interpretation of the American state as inordinately constrained revolves around the fragmentation of public authority, it may of course be that other explanations are more compelling. One such explanation has been widely subscribed to in one form or another since de Tocqueville. The American state is highly constrained because it confronts an especially "strong society," one which features a plethora of well-endowed private associations and an especially dynamic private sector. Yet how much confidence is to be accorded the statement that civil society in America is markedly stronger and better able to constrain the state than it is in most other advanced industrial democracies? What was true in the past is not necessarily so today; if American society does feature a relative abundance of private associations, surely their number alone is not an especially persuasive indicator of a society's capacity to constrain the state; and if the interpretation turns upon the associations' organizational cohesiveness and other resources along with the private sector's dynamism, it is not at all clear that American society is relatively advantaged in these respects. According to another interpretation the weakness of the American state is explicable in terms of its relatively undeveloped capacities. Relative to almost all other advanced industrial democracies the American state's activities are limited in their scope and penetration of the economy and society, but as will be suggested in the next section of this chapter, it is far from certain that variations in public capacities and activities are closely related to state autonomy.

7. However, it is possible that there are some as yet unidentified state variables that can help explain differences in state autonomy. This would not be surprising given how little work has been done on problems of state autonomy.

8. The horizontal axis is not extended farther left because those points on the continuum would not constitute instances of societal opposition to state preferences. The impact of varying degrees of societal support for state preferences upon Type III autonomous actions are not discussed here or in Chapter 3 for a simple but basic reason: they are not thought to have more than a marginal effect upon either the translation of the state's nondivergent preferences into authoritative actions or the use and effectiveness of the Type III autonomy-enhancing capacities and opportunities.

## 8. The Plausibility and Implications
## of the State-Centered Model

1. Just about the only exception to this broad characterization is found in Marx and Engel's writings on the independence of the state from the financial, industrial, and landed elites. Yet, as pointed out in Chapter 5, it is plainly said that this occurs only "by way of exception" and none of their few examples involves a democratic state.

2. Dankwart A. Rustow, "The Study of Elites: Who's Who, When and How," *World Politics,* 18 (1966), p. 708.

3. *The Politics of Aristotle* (Oxford: Oxford University Press, 1946), translated by Ernest Barker, p. 123.

4. John Stuart Mill, *Representative Government,* in *Utilitarianism, Liberty, and Representative Government* (London: Dent, 1910), p. 209.

# Index